THE RUSH TO DEVELOPMENT

THE RUSH TO DEVELOPMENT

ECONOMIC CHANGE AND POLITICAL STRUGGLE IN SOUTH KOREA

MARTIN HART-LANDSBERG

MONTHLY REVIEW PRESS
NEW YORK

Copyright © 1993 by Martin Hart-Landsberg
All right reserved

Library of Congress Cataloging-in-Publication Data

HC
467.5
H37
1993

Hart-Landsberg, Martin.
  The rush to development : economic change and political
struggle in South Korea / Martin Hart-Landsberg.
     p.   cm.
  Includes bibliographical references and index.
  ISBN 0-85345-856-1 : $38.00. -- ISBN 0-85345-857-X (pbk.) : $18.00
1. Korea (South)--Economic conditions--1960- 2. Korea (South)--Economic
policy--1960- 3. Korea (South)--Politics and government--1960- I. Title.
HC467.5.H37 1993
338.95195--dc20   93-9255
                                                            CIP

Monthly Review Press
122 West 27th Street
New York, NY 10001

Manufactured in the United States of America
10 9 8 7 6 5 4 3 2 1

For my daughters, Leah and Rose Hart-Landsberg

Nearly all the friends and comrades of my youth are dead, hundreds of them; nationalist, Christian, anarchist, terrorist, communist. But they are alive to me. Where their graves should be, no one ever cared. On the battlefields and execution grounds, on the streets of city and village, their warm revolutionary blood flowed proudly into the soil of Korea, Manchuria, Siberia, Japan, China. They failed in the immediate thing, but history keeps a fine accounting.

—Nym Wales and Kim San

CONTENTS

8 THE RUSH TO DEVELOPMENT

III THE GATHERING STORM:
CONTRADICTIONS, CONFLICT, & CRISIS

ACKNOWLEDGMENTS

I owe thanks to scholars and activists on both sides of the Pacific for their willingness to answer many questions, share resources, arrange meetings, and offer their own insights into the South Korean experience. In South Korea these people include Lee Kyu Ho, Lee Su-Hoon, Lim Young-il, Mun Ho Gen, Yu Bok Nim, and many members of the Korean Teachers' and Educational Workers' Union and the Masan-Changwon General Federation of Trade Unions. In the United States, I especially want to thank David Satterwhite, Hyuk-Kyo Suh, Linda Jones, and the members of the Korea Support Network. My parents, David and Frances Landsberg, also deserve thanks for clipping and sending me dozens of news articles on the South Korean economy, which provided a wealth of data for testing my ideas.

A number of people made time in their own crowded schedules to read earlier drafts of this book—Eddie Boorstein, Reggie Boorstein, Sam Bowles, Sylvia Hart-Landsberg, Norm Diamond, Mike Lebowitz, Jerry Lembcke, Arthur MacEwan, Michael Munk, and Bob Pollin. Their comments, criticisms, and suggestions were invaluable in helping me to develop and sharpen my arguments. I, of course, am solely responsible for any shortcomings of analysis that might remain after their contributions. Finally, I owe a special debt to Sylvia Hart-Landsberg. Without her constant encouragement and support this book would have never been written.

INTRODUCTION

This is a book about economic and political development in South Korea. While most analysts praise South Korea as a success story, promoting its economic strategy as a model for the third world, I do not believe that the South Korean experience supports their claim. These analysts largely ignore not only the social and economic contradictions generated by South Korea's success but, even more important, the fact that growing numbers of South Koreans oppose the very existence of a separate and capitalist South Korea. Nevertheless, the South Korean experience does offer important lessons, both positive and negative, to those concerned with creating democratic and sustainable development.

Such lessons are always useful, but especially so now, with global trends being interpreted by many people to indicate that there are no workable alternatives to the free-market capitalist approach to development. Even many countries that once claimed to be building socialism, such as the former Soviet Union, Hungary, Czechoslovakia, and Poland, now publicly renounce their respective past national policies and commitments and race to embrace the logic of unregulated markets. Angola and Mozambique have also abandoned, at least temporarily, their respective attempts to create alternatives to capitalism, seeking instead to rebuild their economies through the introduction of various free-market, free-trade policies. Vietnam and China also appear to be moving toward greater accommodation with international capitalism.

There can be no denying that political and economic conditions have often been less than desirable for people living in these as well as the other countries that continue to identify themselves as socialist. There are several explanations for this. First, in contrast to the principles of socialism, governments in these countries created highly centralized political and economic structures, leading to the exclusion of most people from participation in decision-making. Second, rigid centralized planning structures also proved unable to produce desired products in sufficient quantity and quality. Finally, internally generated political and economic tensions were greatly intensified by external pressures, including actual or threatened military aggression as well as U.S organized trade and credit embargoes. In general, this combination of factors led to the political demobilization of large numbers of people, economic stagnation, and in a number of countries the outright rejection of the existing regime and its policies by the great majority of the population.

It is not so difficult to explain why people rejected those structures which they believed to be the cause of their difficulties. But it is not so easy to understand what led so many of these same people to support free-market, free-trade policies rather than the creation of new, more democratic and egalitarian forms of social organization. This growing embrace of unregulated capitalism in the countries mentioned above is puzzling for at least two main reasons. First, the great majority of third world countries, themselves organized by capitalism, suffer from even worse socioeconomic conditions. Second, the introduction of capitalism in the countries of Eastern Europe and the former Soviet Union has fallen far short of the promises made by its proponents. According to United Nations calculations, for example, the economies of Eastern Europe as a whole shrank by 11 percent in 1990, with Poland, Bulgaria, and the former East Germany each suffering declines of approximately 13 percent.

Capitalism's continuing ideological strength in the third world also needs explanation in light of the widespread depression conditions to be found there. Ironically, the crisis in the third world has done surprisingly little to delegitimize capitalism, while the crisis of existing socialism appears to have weakened the quest for alternatives to capitalism in the third world. According to the *Wall Street Journal*, for example:

> Over the past few years, South America has gone through economic and political revolutions as startling, though less publicized, as East-

ern Europe's . . . Capitalism is in vogue. Foreign companies are being welcomed. South American governments are selling state assets, cutting tariffs, curbing public spending and liberalizing economies as they seek to make up for the "lost decade" of the 1980s.[1]

What is most surprising, then, is that even though both capitalism and socialism have proven problematic, free-market, free-trade capitalism appears to be considered by most experts and many people to be the only viable and successful model of social organization. Other responses to the worldwide crisis were certainly possible, including wide-ranging debates over alternative forms of social organization and mass struggles for greater control over the institutions and structures that shape economic planning and production decisions. But, although anticapitalist sentiment remains significant in many countries throughout the world, progressive forces worldwide remain largely on the defensive.

Many explanations can be given for free-market capitalism's ideological triumph in the face of its failures in so many countries and on so many levels. One is that its success is largely due to the efforts of Western capitalist media systems which have the power to shape the terms of debate and thus people's understanding of winning and losing. A second is that the overwhelming economic power of the advanced capitalist countries has enabled them to demand ideological obedience from desperate third world and former socialist governments as a precondition for access to markets and credit. While both of these explanations are valid, I believe that a more complete understanding of capitalism's current ideological strength requires adding another explanation — one that returns us to the topic of this book: the only recently poor nations to have demonstrated the ability to generate *rapid* and *sustained* economic growth are those that are organized under the banner of capitalism, more specifically, the East Asian "newly industrializing countries" (NICs) of South Korea, Taiwan, Singapore, and Hong Kong.

For mainstream analysts, the success of these East Asian NICs is easy to explain: these countries have succeeded because they have organized their economies according to free-market, free-trade principles. Other countries have failed to grow and develop because their governments have pursued statist policies including restrictions on the international movement of goods and capital. Thus, with no existing socialist country apparently able to present itself as an attractive alternative, free-market capitalism appears to many to offer the only viable model for development. Staffan Burenstam makes this point most forcefully in his book, *The Pacific Century*:

> The Asian NICs are delivering a second shock to Marxism. Not only does it remain clear that, contrary to what Marx claimed, advanced capitalism can avoid disintegration; it has also been demonstrated that, contrary to the neo-Marxists' claim, newcomers can rise by means of capitalism. . . . The Marxist (and the socialist) methods have accordingly lost their attraction—even, it seems, among many of their own practitioners.[2]

In an interesting way, the debate over the causes of world economic difficulties, as structured by Western commentators, has come to identify state intervention with socialism. Thus, if free markets and free trade are shown to be "superior" to state intervention, we are supposed to conclude that capitalism is superior to socialism. There is obviously a strong element of truth to the identification of a strong role for public regulation of economic activity with socialism. But, as many on the left have noted in their critiques of existing models of socialist development, state planning and direction of production, finance, and trade do not, in and of themselves, define socialism; worker and community control over political and economic decision-making is also required. The problem, of course, is that it has not proven easy to create the kinds of institutions and structures necessary to promote and ensure such democratic participation in economic and political life.

Even though the market versus state debate is not the same as the debate mainstream analysts like to claim, it is not unrelated. If these analysts can use the experiences of the East Asian NICs to demonstrate that restrictions on market activity are counterproductive for raising standards of living, then support for alternative visions of society based on principles of worker and community empowerment will be difficult to encourage.

Obviously then, the East Asian NICs have considerable significance beyond their relative weight in the world economy. And, given their role in influencing people's understanding of social possibilities, it is very important that we have an accurate understanding of the nature of their political and economic experiences. At issue, then, is the accuracy of mainstream pronouncements on these East Asian NICs. This book, the result of my own investigation into the South Korean experience, stands as both a challenge to their conclusions as well as a reaffirmation of socialist possibilities.

The South Korean Experience
in Broad Brush Strokes

I chose to study South Korea rather than any of the other East Asian NICs for several reasons. First, while all the East Asian NICs have achieved rapid economic growth over the last three decades, South Korea has done far better than the others in establishing a diversified industrial base under national control. Second, because South Korea's industrialization was achieved while having to contend with the largest rural sector and international debt of the four, its experience appears to be the most relevant for other third world countries. I also picked South Korea because its geographic position on the "frontline" of the military face-off between capitalist and socialist forces gives developments there a special international political significance. Finally, I chose South Korea for study because I believe it to be the country which other countries most often seek to emulate. As such, it plays a leading role in the ideological struggle discussed above.

The starting point for my study was the question: how did South Korea achieve its rapid economic transformation? I began my work fully expecting to confirm the conventional wisdom that South Korea had achieved its success following traditional free-market, free-trade policies. It is no exaggeration to say I was shocked to discover how completely this conventional wisdom misrepresented the country's actual experience. It was, for me, a good lesson in the power of ideology.

I found that South Korea's economic growth and industrial transformation was largely the result of highly centralized and effective state planning and direction of economic activity. In fact, the state in South Korea had, from 1961 to 1979, as much control over credit allocation, investment, and trade decisions as did some Eastern European states, for example Hungary. Thus, South Korea's economic experience provides us with another excellent opportunity to investigate and learn more about the dynamics of state planning.

This discovery raised new questions for me: what enabled South Korean state planning to work so effectively when other planned economies had apparently collapsed? And, was South Korea's state-directed, export-led growth strategy generalizable to other countries?

My work led me to believe that South Korea's economic success was to a considerable extent the result of unique historical developments triggered primarily by Japanese and United States imperialism. For example, Japanese and then U.S. policies laid the groundwork for the emergence of a dominating state in South Korea. Thus, when a strong leader, Park Chung Hee, seized power in a 1961 military coup, he was able to quickly create new institutions which allowed him to successfully plan and direct economic activity. As part of this process, a small group of family-owned conglomerates, called chaebol, were promoted to mobilize the country's resources for the purpose of exporting manufactures to the advanced capitalist world, especially the United States.

South Korea was far luckier than most countries, however, in that Park's efforts at state planning and direction of private economic activity were not opposed by the U.S. and Japanese governments. In fact, although for different reasons, both supported South Korean growth with aid and credit as well as access to technology and markets. Without this international support, South Korea's economic strategy is unlikely to have succeeded.

This history casts strong doubt on the claim that South Korea's specific economic strategy can be adopted by other countries with similar economic results. Dominating states, for example, cannot easily be established given the existing power of private corporations in most countries. Moreover, few countries can expect to operate in an international economic environment similar to the one South Korea enjoyed during its period of rapid industrial transformation.

This line of inquiry led me to take up an even more basic question: leaving aside concerns of generalizability, is the South Korean experience an example of successful development? Most commentators appear to be unanimous in answering this question in the affirmative, citing the country's economic record and more recent political liberalization. But, by what criteria do we judge success? Certainly, South Korea's economic record is impressive. However, in studying the growth process that produced this record, I found a reality which strongly challenges the arguments of those who would promote the South Korean economic strategy as a desirable model for other countries to follow.

South Korea's economic experience from 1961 to 1979 is usually described as one long period of problem-free growth. In contrast, I found that the country's economic strategy produced a rapidly growing but unstable and unbalanced economy. More important, decisions made during the 1980s by the United States and Japanese to limit South Korea's access to markets and technology as well as the erosion of state control over chaebol activity, have begun to seriously undermine the effectiveness of South Korea's economic strategy. Rather than offering a model for other countries, it appears that South Korea's economic strategy has finally exhausted its potential.

Perhaps the most important factors calling the South Korean approach to development into question, however, are political: state power was based on military dictatorship, and growth was supported and maintained by policies requiring the suppression of most basic political, civil, and labor rights. Significantly, South Korean growth from 1961 to 1979 did not lead to greater political and social freedom for South Koreans, but quite the opposite. Growth was accompanied by intense exploitation, a cycle was created in which the workers' and farmers' strong resistance was answered with greater repression by the state in its attempt to maintain the conditions necessary for continued growth. This dynamic finally led, over the decade of the 1980s, to the formation of organized groups of workers, women, students, farmers, urban poor, and environmentalists not only opposing the South Korean model, but also capable of mounting effective opposition to the policies the government believed necessary to sustain it. In short then, without substantial change in the organization of the South Korean political economy, the country seems headed for a serious crisis.

The South Korean government has long argued the necessity of a dictatorship to raise the country out of poverty. Many Western experts have supported this notion, arguing that it was a trade-off supported by the population itself. I do not believe that this is true nor do I believe that effective planning and social regulation of economic activity requires a dictatorship. Of course, such a statement raises a new set of questions: what kinds of institutional arrangements will best promote mass participation in goal formulation and policy decision-making? What are the implications of various forms of participation for planning systems, strategies of growth, the organization of production, and relations with other countries?

The South Korean people may well provide answers to these questions. Here again, my investigation of the South Korean experience uncovered an unexpected reality. Mainstream analysts present South Korea as a society seeking to model itself on principles of Western capitalist democracy. The only admitted exceptions are described as a small group of radical students, who are often shown in newspaper photographs without accompanying stories, throwing bombs or fighting against riot police.

Actually, there is strong, widespread political activity opposed to the present system, and it is rooted in similar activity throughout this century. Many Korean industrial workers and peasants had become highly politicized during the period of Japanese occupation from 1910 to 1945. With the surrender of Japan at the end of World War II, these working people formed the nucleus of a well-developed popular movement which sought to create a new unified Korea based on socialist principles. The most significant base of support for the newly declared Korean People's Republic was an organization of workers who directly controlled and managed almost all the country's industrial enterprises. As Edwin Pauley, one of President Truman's closest advisors, reported after a tour of Korea, "Communism in Korea could get off to a better start than practically anywhere else in the world."[3]

This movement was crushed in southern Korea by U.S.-led repression in the period before the establishment of a separate, pro-capitalist South Korea; by a right-wing South Korean government before the Korean War; by joint efforts of the two governments during the Korean War; and by successive years of military dictatorship after the Korean War. Park Chung Hee who instituted the system of planning mentioned above, announced that anticommunism was the first priority of his government. He sought legitimacy for his military dictatorship by pursuing rapid economic growth.

In spite of South Korea's economic success, the government and its growth strategy continue to enjoy little support among most industrial workers, farmers, and students. In fact, the very dynamics of growth have slowly worked to rebuild a working-class-led opposition movement that is now beginning to reclaim its early radical history and vision. This vision is not tied to the creation of a liberal-reformed capitalism, but rather to a radically different, socialist-oriented political economy where political and economic power would be held by working people and expressed through new structures of planning and production.

This movement has yet to create a well-developed political formation to represent its interests or concretize its vision. But progress is evident in the coalitions of environmentalists, women, farmers, religious activists, students, urban poor, cultural groups, and workers pursuing this task. Careful study of this process offers an excellent opportunity to learn more about the dynamics of movement-building and structural transformation. Although not providing complete answers to all of the questions posed above, the study of South Korea has convinced me that capitalism's present dominant position is far from secure. The human costs associated with its own motion continue to generate resistance to it and interest in alternative approaches to development.

Part I of this study of South Korean capitalism begins with an examination of the role of the South Korean state in the country's rapid economic growth and industrial transformation. Chapter 1 sets the stage for this examination by briefly highlighting and comparing South Korea's post-1961 economic record with that of other third world countries, and then presenting and refuting free-market, free-trade explanations for the relative success of South Korea and other East Asian NICs.

Having established in general terms the important role active state intervention has played in economic growth, Chapter 2 begins a detailed examination of South Korean state activities by describing the specific structures and operational dynamics of South Korea's planning network. Chapter 3 examines policy implementation, focusing on how the South Korean state used its control over finance as well as nonfinancial public enterprises to direct domestic economic activity. Chapter 4 also considers policy implementation. It shows the way state regulation of international economic activity served as a necessary complement to domestic initiatives. These chapters make clear that South Korea's celebrated economic record owes considerably more to active state intervention than to free-market forces, thereby affirming the possibility of effective social regulation of economic activity.

Part II broadens the examination of South Korean capitalism to include the social forces that shaped South Korea's military dictatorship and state policies as well as the social, political, and economic consequences of the resulting growth. Chapters 5 and 6 provide the historical framework for this examination by highlighting how foreign interests, first Japanese and then United States, advanced a process leading to the intensification of class struggle, the division of Korea, and the establishment of a capitalist-oriented South Korea ruled by military dictatorship.

Chapter 7 then examines the considerable influence of Japan and the United States on the state structures and policies of South Korea's military dictatorship as well as the performance of the South Korean economy. These chapters reveal that South Korea's economic growth depended heavily on United States and Japanese actions as well as efficient national state planning, thereby making it highly unlikely that other countries could simply replicate the South Korean experience.

With this international perspective providing a framework, Chapters 8 and 9 analyze and evaluate the South Korean experience from 1961 to 1981. Developments examined include the consolidation of the Park regime and adoption of an export-led growth strategy, the resulting rapid industrialization and economic and social instabilities, the growing concentration of economic power and wealth by the chaebol, the intensification of dictatorship and political repression, and the renewal of political opposition. We see that the South Korean approach to development—by placing exports over domestic needs, profits over wages and working conditions, dependence on the United States and Japan over national independence, and thus by necessity the interests of the few over the rights of the many—demanded unacceptable sacrifices from the South Korean people. These two chapters present a strong challenge to those who would promote South Korea's industrial transformation as a "textbook case of successful development."

Part III highlights the unraveling of the South Korean growth strategy over the decade of the 1980s and the resulting economic disorder and political struggles. South Korea's economic success from 1961 to 1981 was largely due to the ability of the state to control the chaebol, international trade and investment activity, and the South Korean population. However, as a result of contradictions inherent in the South Korean growth process, economic and political forces have begun to seriously undermine state power in each of these spheres, thus imperiling the state's ability to sustain its chosen approach to development.

Chapter 10 highlights the way South Korea's economic success greatly accelerated trends whose effect was to weaken the position of the South Korean state in its relations with the chaebol and the United States and Japan. Similarly, Chapter 11 highlights how growth itself worked to strengthen mass movements, leading to their more effective opposition to oppressive state policies designed to maintain growth. These two chapters together demonstrate that, while mainstream analysts and government leaders may continue to praise the South Korean approach to development, the South Korean people face growing economic difficulties in addition to continuing political repression. Chapter 12 concludes the book by examining the rise of an increasingly powerful left movement, led by the working class, and its struggle to win majority support for the creation of a new political economy based on socialist principles of popular empowerment.

PART I:

THE STRUCTURE AND DYNAMICS OF SOUTH KOREAN STATE PLANNING

CHAPTER 1

ACKNOWLEDGING THE PRIMACY OF STATE INTERVENTION

South Korea's reputation for economic success is based on a record of sustained economic growth and industrialization which few countries can match. Making this record even more impressive (and South Korea an even more attractive model for other countries), is the fact that before the early 1960s South Korea was itself a poor country on the verge of becoming poorer. As a way of introducing the South Korean experience and providing background for the discussion to follow, I offer below a brief overview of South Korea's industrial transformation.

U.S. advisors to the newly established South Korean government began with high hopes for the country's future. Tony Michell, an economist who has worked as a consultant for the South Korean Economic Planning Board and has written about the country's economic rise for the International Labor Organization, describes early U.S. thinking as follows:

> From 1949 onwards the United States encouraged the idea that the Republic of Korea could become a model of capitalist development, it would be successful not only economically but also socially and would provide objective proof that capitalism is more effective than socialism.[1]

But by 1960 most U.S. policymakers were prepared to give up on South Korea, calling the country a "hopeless case."[2] South Korea was then still largely a rural and agriculturally based country. Only 24.4 percent of the population of 24.9 million lived in cities of over 50,000 people. Agriculture accounted for almost 40 percent of Gross Domestic Product (GDP) and employed approximately two-thirds of the work force. The population was also poor. Designated as a low income country by the World Bank, South Korea had a per capita income of $82 (in 1960 prices), approximately the same as estimates of the Japanese per capita income in 1868 (also in 1960 prices).[3] This per capita income placed South Korea below Ghana, Senegal, Liberia, Zambia, Honduras, Nicaragua, El Salvador, and Peru.[4]

South Korea's economic weakness at this time is probably best highlighted by the country's international trade position. Imports of goods and services equaled 13 percent of Gross National Product (GNP), while exports of goods and services were equal to only 3 percent of GNP. Moreover, reflecting South Korea's limited industrial base, almost 90 percent of exports were primary commodities: agricultural, forestry, and fishery products (56 percent) and fuels, minerals, and nonferrous metals (30 percent).[5]

The country's large trade deficit was covered and economic growth was sustained only because of massive U.S. aid which financed approximately 70 percent of South Korea's total imports between 1953 and 1962.[6] With the U.S. government determined to reduce its aid to South Korea, it is not surprising that most U.S. economists had a pessimistic view of South Korea's economic future. South Korea's situation had been even more discouraging when compared with developments in North Korea, which had, at that time, grown rapidly.

Beginning with Park Chung Hee's May 1961 military coup, however, South Korea's economic conditions began a dramatic turn around. Within twenty years, according to World Bank rankings, South Korea rose from a low-income country to the top third of all middle income countries. Its per capita income in 1980 had risen to a level three times the average of the above-mentioned four African countries and more than two times that of the four Latin American countries.[7]

The following tables, drawn from World Bank data, help illustrate the enormity of this economic achievement.[8] Table 1.1 shows South Korea's rapid growth in production. We can see that its rate of growth of production in all categories was significantly faster than the average rate of growth for all middle income oil importers. Table 1.2 shows the enormous impact this growth had on the industrial structure of the South Korean economy. In fact, by 1980 South Korea had

TABLE 1.1
Growth of Production
(by percent)

	Middle-income oil-importing economies	South Korea
GDP		
1960-70	5.8	8.6
1970-80	5.6	9.5
Agriculture		
1960-70	3.5	4.4
1970-80	2.8	3.2
Industry		
1960-70	7.8	17.2
1970-80	6.6	15.4
Manufacturing		
1960-70	7.5	17.6
1970-80	6.2	16.6
Services		
1960-70	5.7	8.9
1970-80	5.7	8.5

Source: *World Development Report*, 1982.

a structure of production close to that of the average for all middle-income oil-importing countries. Not surprisingly, such changes also affected the occupational status and geographic location of the great majority of South Korean citizens. Table 1.3 highlights the rapid employment shift out of agriculture and into industry. Table 1.4 shows the resulting urbanization of the population.

Exports of manufactures were the driving force behind South Korea's rapid industrial transformation. The country's export success is highlighted by the comparative figures presented in Table 1.5. The shift in the composition of trade to manufactures can be seen in Table 1.6. Finally, Tables 1.7 and 1.8 show that even though South Korea's economic performance slowed in the 1980s, it continued to exceed the average gains made by both middle- and upper-middle income countries in production and exporting.

By 1985, South Korea had, as shown in Table 1.9, achieved a

TABLE 1.2
Structure of Production:
Distribution of Gross Domestic Product (by percent)

	Middle-income oil-importing economies	South Korea
Agriculture		
1960	23	37
1980	15	16
Industry		
1960	32	20
1980	37	41
Manufacturing		
1960	23	14
1980	23	28
Services		
1960	45	43
1980	48	43

Source: World Development Report, 1982.

level of per capita GNP greater than that of the four larger non-East Asian "newly industrializing countries" (NICs) and considerably above that of the average for middle-income countries. In fact, South Korea's GNP in 1985 was larger than that of half the members of the Organization for Economic Cooperation and Development (OECD), the influential grouping of the twenty-four most advanced capitalist countries.[9]

While South Korea's overall level of development is still below that of most OECD member countries, its relative international standing in terms of GNP, industrial production, and trade volume is now widely recognized. As a result, the OECD is actively considering South Korea for membership. If the offer of membership is made, as many expect it to be, and accepted, South Korea would become the organization's first new member since 1973.[10]

The economic record presented above, although one-dimensional and one-sided, shows why so many analysts and government leaders consider South Korea to be a model of successful development. Equally significant, the great majority of these analysts and

TABLE 1.3
Structure of Employment:
Labor Force Distribution (by percent)

	Middle-income oil-importing economies	South Korea
Agriculture		
1960	59	66
1980	42	34
Industry		
1960	16	9
1980	22	29
Services		
1960	25	27
1980	36	37

Source: *World Development Report,* 1982.

TABLE 1.4
Urbanization

	Middle-income oil-importing economies	South Korea
Urban population as percent of total population		
1960	37	28
1980	50	55
Average annual growth rate		
1960-70	4.2	6.4
1970-80	3.8	4.7
Percentage of urban population in biggest city		
1960	28	35
1980	28	41
Percentage of urban population in cities of over 500,000		
1960	36	61
1980	48	77

Source: *World Development Report,* 1982.

leaders are convinced that South Korea's success is due to the government's faithful application of free-market, free-trade policies. Because this interpretation of the South Korean experience is almost universally accepted—and wrong—I conclude this chapter by presenting and then refuting conventional market-based explanations for South Korea's economic accomplishments.

The Conventional Wisdom: Market Power

Most economists attempt to explain South Korea's achievements by comparing the common economic policies and success of South Korea, Taiwan, Singapore, and Hong Kong with the common economic policies and difficulties of Brazil, Mexico, Argentina, and India. The four East Asian NICs are viewed as countries that have grown rapidly because they followed a strategy of export-led development based on free-market, free-trade policies. The non-East Asian NICs, on the other hand, are considered to have failed to develop because they adopted an inward-looking, import-substitution industrialization strategy, based on state regulation of domestic and international economic activity.

For example, after examining "why the economic fortunes of Latin America and Asia have diverged so dramatically," the *Far Eastern Economic Review* concluded that:

> there is now a near-universal realization by Latin Americans themselves that their problems were rooted in a tolerance of high inflation, their championing of import substitution rather than export-led growth [as in Asia], and the adoption of a large role for the state.[11]

Before critically examining this conventional wisdom, we consider an influential study, *Adjusting to Success: Balance of Payments Policy in the East Asian NICs*, by two well-known economists and international advisors, Bela Balassa and John Williamson. This study, which compares the performance and policies of the four above-mentioned East Asian NICs with those of the three Latin American NICs and India, finds that the East Asian NICs have far out-performed the other countries in both GNP and per capita GNP growth rates. Moreover this success was associated with extremely rapid export growth.

TABLE 1.5
Growth of Merchandise Trade:
Average Annual Growth Rate of Exports (by percent)

	Middle-income oil-importing economies	South Korea
1960-1970	7.1	34.1
1970-1980	4.1	23.0

Source: *World Development Report*, 1982.

TABLE 1.6
Structure of Merchandise Exports:
Percentage Share of Merchandise Exports

	Middle-income oil-importing economies	South Korea
Fuels, minerals, metals		
1960	14	30
1979	10	1
Other primary commodities		
1960	10	56
1979	20	10
Textiles and clothing		
1960	16	8
1979	8	31
Machinery and transport equipment		
1960	29	—
1979	29	20
Other manufacturers		
1960	31	6
1979	33	38

Source: *World Development Report*, 1982.

TABLE 1.7
Growth of Production:
Average Annual Growth Rate (percent)

	Middle-income economies		Upper-middle-income economies		South Korea	
	1965-80	1980-87	1965-80	1980-87	1965-80	1980-87
GDP	6.2	2.8	6.7	3.4	9.5	8.6
Agriculture	3.4	2.5	3.4	2.6	3.0	4.4
Industry	6.0	2.9	5.8	3.7	16.5	10.8
Manufacturing	8.1	3.0	9.2	4.1	18.7	10.6
Services	7.3	3.1	8.2	3.8	9.3	7.7

Source: *World Development Report*, 1989.

For example, the East Asian NICs' share of third world exports of manufactures rose from 23.8 percent in 1963, to 45.9 percent in 1973, and to 53.5 percent in 1984. Over the same period, Latin American NICs registered only a slight gain from 7.8 percent to 12.2 percent. India suffered the biggest single decline, with its share of exports falling from 19.5 percent in 1963 to less than 3 percent in 1984. South Korea's record perhaps best illustrates the export-led rise of the East Asian countries. In 1963, South Korea accounted for only 1.1 percent of all third world exports of manufactures, a level exceeded by all of the non-East Asian NICs. By 1984, however, South Korea had an export share of 18.1 percent, placing it far ahead of all those countries it had previously trailed, and second only to Taiwan which had an export share of 18.8 percent.[12]

What determined the economic success of the East Asian NICs and the failure of the others? According to Balassa and Williamson, it was differences in policy choices by the respective governments. In short, the former countries were practitioners of neoclassical thinking—reliance on free markets and free trade—while the latter were committed to statist policies. More specifically, the following policies are seen by the authors to have been critical in accounting for the differences in economic performance:

1. East Asian governments neither promoted or discriminated against export activity. "In contradistinction to most developing countries, including the large Latin American countries (with the

TABLE 1.8
Growth of Merchandise Trade:
Average Annual Growth Rate of Exports (by percent)

	Middle-income economies	Upper-middle-income economies	South Korea
1965-80	2.4	1.0	27.2
1980-87	5.5	5.6	14.3

Source: *World Development Report*, 1989.

TABLE 1.9
GNP Per Capita
(in current U.S. dollars)

	1980	1983	1985	1987	1989
Argentina	2390	2070	2130	2390	2160
Brazil	2050	1880	1640	2020	2540
India	24	260	270	300	340
Mexico	2090	2240	2080	1830	2010
Middle-income economies	1580	1310	1290	1810	2040
South Korea	1520	2010	2150	2690	4400

Source: *World Development Report*, various issues.

partial exception of Brazil) and India, the East Asian NICs have not discriminated against exports. Rather, on the average, they have provided similar incentives to sales in foreign and domestic markets."[13]

2. East Asian governments created a stable economic environment. "The stability of policies in the East Asian NICs meant that exporters could make plans for the future with confidence."[14]

3. East Asian governments limited their interference in economic activity. "More generally, the scope of administrative controls was much more limited in the four East Asian NICs than in Latin

America and, even more, India. In the latter case, there were pervasive controls on investment, prices, and imports, and decisions were generally made case by case, thereby creating uncertainty for business and opportunities for corruption, which has remained comparatively limited in East Asia."[15]

4. East Asian governments did not allow the creation of powerful trade unions or become involved in excessive labor market regulation. "In contrast, labor unions were powerful and labor markets extensively regulated in Latin America (rather less so in Brazil) and in India."[16]

5. East Asian governments refrained from overregulating capital markets. "Capital markets, too, were freer in the East Asian NICs than in Latin America and in India."[17]

6. Finally, East Asian governments followed conservative, antiinflationary fiscal policies. "Fiscal policy presents another contrast between East Asia and Latin America. Fiscal prudence has augmented domestic savings, has avoided a need to resort to the inflation tax, has contributed to the maintenance of moderate but positive real interest rates, and has dampened the sort of fears that helped fuel capital flight in Latin America."[18]

If one principle stands out in the above presentation of policy differences between countries, it is the role of the state. In East Asia, states are alleged to have confined their activities to creating an attractive and stable business environment for entrepreneurs. Supposedly free capital and labor markets gave these entrepreneurs the ability to respond to international market signals, thereby enabling each country to take advantage of its international comparative advantage and begin a process of sustained export-led industrialization. In the case of the less successful NICs, states are said to have attempted to shape and control economic activity to the detriment of their respective economies.

This belief that the economic record shows that success depends on the free workings of market forces as opposed to active state planning and economic intervention is held by the great majority of economists. For example, in a comparative study of Japan and the Asian NICs, E. K. Y. Chen argues that in all of them, "State intervention is largely absent. What the state has provided is simply a suitable environment for the entrepreneurs to perform their functions."[19]

The economic experience of the East Asian NICs is also advanced to discredit those who would support socialism over capitalism as the preferred engine of growth for the third world. Mainstream economists have mistakenly confused Marxist theories of imperialism with the position that third world economic problems can be completely explained by the degree to which a country is integrated into the global capitalist system. This position was at one time popular in many countries, especially in Latin America, where many intellectuals believed that sustained growth and industrialization was impossible as long as a country remained part of the international capitalist trading system.

On the ideological defensive for much of the 1960s and 1970s, mainstream economists now confidently argue that the historical record summarized above proves this anticapitalist position, and thus the Marxian critique of capitalism, to be false. The Latin American NICs and India (and to an even greater extent the former socialist countries of Eastern Europe) pursued development through active state policies designed to limit the role of domestic and international market forces. Their economies have performed poorly. The East Asian NICs pursued development by freeing up market forces to participate more effectively in the world capitalist system. Their economies have grown rapidly. End of argument.

The ideological importance of the East Asian success is real. Drawing strength from their economic record, free-market theorists are battering down all opposition. If free-market policies are at the heart of the East Asian success, then, according to these theorists, any country willing to embrace similar policies can also expect to enjoy success. As Donald Keesing, writing in a World Bank working paper, makes clear:

> application in new settings of the combination of what is now known and recommended—particularly in countries well along in the process of development—gives very encouraging results, even if it does not turn other countries into success stories on the same scale as Korea.[20]

There seems to be an amazing consensus concerning the reasons for economic success and failure. Yet, as we will see next, this received wisdom, which identifies economic success with free-market, free-trade policies and economic failure with active state economic intervention, seriously misrepresents reality. The following brief overviews of the role of the state in South Korea and Taiwan show that while both countries have export-driven economies, in neither country has the decision to focus on exports or the allocation of capital to sectors or firms primarily been market determined; economic activity in both countries has largely been planned and driven by a powerfully organized state apparatus.

In fact, based on the experiences of these two powerful East Asian NICs, it is more likely that the economic problems of Latin America and India are the result of insufficient or ineffective state regulation of capitalist activity rather than overly aggressive state intervention. This is an especially important conclusion in light of current developments in Eastern Europe and the countries of the former Soviet Union, where many policymakers advocate dismantling all state controls over credit allocation, trade, and investment in order to follow what they incorrectly believe to be the East Asian path to success.

The Challenge to Conventional Wisdom: An Overview of the State in the South Korean Economy

In South Korea, as in Taiwan, the state, rather than market forces, has played the central role in structuring the economy and shaping growth. As Alice H. Amsden effectively demonstrated in her book, *Asia's Next Giant: South Korea and Late Industrialization*, South Korea is a country "that grew very fast and yet violated the canons of conventional economic wisdom."[21] Amsden's important contribution to the literature on South Korean development was to show that the major post-1961 investment and resource allocation decisions that powered South Korea's industrial transformation were made by the state, not private entrepreneurs, and in response to state-formulated growth priorities, not profit-maximizing market signals. Furthermore, production itself was highly centralized as a result of state policy and organized by a few large family-owned conglomerates called chaebol.

Control over the country's financial system has been the single most important factor enabling the state to successfully direct the economy. One of Park Chung Hee's first acts after taking state power in 1961 was nationalization of all major commercial banks. Government planners were then able to use their control over both the allocation and cost of capital to direct firm activity into areas considered strategic for industrial development.

By the mid-1960s, the government decided upon exports as a priority activity for all firms. This emphasis was hardly a response to an individual firm's profit-maximizing behavior. As Byong-Nak Song, an economist with experience at both government planning agencies and research institutes, explains:

> Under the government export promotion strategy, "survival of the fittest" among competing firms was not determined in the marketplace, but through discretionary government actions. "Fitness" was judged in terms of the ability to expand exports, rather than based on profitability. If determined "unfit," firms were likely to face bankruptcy. Such firms were under constant threat of tax investigations and other punitive sanctions. On the other hand, firms that efficiently used their government-backed loans to expand exports were implicitly considered fit and favored with even further support.[22]

The government's commitment to exports did not, however, signify a commitment to free-trade principles. The state made regular use of a variety of techniques to control and limit imports. For example, all importers had to be licensed by the government, and permission to import was usually granted only under terms that specified type and quantity of product and often restricted the country of origin. Even goods listed as "automatically approved" for import were subject to a maze of special laws, regulations, and hidden taxes which the government used to restrict their entry. The effectiveness of these controls is highlighted by the fact that in 1990 less than 3 percent of South Korean imports could be classified as luxury goods.[23]

Equally important, government export promotion was undertaken as part of a comprehensive effort to promote national industrial development. While most international development experts routinely advise countries that they must choose between either an export-oriented or import-substitution-oriented development strategy, South Korea has used both strategies simultaneously. The government regularly targeted new areas for development by encouraging the establishment of domestic firms to replace imports. These new firms were protected by both trade restrictions and strict limits on foreign direct investment and, when judged capable, were required to export as well as meet domestic needs.

An excellent example of this development approach was the government's 1973 program to establish new heavy and chemical industries for both import-substituting and export-generating purposes. The government directed firms into these targeted areas with, among other things, subsidized capital. Subsidized loans grew from approximately 30 percent of total credit over the 1965-70 period, to over 43 percent over the 1971-75 period, to an estimated 80 percent of manufacturing loans in 1978.[24] The government's success is illustrated by the fact that these newly established industries not only reduced the country's dependence on key foreign imports, they also increased their share of total exports from approximately 13 percent in 1970 to nearly 60 percent by 1985.[25]

The government was also not hesitant about undertaking key investment activities itself, through public enterprises, as in the case of petroleum, chemicals, and iron and steel. As a result, investment in public enterprises rose from 19 percent of total investment in 1970 to over 33 percent in 1975.[26] That year, in fact, twelve of the sixteen biggest firms in the country were government owned.[27] And, in contrast to the claims of most mainstream economists, the government's activities regularly pushed its budget into deficit.[28]

The government did eventually decide, as part of its heavy chemical industrialization program, that production should be primarily carried out by private firms. The resulting market environment, however, has little in common with mainstream visions of free-market competition. As part of the decision to establish new capital intensive industries and launch new exports in areas such as automobiles, shipbuilding, and computers, the government selected a small group of chaebol to dominate production. Supported by government licensing and credit subsidies as well as foreign trade and investment restrictions, the combined sales of the top ten chaebol relative to GNP soared from approximately 15 percent in 1974 to over 67 percent by 1984.[29] By 1988, the combined revenues of the top four chaebol—Samsung, Hyundai, Lucky-Goldstar, and Daewoo—equaled approximately 47 percent of Korea's total GNP.[30]

Finally, the South Korean government supported the rapid

growth of the chaebol and exports through a highly interventionist labor policy. To create a low cost but productive labor force, workers were kept disorganized and on the defensive for most of the 1960s and 1970s by government control over the only legal labor federation; a maze of ever more restrictive labor laws; and increasingly violent intervention into labor disputes by the Korean Central Intelligence Agency and special labor police. Government efforts to contain growing labor militancy in the 1980s were expanded to include frequent mass arrests and several major military assaults against workers, twice involving tens of thousands of riot police in combined air, sea, and land operations.

In summary, South Korea's rapid export-driven growth is not the result of free-market, free-trade policies, but rather effective government intervention in all aspects of the economy, including market entry and exit decisions, the allocation and price of capital, international trade and investment decisions, and labor market conditions. As we will see next, the same is true about Taiwan.

The Challenge to Conventional Wisdom: An Overview of the State in the Taiwanese Economy

The general picture of state involvement in economic affairs in Taiwan is similar to what was described in South Korea. But Taiwan's specific experience differs from South Korea's largely because the Taiwanese government and ruling Kuomintang Party (KMT) were dominated by Chinese who fled the mainland in 1949 and not by those Taiwanese who were already living in Taiwan. Fearful of sharing economic power and thus undermining their own political power, the national Chinese ruling elite chose to emphasize direct state production rather than the promotion of Taiwanese-owned conglomerates.

As a result of this policy, state enterprises accounted for almost 57 percent of industrial production in the early 1950s. Although that percentage has steadily declined to its present value of 20 percent, state production still dominates the country's strategic industries, including petroleum, steel, railways, electric power, shipbuilding, and telecommunications. A true picture of the state-party hold on the economy, however, also requires including the economic contribution of some fifty important companies owned in one form or another by the KMT itself. Combined state and party assets have been estimated as being equal to approximately half of the country's total corporate assets.[31]

The government also controls the financial sector through its ownership of almost all the country's banks. According to Robert Wade, an expert on the Taiwanese economy, "even as late as 1979 the four private banks had only 5 percent of the deposits and branches of the commercial banks as a whole and the biggest of the private banks was only nominally private."[32] Operating through this state-controlled system, the Central Bank of China has been able to direct the greatest share of funds to the large state and party-owned enterprises; state enterprises alone received some thirty percent of all bank loans in 1983.[33]

The government has used its enormous economic power to aggressively transform the country's industrial structure. Activity in the 1950s was organized around state and mainland import-substitution activity protected by closed markets, subsidized credit, and sectorial allocation of foreign exchange. Industries developed during this period ranged from textiles and apparel to cement and fertilizer. When the Taiwanese government began promoting exports in the early 1960s, it continued, much in the same way as South Korea, to advance a complementary import-substitution program. For example, it continued its promotion of petrochemicals and directed the establishment of basic metals production, aluminum production, shipbuilding, automobile production, and nuclear power.

In the 1970s, the government launched a second import-substitution drive to create the infrastructure necessary to support new, more technologically advanced firms. The ten major projects included new state-owned shipyards, petrochemical facilities, and an integrated cold-rolling iron and steel mill. The government also increased its support for production of precision engineering products, electrical and nonelectrical machinery, and metal manufacturing. State initiatives for the 1980s included modernization of telecommunications, upgrading of textile, auto, and computer production, and semiconductor development.

Exports have, of course, played a leading role in spurring Taiwan's growth. They were encouraged by the government in two different ways. By deliberately denying the great majority of small-and medium-sized Taiwanese businesses access to credit or the domestic market, the government left these businesses with no choice but to export. At the same time, the government actively used tax, labor, and credit policies to attract export-oriented foreign multinational corporations. In fact, the Taiwanese government often combined these two approaches by actively encouraging the creation of OEM ("original equipment manufacturer") arrangements which had Taiwanese firms producing products to be marketed by foreign buyers such as K Mart, Sears, IBM, and General Electric.

As with South Korea, however, support for exports did not mean that the Taiwanese government operated on the basis of free-trade principles. Only exporters have enjoyed a relatively open trade regime, normally being allowed to import the equipment and materials they need at world market prices. More generally, the government has used an extensive system of trade management to control imports.

All imports are classified into three groups: prohibited, controlled, and permissible. The controlled list includes luxury goods, goods subject to government monopoly procurement, and goods considered important to national security. Such goods cannot be imported without prior government approval and licensing. Goods not labeled prohibited or controlled are considered permissible and, theoretically at least, automatically eligible for an import license. However, even permissible goods can be restricted, often on the basis of both country of origin and importing agency. One mid-1970s study found the following goods listed as permissible but restricted in their import because of origin restrictions: yarns, artificial fibers, fabrics, some manufactured foodstuffs, chemicals, toilet preparations, machinery, and electrical apparatus. These were, of course, all products currently being produced in Taiwan.[34]

Even permissible goods that meet origin and agency restrictions can be restricted. All import requests must be referred to the Industrial Development Bureau which operates a hidden list system based on government priorities for national industrial development. If the import in question is considered likely to undermine national industrial policy, the government can simply refuse to grant a license. Domestic producers of petrochemicals, chemicals, steel, and certain machinery and components have all been protected in this way. Imports in these areas are allowed only if the government is assured that domestic firms cannot deliver the product within reasonable specifications of quality and price. If such a situation is found to exist, the government will also normally take action to upgrade domestic production.[35]

Finally, the government has also actively intervened in the labor market. To ensure that all firms, but especially foreign multinational exporters, have access to low-cost labor, the state enforced a highly restrictive labor code which denied the right to unionize to almost 80 percent of the work force; established and tightly controlled the only legal labor federation; and, governing under conditions of martial law until 1987, outlawed all strikes.

As in the case of South Korea, the Taiwanese experience described above is hard to reconcile with mainstream pronouncements that growth was the result of the operation of free labor and capital markets, free trade, and minimal government intervention into economic affairs.

First Lessons

Both South Korea and Taiwan are market economies in the sense that most production is organized by private producers in pursuit of individual profits. But, in both countries, control over credit, market entry, trade, and key industrial inputs like steel, give the state sufficient leverage to dictate policy to private capital. In other words, state policy and production shaped the structure and dynamic within which market activity occurred.

The role of the state in the Latin American NICs has been quite different. For example: while governments did place controls on imports, these controls were usually designed to localize production in response to existing market demand, not initiate or advance a plan of economic restructuring. One result was the rapid growth of a luxury consumption-goods industry rather than the establishment of an integrated industrial base.

Similarly, by not controlling or directing investment decisions and capital markets, Latin American governments allowed firms producing in protected markets to use their high profits for speculative rather than productive activities. Moreover, even when Latin

American governments did decide to promote exports, incentives to targeted industries were rarely combined with national industrial policies designed to create complementary centers of domestic production and technology. Export producers were, as a result, usually forced into dependence upon foreign multinational corporations, thereby greatly reducing their ability to further the industrial development of the country.

In short, Latin American states, as opposed to South Korea and Taiwan, have shown far less concern over who produces what products and whether speculative activity dominates industrial activity. Thus, in a reversal of the conventional wisdom presented earlier, I find it far more likely that the superior economic performance of South Korea and Taiwan relative to that of the Latin American NICs reflects their more extensive use of state regulation of trade, investment, and credit, rather than their reliance on free-market forces.[36] In making this argument, I do not mean to claim, however, that development is simply a matter of strengthening the economic powers of the state or that South Korea and Taiwan should be taken as models to be emulated by other countries. For one thing, strong states are not created by simple policy initiatives. The strength of the state in both South Korea and Taiwan, for example, is the result of specific and complex historical forces. And, on the negative side, such forces led to states made strong through military dictatorship and political repression. Moreover, both South Korea and Taiwan now face serious internal and external problems which threaten to undermine their future growth.[37]

It seems reasonable to conclude at this point that development is at least compatible with, if not contingent upon, strong social regulation of economic activity. What must be better understood are the dynamics that shape the national and international social relations which give rise to and help structure that regulation. Hopefully, the following examination of the South Korean experience will give us greater insight into that process and thus ways we can influence it for the better.

CHAPTER 2

THE STRUCTURE AND FUNCTION OF STATE PLANNING

Having discussed the pattern of state intervention in both South Korea and Taiwan, I now move beyond generalities to highlight the organization and operation of the South Korean state planning network created by Park Chung Hee after his 1961 military coup. To provide a context for this presentation, I begin with a brief historical overview of South Korea's pre-1961 experience with economic planning.

The Historical Roots of
South Korean State Planning

South Korea, officially known as the Republic of Korea, was formally established on August 15, 1948, with Syngman Rhee as the country's first president. Because the division of Korea and creation of a separate nation in the south was largely the result of U.S. efforts and achieved over the objections of the great majority of Koreans, Rhee's government enjoyed little popular support but considerable U.S. backing.[1]

The U.S. government signed its first aid agreement with the South Korean government in December 1948, but it was only after the Korean War that U.S. aid contributions became sizeable. From 1953 to 1962, for example, U.S. aid totaled approximately 75 percent of South Korea's fixed capital investment and 8 percent of its GNP.[2] Rhee and the United States had, however, serious disagreements over what constituted appropriate economic policy and thus how the aid should be used.

The United States, anxious to keep its aid burden to a minimum, supported a program of economic stabilization built around higher taxes, reduced government spending, especially on defense, and a lower exchange rate to stimulate exports of basic primary commodities. Rhee, in contrast, viewed such a program as political suicide. Responding to his own political interests, Rhee preferred an expansionary fiscal policy—with U.S. aid covering the budget deficit—since such spending allowed him to stimulate growth and create an attractive business climate for friends. This policy, coupled with an overvalued exchange rate and low interest rates, encouraged more U.S. aid, thereby giving Rhee greater ability to reward his friends.

For example, favored textile and flour producers were granted access to imported commodities such as cotton or wheat almost duty free, enabling them to make super profits on the domestic sale of their products. Other loyal businessmen were rewarded with access to scarce dollars, enabling them to make quick profits through the importation and then resale of products, such as fertilizer, which were in short supply on the domestic market. Still other businessmen benefited from loans at subsidized interest rates, special tax exemptions, or preferential contracts for large-scale government projects.[3]

Not surprisingly, early U.S. attempts to prod the South Korean government into constructing detailed economic plans that could then be monitored met with little success. As economists David Cole and Young Woo Nam explain:

> [Rhee and his followers] rejected the idea of overall planning and were not interested in trying to define the longer-run objectives or an integrated set of policies. This probably reflected a belief on their part that they could retain more flexibility and achieve better results in negotiations with donors by proceeding on an ad hoc basis. . . . To have agreed to [an economic plan] would have exposed the government to serious political risks.[4]

South Korea's dependence on U.S. aid was too great, however, and U.S. advisors finally succeeded in forcing Rhee to introduce an anti-inflation stabilization plan beginning in 1956. Internal and external pressures also forced Rhee to accept the creation of a new planning-oriented ministry, the Ministry of Reconstruction (MOR). The MOR was formed in 1955, initially working with U.S. aid advisors to develop and implement the annual stabilization plans demanded by the U.S. government.

In 1958, the Economic Development Council was created by the MOR and given responsibility for developing a long-term economic plan for South Korea. A Three Year Economic Plan was, in fact, drafted and presented for government consideration in April 1959. Although the plan was never implemented, the process itself proved to be significant: economists were trained in the art of planning; statistical gathering procedures were improved; and various ministries gained practice in working together.[5]

The plan was never implemented because not long after its adoption by the cabinet, Rhee's government collapsed. The U.S.-mandated stabilization plans, coupled with aid cuts, triggered a serious slowdown in investment and growth beginning in 1958. Rhee was finally driven from office by a student-led movement unhappy with the economic situation and outraged by his corruption and manipulation of the results of the 1960 election.

Syngman Rhee's replacement, Chang Myon, proved much more agreeable to United States policy dictates, but too weak to provide the leadership necessary to stabilize either the country's economic or political situation. Significantly, however, the planning process was begun once again. The MOR was instructed by the new government to continue its past efforts and draft a five-year plan to guide the economy. More important than the plan that emerged was the general agreement of those involved that successful planning required the creation of a new super-planning ministry which would combine planning responsibilities with control over the budget and foreign capital flows. As we will see later, this proposal was eventually adopted by the military government of Park Chung Hee in the form of the Economic Planning Board.[6]

Before Chang Myon had the opportunity to act on the plan or planning recommendations of his MOR, his regime was overthrown by a military coup. During the ten months that he was in power, approximately 2,000 street demonstrations took place, involving about 1 million people.[7] Demands for direct negotiations with the North for reunification of the country reflected continuing popular rejection of the U.S.-initiated project of a separate, pro-capitalist South Korea. The South Korean military, having just fought a war to maintain the separation of North and South Korea, obviously feared the direction that the political events were leading. And when North Korean students accepted an offer by South Korean students to hold talks with the aim of increasing ties between the two countries, military leaders made plans for a takeover. On May 16, 1961, four days before the meeting and two days after a large rally in Seoul calling upon the South Korean government to endorse the talks, a small group of army officers, led by Park Chung Hee, carried out a *coup d'état*.

Active in army intelligence, Park knew that North Korea, with its interventionist state, was growing far more rapidly than South Korea and that without strong action to halt the economic slide and increasing opposition to the country's political economy, reunification of the peninsula might well occur—and on terms favorable to socialism and the North. Determined not to let this happen, Park moved quickly to establish control over political events by dissolving the National Assembly and all political parties; outlawing all demonstrations; abolishing existing trade unions; taking control of the press; passing new anticommunist laws that broadened the power of the state to arrest opponents; and creating the Korean Central Intelligence Agency (KCIA) to monitor and, when necessary, directly influence political developments.

Simultaneously, he also took action to gain control over the economy, including the creation of powerful new ministries as well as business and trading associations.[8] As the previous brief discussion of economic planning shows, Park's success in creating, almost overnight, the institutions and structures necessary for planning had much to do with developments that predated his takeover. Perhaps most important, these developments enabled Park to draw upon the practical knowledge and ideas of an existing group of economists who were already experienced with and committed to planning. The focus of the rest of this chapter will be on the actual organization and logic of the South Korean state planning apparatus.

The Planning Network: State Bodies

Park Chung Hee relied heavily upon five key state planning bodies to direct economic activity: the Economic Planning Board, the president's Economic Secretariat; the Ministry of Trade and Industry; the Ministry of Finance; and the Ministry of Construction. I will briefly consider each in turn, in order of their overall importance in the planning process.

Economic Planning Board

The Economic Planning Board (EPB) has been South Korea's most important planning body. *Business Korea*, a leading South Korean business publication, recently described it as follows:

> The EPB, which celebrated its thirtieth anniversary late last month, has no match in capitalistic nations in terms of its power and influence over the economy. Some compare it with the Japanese Economic Planning Ministry, but the role of its Japanese counterpart is much smaller than that of the EPB. The only possible comparison to the EPB may be central planning agencies in socialist nations.[9]

Created in July 1961 by joining together the Ministry of Reconstruction, the Bureau of the Budget, and the Bureau of Statistics, the EPB was given not only the responsibility to direct planning but also, by virtue of the fact that it controlled the national budget and thus government spending priorities, the ability to implement its plans.

To strengthen its planning and implementation powers, the EPB was also given the power to regulate foreign borrowing through its control over the issuance of mandatory government repayment guarantees as well as direct investment through its control over an investment screening process. The EPB was also granted the authority to regulate the prices of a number of domestically produced goods and services deemed essential by the government.

The EPB's power to shape and implement its plans was further strengthened by the fact that its chief minister also served as chair of the Council of Economic Ministers. Control of the Council of Economic Ministers by the EPB, where overall planning activities take place, was enhanced by its power to reduce the funding levels of any ministry that refused to comply with its program of action. In 1963, after the institution of civilian government, the head of the EPB was also given the title of deputy prime minister.

The President's Economic Secretariat

After his election as president in 1963, Park created his own special planning agency, the president's Economic Secretariat. Over time, with the President's support, the head of the Economic Secretariat came to exercise considerable influence over economic decision-making. In fact, beginning in the early 1970s, the economic secretary's influence on policy often rivaled that of the head of the EPB.[10] The president's Economic Secretariat ensured that the president himself was able to monitor and directly exert, if necessary, control over the planning process. We will see its importance later, especially when discussing the development and implementation of the 1973 heavy and chemical industry plan.

During the first half of the 1980s, under President Chun Doo Hwan's rule, the influence of this office on policy was greatly expanded once again. Reflecting this trend, President Roh Tae Woo recently upgraded the position of chief presidential aide for economic affairs (formerly the economic secretary) from the level of vice minister to that of minister. Similarly, a number of new committees such as the Social Infrastructure Investment Planning Task Force and the High-Speed Railway Task Force, which at one time would have come under the jurisdiction of the EPB, were placed under the direct control of the chief presidential aide.[11]

Ministry of Trade and Industry

Next in importance in the planning process was the Ministry of Trade and Industry (MTI). The MTI was responsible for export promotion and import controls, industry development plans and investment applications, project and firm designation, and trade licensing. Given the importance of foreign trade and manufacturing, this ministry was absolutely crucial to the successful implementation and direction of South Korea's economic policy. Over time, while some of MTI's responsibilities were given to new ministries such as the Ministry of Energy and Resources, its overall power has grown in significance because of its control over a number of quasi-governmental organizations dealing with trade and industry (to be discussed below).

Ministry of Finance

The Ministry of Finance also played a major role in South Korea's planning and policy implementation. Most important, it was responsible for regulating and supervising all domestic and foreign financial institutions. It also administered the foreign exchange plan and controlled tax as well as tariff assessment and collection. The ministry's importance increased in 1981 when it replaced the EPB as the ministry in charge of regulating foreign loans and investment.

Ministry of Construction

The Ministry of Construction was responsible for national material planning and the construction of all industrial estates, cities, highways, and ports. Because the government promoted the country's rapid industrial development through an aggressive program of infrastructure expansion, this ministry also played a significant role in directing the country's economic growth.

The Planning Network: Quasi-State Organizations

The actual size of the central bureaucracy, about 12,000 in the mid-1970s, remained rather small and stable, despite the enormous industrial transformation of the economy from 1967 to 1979.[12] The planning structure did grow, however, largely through the creation and use of a number of quasi-governmental organizations under the authority of one or more of the ministries highlighted above, usually the MTI. In fact, the growing significance of these organizations has greatly expanded the power of the MTI relative to other ministries, including the EPB.

These quasi-state organizations appear to give the government substantial control over the economy while ensuring that policy planning remains flexible and realistic. For example, they provide the state with a means of monitoring business activity and ensuring compliance with its policies. To illustrate their role in the South

Korean economy and planning process, I will highlight three of the most important: producer associations, the Korea Trade Promotion Corporation (KOTRA), and the Korea Foreign Traders' Association (KFTA).

Producer Associations

As part of Park's 1961 economic reorganization, the government required all incorporated businesses to join one of sixty-two business associations. These associations continue to function as intermediaries between the MTI and individual businesses and help ensure a steady flow of information between government and business.

When the government became interested in highlighting strategic industries in the late 1960s, it ordered relevant associations to join together to form new, more inclusive organizations. For example, the Korean Federation of Textile Industries (KOFOTI) was formed in 1967, uniting all textile-related producer associations. Similarly, the Korea Society for the Advancement of the Machine Industry (KOSAMI) was established in 1968 to cover the machinery industry.

Producer associations have been used by the government for three main purposes. First, the MTI has used them for purposes of industrial licensing. As Alice H. Amsden notes, "In the 1960s and 1970s, the government became the premier entrepreneur by using its industrial licensing policies to determine what, when, and how much to produce in milestone investment decisions."[13] By controlling entry into these associations, the MTI was able to monitor and regulate business activity.

Second, the EPB has used these associations to negotiate annual price controls on selected goods and services. The government can easily set prices in industries such as railways, transportation, electricity, coal, oil refining, and chemical fertilizers, where production is dominated by state-owned firms. However, through these associations, the EPB also has the power to negotiate, on an annual basis, ceiling prices for many privately produced goods. Producers affected by government-mandated price requirements are required to report price increases to the EPB and other relevant authorities within three days of a price increase. If the rise is deemed excessive, the government can use a number of different possible laws (Price

Stability Law, Monopoly Regulation and Fair Trade Law) and force a rollback as well as punish the offenders.[14] Since 1976 the annual number of items under price control has ranged from forty-six to 193.[15] Some of the 110 commodities whose prices were still being controlled in 1986 were flour, sugar, coffee, electricity, gas, steel, chemicals, synthetic fibers, paper, drugs, nylon stockings, automobiles, and televisions.[16]

Finally, as noted above, the government has also used these associations to promote the growth of industries deemed strategic for the country's development. For example, the government used the Korea Society for the Advancement of the Machine Industry (KOSAMI) to provide "maximum administrative and financial support" for the manufacture of certain machinery items intended to replace imports. KOSAMI was given a fund to support investment in targeted areas of the machinery industry and low-cost loans for buyers of locally produced machinery. In 1982, this organization included nineteen different associations of manufacturers formed under the 1961 legislation. Although supposedly a private "nonprofit" organization, KOSAMI's staff size and selection is controlled by the MTI, and it has been audited by the Board of Audit and Inspection whose area of responsibility includes only state agencies.[17]

Korea Trade Promotion Corporation

The Korea Trade Promotion Corporation (KOTRA), established in 1962 as a nonprofit organization, played an important role in the government's early export efforts. KOTRA functioned as the MTI's overseas representative, and its officials traveled around the world looking for markets for existing products as well as investigating possibilities for the profitable development of new products.

KOTRA currently maintains over eighty-five Korean trade centers throughout the world. Using this network, it serves the government by monitoring all tariff and non-tariff barriers on goods from South Korea on a month-by-month basis and advising those businesses that might be affected by these barriers. Finally, it advises the MTI on possible overseas ramifications resulting from any modifications in South Korean trade policy.

The organization's role in export promotion diminished in the mid-1970s, however, when the chaebol established their own general trading corporations and worldwide network of trading centers. KOTRA now concentrates its efforts on supporting government initiatives, such as establishing direct trade relations with socialist countries, aiding the export efforts of small- and medium-size enterprises, and assisting foreign businesses wishing to import South Korean products.

Korea Foreign Traders' Association

The Korea Foreign Traders' Association (KFTA) was founded in 1946 with over one hundred companies as a purely private organization.[18] While still officially considered a private "non-profit" organization, it has functioned since 1961 as part of the government's planning network. As Tony Michell describes:

> The head is vetted by MTI and during the 1981-82 drive to cut the number of civil servants, the quota cuts for MTI and related agencies included some ordered in (KFTA). Its budget amounts to 100 million dollars per annum, and is described by one very senior government official as "all government money anyway"; it is often spent at the discretion of the central administration.[19]

In 1966, KFTA assumed control over the Korea Commercial Arbitration Board, which deals with disputes arising from international trade. It was reorganized and strengthened again in 1969 and given the right to levy a tax based on the value of imports into the country. The money from this tax allows the organization to engage in a number of activities of use to member firms, including trade and insurance assistance, as well as sponsoring South Korean participation in various bilateral economic councils, such as the Korea-Japan Economic Committee.

KFTA's most important role, however, is its use by the government to control trade activity of individual businesses. For example, all importers and exporters must be licensed, and only KFTA is empowered to grant such trade licenses. KFTA thus determines, in response to MTI policy, which firms will be allowed to engage in international activity, in what products, and with what countries. It also is responsible for monitoring an individual firm's compliance with existing government regulations concerning trade.

Discipline in Planning

While the ministries and quasi-state organizations described above formed the basic structure of South Korea's planning network, it was military discipline that ensured that they would function as a coherent whole in response to state directives. This discipline was imposed in a number of ways. For example, military leaders instituted a system of weekly meetings where top economic planners were required to brief them on the state of the economy. They also introduced "planning and control offices" in every major ministry. Each individual "office" was required to make quarterly reports on the status of the planning process in its assigned ministry to the nationally centralized Office of Planning Coordination, which in turn reported its findings directly to the prime minister and through him to the president. The military also introduced a series of reforms which, by centralizing the recruitment and placement of administrative personnel, gave them greater oversight and control over the entire state bureaucracy.[20]

Park, in fact, took full advantage of military discipline and relationships to establish his own chain of command which operated from the highest level of the bureaucracy down to the shop floor. As George Ogle, a keen observer of South Korean politics, explains:

> To make sure that commands were heard and obeyed the whole way down to the plant floor, Park had military comrades appointed as president or vice president of companies, as members of the boards of directors, as heads of the personnel department and to other key positions. To complement the military presence in industry, about 38 percent of non-economic jobs in government also went to military appointees. This permitted Park a direct and personal supervision of the entire industrial and political complex.[21]

Finally, as a direct check on the independence of the economic bureaucracy, Park established the Board of Audit and Inspection in 1963. This agency reports directly to the president and is free to "descend on any government or quasi-government organization without warning and conduct a detailed inquiry into financial and other activities; 51,468 corrupt officials (or 10 percent of all government employees) were punished for irregularities in 1976."[22]

As we have seen, the South Korean planning system offered the state the means to both generate plans as well as monitor business compliance. In the following two chapters I will show how it was used by the Park regime, along with other policy instruments, to direct the country's rapid growth and industrial transformation.

CHAPTER 3

POLICY IMPLEMENTATION: STATE DIRECTION OF NATIONAL ECONOMIC ACTIVITY

While most economists recognize the existence of the planning structure described in the previous chapter, almost all discount its significance in terms of actual state direction of economic activity. For example, Paul Kuznets, an economist and East Asian specialist, has written:

> The coincidence of rapid growth and economic planning, and the primacy of the Economic Planning Board in the circle of economic ministries have led some observers to misconstrue the function of planning and overemphasize the role of government in the Korean economy. Planning does not entail government control of resource allocation, but rather involves a set of activities designed to sustain rather than to repress market functions. The government acts by providing information, reducing risks, and altering incentives rather than by fiat or by assuming market or enterprise functions.[1]

This statement seriously misrepresents the purpose and practice of planning in South Korea. As we will see, planning was undertaken to guide ongoing state efforts to diversify and strengthen the country's industrial base to achieve maximum rates of economic growth. In this chapter, we will examine how the government used its control over finance as well as state production to move economic activity along lines specified by its plan, often assuming both market and enterprise functions in the process.

State Control over Finance

State direction of credit has been the government's most powerful instrument of industrial policy. According to Leroy P. Jones and Il Sakong, who authored a landmark study on the government-business relationship in South Korea: "Government control of the banks is . . . the single most important economic factor explaining the distinctly subordinate position of the private sector."[2]

Although banks in South Korea were privately owned at the time of the 1961 military coup, they did not remain so for long. One month after the coup, the government arrested fifty-one business leaders on charges that they were "illicit fortune accumulators" and threatened to confiscate their assets. Soon after, however, a deal was struck. In exchange for paying sizable fines, the government agreed to exempt the businessmen from prosecution and returned all of their assets, with one major exception—their commercial bank shares.[3]

As a result, from 1961 until 1981, when a managed program of financial privatization was begun, the South Korean government enjoyed total control over the country's financial system, primarily through its ownership of all five nationwide commercial banks, all six special banks, and two of the country's three major nonbank financial development institutions. The Ministry of Finance was thus able to set interest rates, credit ceilings, and loan priorities as well as make budget, salary, and hiring-and-firing decisions at each individual bank.[4]

Also, recognizing that its control over the price and allocation of credit could be undermined by international capital flows, the government moved quickly to control private access to foreign capital: it amended the Foreign Capital Inducement Law in 1962 to require that all foreign loans be approved and guaranteed by the government. While this measure responded to foreign demands for insurance against possible default, it also gave the government, through the Economic Planning Board, the ability to decide which enterprises would have access to foreign capital. The government also took steps to control the outflow of money as well. Legislation was passed which made any illegal transfer overseas of $1 million or more punishable with a minimum sentence of ten years imprisonment and a maximum sentence of death.

Finance and Economic Restructuring

Credit has been a powerful lever shaping industrial activity in South Korea because of the government's aggressive and focused lending policies. During the formative stages of the country's industrial growth, for example, the government used an expansive credit policy to facilitate a rapid increase in export activity. As a result, debt-equity ratios of manufacturing firms rose rapidly from 1.2 in 1966 to 3.9 in 1971.[5] Firms were encouraged to borrow to expand their operations in two ways. By guaranteeing a stable source of funding for firms undertaking targeted activities, the government was able to greatly reduce the risk associated with new ventures. By subsidizing the price of credit, the government was able to significantly reduce the cost of investment and thus increase the expected rate of return for the targeted activity.

Looking at cost of capital, Jones and Sakong point out that:

> Throughout the post-war period, interest rates on domestic loans have been regulated, generally at levels well below their equilibrium values . . . The general picture . . . shows that: first, the general bank rate has typically been half of the [unregulated] curb market rate; and second, the real bank rate has often been negative and generally below even the most conservative estimates of the opportunity cost of capital. The result has been excess demand followed by the necessity of non-price rationing devices.[6]

When the United States and the IMF pressured the South Korean government to accept a stabilization program in 1965 which included a doubling of domestic interest rates, the government responded by increasing the inflow of foreign funds to selected firms. With the cost of foreign borrowing far lower than the domestic cost of funds, in fact negative in real terms, the government was able to ensure, at the cost of a rapid growth in foreign debt, that favored firms and activities would continue to receive access to credit at preferential prices.[7] Interest rate differentials for the period from 1966 to 1970 highlight the significance government credit allocation decisions had for a firm's decision-making and profitability: annual average domestic bank-lending rates were 24.4 percent; annual average unregulated curb market rates were 54.2 percent; and annual average foreign interest rates were 6.4 percent. The interest rate differential between domestic and foreign bank lending rates was 12.9 percent, even after adjusting for exchange rate movements.[8]

Not surprisingly, the government used its monopoly over finance to shape overall business activity along lines specified by its plan. There was no middle ground: firms willing to operate within the logic of the government's plan could look forward to significant financial support. Those who refused were left with no choice but to seek funds in the very expensive curb market.

By the mid-1960s, the government had declared exporting and certain import-substitution activities that were seen as export-supporting to be priority activities. And, as the South Korean economist Byung-Nak Song describes:

> The export targets agreed upon between the government and individual firms were taken by businessmen as equivalent to compulsory orders. Firms which failed to achieve their export targets without a plausible excuse ran the risk of heavy administrative sanctions from the government. During the 1960s, the export promotion strategy was dominated by the government, which was the primary decision-maker in "Korea, Inc."[9]

In response to government initiatives, exports became increasingly central to all economic activity. For example, manufactured goods produced for export rose from 8 percent of final demand in 1963, to 22 percent in 1966, and to 40.1 percent in 1973. Employment in the production of manufactures for export rose from 6.4 percent of total manufacturing employment in 1963, to 16.5 percent in 1966, and to 34.5 percent in 1973.[10] From 1965 to 1975, the ratio of exports to GNP more than tripled and manufacturing's contribution to GNP more than doubled.[11]

The resulting industrial transformation of the South Korean economy is perhaps best illustrated by the changing composition of South Korean exports. The top six exports in order of dollar value in 1961 were basic ores, iron ore, fish, raw silk, vegetables, and swine. In 1971 they were clothing, plywood, other manufactures including wigs and toys, electrical machinery, raw silk, and basic ores. In 1976, they were clothing, footwear, fabrics, electrical machinery, plywood, and telecommunications equipment.[12]

However, even while sales of basic labor-intensive manufactures—such as textiles and clothing, electronic parts and components, and footwear—continued to drive South Korea's export-led economy well into the 1970s, state officials began planning early in the decade for yet another major restructuring of the economy. In spite of the country's export success, South Korea was still running a trade deficit. Moreover, other third world producers with even lower wage costs were also beginning to export basic labor-intensive manufactures in competition with South Korean firms. The government's response was its 1973 Heavy and Chemical Industrial (HCI) Plan. Designed to both upgrade and diversify South Korean exports, as well as reduce the country's import dependence, the plan targeted the development of six new industries: iron and steel, petrochemicals, electronics, machinery, shipbuilding, and transport equipment.

As before, the state relied heavily, although not solely, on financial incentives to achieve its desired ends. More specifically, the government made use of a number of different targeted policy loans to encourage investment in these new industries. In 1978, these policy loans accounted for approximately 45 percent of total domestic credit and 75 percent of total bank loans.[13] Among the most important were export loans, Machinery Industry Promotion Fund loans, and National Investment Fund loans.

The National Investment Fund, for example, was set up in 1973 specifically to fund heavy and chemical industries. Between 1974 and 1980, the heavy, chemical, and power industries combined received 80 percent to 90 percent of all of its loans.[14] As a result of this policy, heavy and chemical-goods producers enjoyed not only greater access to capital, but also had significantly lower costs than did producers of light manufacturers, in some years as much as 35 percent lower.[15]

One measure of the government's success in implementing its plan was the resulting structural change in the South Korean economy. As shown in Table 3.1, from 1975 to 1980, the industrial center of the South Korean economy, in terms of both gross output and value added, shifted from light to heavy and chemical manufacturing industries. The same was true for exports: the share of heavy and chemical goods in merchandise exports rose from 14 percent in 1971 to 38 percent in 1979, and to 60 percent in 1984.[16]

Significantly, South Korea's Heavy and Chemical Industrial Plan was opposed by most Western advisors, including those at the World Bank, who believed that South Korea's international comparative

TABLE 3.1
Structural Change in Manufacturing
(in percentage terms)

	Gross output				Value added				Employment			
	1970	1975	1980	1983	1970	1975	1980	1983	1970	1975	1983	1983
Light industry	28.4	29.5	24.7	22.1	12.8	14.5	13.7	13.6	9.2	13.5	13.8	13.0
Food, beverages, and tobacco	15.9	14.4	10.8	9.6	6.2	6.3	6.2	5.9	2.5	2.8	2.9	3.0
Textiles and leather	7.1	9.9	8.4	7.0	3.8	5.5	4.9	3.9	4.0	7.9	7.4	6.5
Lumber and wood products	1.4	1.2	1.0	0.9	0.7	0.5	0.4	0.4	0.6	0.6	0.7	0.6
Paper printing and publishing	1.4	1.4	1.6	1.8	1.1	1.3	1.4	1.4	0.6	0.7	0.9	0.9
Nonmetallic metal manufacturing	1.4	1.5	1.9	1.8	1.1	1.3	1.4	1.4	0.6	0.7	0.9	0.9
Miscellaneous manufacturing	1.2	1.1	1.0	1.0	1.0	0.9	0.8	0.8	0.9	0.7	1.1	1.1
Heavy and chemical products	11.9	20.9	26.3	27.9	7.2	11.6	14.5	15.9	3.2	5.7	7.9	9.2
Chemical and chemical products	5.9	10.8	12.6	11.8	4.0	5.9	6.7	6.3	1.2	1.9	2.5	2.7
Primary metal manufacturing	2.0	3.4	5.1	5.0	0.7	1.0	1.7	1.8	0.4	0.5	0.7	0.9
Metal products and machinery	4.0	6.7	8.6	11.2	2.5	4.7	6.1	7.9	1.6	3.3	4.7	5.6

Source: World Bank, Korea: *Managing the Industrial Transition*, vol. 2, p. 3.

advantage continued to remain with light manufacturing. Park disagreed and, to protect his initiative from these advisors, he had his economic secretariat rather than the more Western-influenced EPB undertake the actual development of the plan. This, then, was a plan decided upon by the president and implemented though direct and active government intervention.

Despite its initial opposition, even the World Bank has been forced to declare South Korea's industrial transformation an economic success. In its 1987 report on South Korea, it summarized the results of Park's HCI plan as follows:

. . . Korean comparative advantage has clearly emerged over the last 10 years in shipbuilding, electrical equipment, metal products, and iron and steel—all extensions of the HCI sector. Although costly to establish, these capital-intensive industries have now reached the level of international competitiveness, and may legitimately be described as successful infant industries. . . . More broadly, the initial transition to capital-intensive exports owes its success and speed to the interventions of the 1970s in establishing industries of sufficient scale to be internationally competitive.[17]

My intention here is not to engage in a thorough analysis of South Korea's Heavy and Chemical Industry Plan. While it helped lay the groundwork for South Korea's economic growth during the 1980s, the plan was, as we will see in Chapter 9, far from an unambiguous success in economic much less social and political terms. Rather, my aim is to show how the government aggressively used its control over credit in concert with other instruments of state policy such as licensing, state production, and trade and foreign investment restrictions to shape the broad outlines of the South Korean economy.

Finance and Industrial Organization

Credit policy was also used to shape the country's industrial organization. Because South Korean planners believed that large firms were better able to respond to state initiatives as well as easier to monitor than small firms, state policy promoted the development of an economy dominated by large producers.

Government preference for large firms was often translated into policy in the following way: the MTI would grant a firm approval for an industrial project. Typically, the project would be financed by one-fifth equity and four-fifth loans. If the firm succeeded at the project, often with additional assistance on the part of the government, it would normally be granted approval for yet another project. That project too would be financed largely by new government-provided credits. In this way, a firm, if favored by the government, could rapidly grow and expand its activities from one area into many others with very little original start-up money.

One result of this policy can be seen by looking at changes in employment size per enterprise over the 1970s. From 1973 to 1978, the average number of employees per enterprise grew from approximately fifty in 1973 to seventy-two in 1978.[18] Large firms, those employing over 300 workers, increased their average employment size over this same period from approximately 883 workers to 984 workers.[19] By 1978, these large firms were employing over half of all manufacturing employees and producing about two-thirds of manufacturing output.[20]

To strengthen their ability to implement desired policies, state planners combined support for large-scale production with limited market competition. Table 3.2 shows that from 1970 to 1977, there was a significant increase in the percentage of commodities sold in terms of market value, by monopoly producers. While this trend reversed from 1977 to 1982, it did not signify greater state commitment to free-market competition. Rather, reflecting government determination to maintain the upper hand in its dealings with individual producers, oligopoly was favored to become the dominant form of economic organization.

One natural result of this policy was a rapid growth in aggregate concentration. According to World Bank figures, the top one hundred South Korean manufacturing firms accounted for 40.6 percent of total manufacturing sales in 1970, 43.6 percent in 1972, 44.9 percent in 1977, and 46.8 percent in 1982. By contrast, the top one hundred manufacturing firms in Japan accounted for only 28.4 percent of total sales in 1975 and 27.3 percent in 1980.[21] In short, South Korean industrial development produced one of the highest levels of economic concentration in the capitalist world.

By far the most important characteristic of South Korea's industrial organization is ownership of these dominant firms by a few large family-run conglomerates, called chaebol. With government industrial policy supporting the expansion of existing business groups rather than the establishment of new independent firms, the average number of firms per chaebol rose steadily from 4.2 percent in 1970 to 14.3 percent in 1979.[22] The *Far Eastern Economic Review* describes the end result of this state-supported dynamic as follows:

> Virtually the whole economy has fallen under the domination of about 50 business groups locally called chaebol. . . . Producing and marketing everything from bread to aircraft engines (Samsung), from razor-blades to TV sets and from toothpaste to micro-chips (Lucky-Goldstar), from automobiles to ships and from housing units to furniture (Hyundai),

TABLE 3.2
Market Structure of South Korean Manufacturing
(by percent)

	1970	1974	1977	1982
Monopoly[a]				
Commodities	29.6	30.8	31.6	23.6
Sales	8.7	12.7	16.3	11.4
Duopoly[b]				
Commodities	18.7	17.9	20.1	11.1
Sales	16.3	12.6	11.0	6.6
Oligopoly[c]				
Commodities	33.2	34.2	32.0	47.4
Sales	35.1	38.6	33.9	50.6
Total noncompetitive				
Commodities	81.5	82.8	83.7	82.1
Sales	61.1	63.9	61.2	68.6
Competitive				
Commodities	18.5	17.2	16.3	17.9
Sales	39.9	36.1	38.8	31.4

[a] Firm concentration exceeds 80 percent.
[b] Top two firms produce more than 80 percent.
[c] Top three firms produce more than 60 percent.

Source: *Korea: Managing the Industrial Transition* (Washington, D.C.: World Bank), vol. 2, p. 30.

they have literally left no stone unturned in their expansion and control of domestic industries and markets.[23]

The top ten chaebol, the 1989 dollar value of their sales, total employment, and main products—are listed in Table 3.3. To illustrate their dominance over the South Korean economy, the four largest, sometimes called the super chaebol, had combined sales equal to approximately 45 percent of South Korea's total GNP. Of course, as noted above, each chaebol is composed of numerous firms involved in a variety of business activities. Samsung, for example, has forty-eight principle affiliates, Hyundai has forty-two, Lucky-Goldstar has sixty-two, and Daewoo has twenty-four.[24]

TABLE 3.3
South Korea's Ten Largest Chaebol

Company	1989 sales (billions $)	Number of employees	Major products
Samsung	34.3	160,596	Electronics, semiconductors, aerospace, food, machinery, apparel, trading, insurance, advertising
Hyundai	32.5	142,630	Construction services, autos, shipbuilding, electronics, heavy machinery, furniture, trading, insurance, advertising
Lucky-Goldstar	23.1	88,403	Electronics, semiconductors, telecommunications, oil and petrochemicals, chemicals, trading, insurance, advertising
Daewoo	18.1	120,000	Electronics, machinery, auto parts, shipbuilding, aerospace, trading, financial services
Sunkyong	9.4	17,985	Oil refining, petrochemicals, polyester products
Ssangyong	7.5	16,870	Cement, auto parts, machinery, trading, financial services
Hyosung	5.2	24,000	Trading
Hanjin	4.8	26,683	Transportation
Korea	4.6	18,291	Petrochemicals, advertising, explosives, financial services
Kia	4.4	23,733	Auto parts

Sources: Sam Jameson, "Families Still Keep Grip on S. Korea's Conglomerates," *Los Angeles Times*, 10 December 1990; "Korea's Powerhouses Are Under Siege," *Business Week*, 20 November 1989: 52; Richard M. Steers et al., *The Chaebol: Korea's New Industrial Might* (New York: Harper and Row, 1989), p. 36.

Finance, the Chaebol, and Industrialization

The economic rise of the chaebol was closely tied to the government's heavy and chemical industrialization drive because, among other reasons to be discussed later, the government found the chaebol form of organization ideally suited to carry out its plans for a rapid expansion of production. Most chaebol are still owned and controlled by their original founder and/or his family. Hyundai, for example, is owned and run by Chung Ju-Yung and his family. Similarly, Samsung is run by the family of the founder Lee Byung-Chull, and Lucky-Goldstar is controlled by the interrelated Koo and Huh families. Such family control is often maintained by the establishment of a "cultural foundation" through which a large percentage of the stock of each company in the chaebol is owned.[25]

Even though the chaebol may have dozens of subsidiaries, each with its own president, they remain operationally unified under the directives of the chairman because of this tight system of family control. This command structure, in addition to a unified planning and coordination office, gives the chaebol, through its chairman, the ability to respond quickly to new opportunities and draw on the collective resources and experiences of all member companies. Thus, from the government's point of view, these business groups were an ideal vehicle for promoting the country's rapid expansion into new capital-intensive areas of production. Kim Suk Won, chairman of the Ssangyong Group, describes this system of state selection and direction of chaebol activity as "comparable to the government development plans of socialist countries."[26]

A Case Study: Shipbuilding

Shipbuilding offers an excellent example of how the chaebol were able to serve the state as an effective instrument of industrial policy. The initial impetus for South Korea's advance into shipbuilding came from President Park Chung Hee, who pressured the head of Hyundai to expand his business group's activities to include shipbuilding.[27] At the time, Hyundai had no shipyard or experience in shipbuilding. Moreover, no shipyard in South Korea had ever built a vessel larger than 10,000 tons.

Hyundai's first shipbuilding contract was signed in 1972, with a Greek ship owner, for the construction of two tankers, each over

240,000 tons; delivery dates were set for July and December 1974.[28] This success was possible largely because of government efforts which included financial support for the construction of the shipyard and extensive financial guarantees for the first contract.[29]

The newly formed Hyundai Shipbuilding and Heavy Industries began work in 1973 but was late in meeting its deadlines. Unfortunately, by the time the ships were ready for delivery, the shipping market had collapsed; only one ship was accepted. Hyundai was again late with two very large crude carriers ordered by a Japanese company and then again with an order for two more carriers for a Hong Kong firm. All four vessels were refused by the contracting parties.

By 1975, Hyundai Shipbuilding and Heavy Industries found itself holding several tankers and facing financial disaster. But having supported the venture from the beginning, the government continued to offer the company assistance. Most important, it gave orders that all oil imported from the Middle East had to be shipped in South Korean-owned ships. After some initial resistance, the Korea Oil Corporation (a government-Gulf Oil Company joint venture) began using Hyundai's tankers.[30]

Not long after, Hyundai established its own general trading company, the Hyundai Merchant Marine Company, which in 1976, purchased all of Hyundai's unsold ships for its own use. This decision to enter the merchant marine business was supported by the government's decision to launch a new system of General Trading Companies (GTC). This system, to be described in more detail later, was designed to push exports. If companies met export requirements designated by the government, they would be granted GTC status and receive a number of special privileges, the most important of which was access to credit at especially low interest rates. Hyundai's merchant marine company not only saved Hyundai's shipbuilding venture, it also gave the chaebol an important advantage in the race to boost exports and win GTC status.

Hyundai began construction of its first ship in 1973 and its shipbuilding affiliate survived largely due to government policies such as those mentioned above. Yet, less than a decade later, Hyundai became the world's largest shipbuilder.[31] In trying to answer the question of how it was possible, even accounting for extensive government support, that a company with no previous shipbuilding experience could grow so quickly and maintain its forward motion in an industry widely known for instability, we come to appreciate the economic advantages of the chaebol business structure.

For example, even though Hyundai Shipbuilding and Heavy Industries had no direct experience in shipbuilding, the Hyundai group was able to compensate for this shortcoming by drawing on the engineering and construction expertise of Hyundai Construction, the workplace organizational knowledge of Hyundai Motors, and the production control experience of Hyundai Cement. Within the unified command structure of the chaebol, engineers, supervisors, managers, workers, and funds were easily transferred from subsidiary to subsidiary as needed.[32] Moreover, the chaebol structure allowed Hyundai to balance off losses in shipping with gains from other subsidiaries, such as those producing automobiles or electronics.

Finance, the Chaebol, and Exports

As noted above, the government had been successful in harnessing the chaebol, through the General Trading Company system, to boost the nation's export efforts. The system was started in 1975, with the MTI awarding GTC status to trading companies if they successfully met certain government standards in terms of company size, number of overseas branch offices, and, most important, annual export performance. Within a year, thirteen trading companies had qualified. Four, however, eventually lost their status because of poor performance, the last in 1985.

To force these trading companies to maximize exports, the government continually raised the minimum export requirement. Even though this policy kept the costs of participation high for those firms involved, the rewards were substantial. Successful trading companies gained access to bank loans at extremely low interest rates, the right to import selected products for resale, and membership on special committees that advised the Economic Planning Board.[33] One measure of the system's success: the share of exports handled by the ten largest general trading companies rose from 13.6 percent in 1976 to 51.3 percent in 1983.[34]

Not surprisingly, it was the largest business groups, such as Samsung and Hyundai, that had the resources to launch trading companies able to win GTC status. Employing the added financial benefits associated with GTC status to strengthen the economic position of the entire business group, these chaebol were able to rapidly out-perform their non-chaebol competitors. As George E. Ogle has commented: "The GTC system, the switch to heavy industry and the giant leap forward by the chaebol, all went hand in hand."[35]

Chaebol domination of economic activity exposes yet another misconception that mainstream economists have about the South Korean economic experience. Not only did these economists understate the economic role of the state, they have also seriously overstated the importance of free-market competitive entrepreneurship. As we have seen, South Korea's economic rise and industrial transformation was powered by a few, large business groups whose growth and activities can best be explained with reference to state directives and initiatives, the most important being financial.

Finance, Wealth, and Power

While control over finance enabled the state to shape chaebol and thus private sector economic activity, it also served as a powerful instrument of political control and personal enrichment for state leaders. This point is probably best illustrated by the following example: under the rule of President Chun Doo Hwan, Park Chung Hee's successor, it became standard practice for the large chaebol to make "donations" to the work of the Ilhae Foundation and the New Village Movement. The first, organized ostensibly to conduct research on questions related to reunification, was controlled by Chun himself. The second, allegedly organized to support rural development, was run by Chun's younger brother.

This corporate giving was commonly understood to be a payoff directly to the president and his brother to ensure good chaebol working relations with the government. It was not voluntary, however, as Yang Chang Mo, the head of the Kukje-ICC group, was to discover. In 1984, he gave only $400,000 to the New Village Movement, while the leaders of the other large chaebol each gave over $1 million. Mr. Yang also refused to make any contribution to the Ilhae Foundation.

At the time, Kukje-ICC was the seventh-largest business group in South Korea, with 21-member companies in areas such as steel, textiles, machinery, footwear, tires, and overseas construction. In 1983, it had trade revenues of $3 billion and a network of forty overseas branches that did business with one hundred countries. But like other businesses in South Korea, Kukje-ICC had grown rapidly through funds borrowed from the government-controlled banking system. While subsidized credit was put to great advantage by the chaebol, it was also their Achilles' heel. As one South Korean banker explained: "Anytime the government chooses to close a company or break it up, it can do so. All it has to do is call the so-called Korean commercial banks, which it controls, and tell them not to refinance a company's debt."[36]

In this case, President Chun, angered by Mr. Yang's actions, ordered Kukje-ICC's four main creditor banks to stop honoring the chaebol's checks. Within a few weeks, Kukje-ICC, with no alternative financing available, was forced to declare bankruptcy. The banks took control of all the company's assets and, under government direction, proceeded to sell them at discounted prices to the other more politically loyal chaebol. The efficiency of this system was clear: A major chaebol collapsed, but no plants were idled or workers unemployed. The government, through its control over the financial system, simply reassigned assets from one chaebol to another.

Well aware of their financial vulnerability, most chaebol have sought to increase their economic and political independence from the state by pushing for deregulation and privatization of the South Korean banking system.[37] In fact, the combination of chaebol and U.S. government pressure has forced the South Korean government to loosen its direct control over the country's financial markets. In 1981, for example, the government began selling its shares in the five nationwide commercial banks.

To minimize its loss of control to the chaebol, the state restricted its privatization program in a number of ways, such as limiting single shareholders (except for joint venture banks) to a maximum 8 percent of total ownership. These efforts had not been completely successful, however, and the chaebol were clearly able to increase their financial strength through the 1980s. But while this development indicates a change in the balance of power between the state and chaebol, it did not mean that the state had completely lost its ability to control the price or allocation of bank credit. For example, bank lending and deposit rates continue to be regulated by the state through so-called "window-guidance" from the Bank of Korea. Moreover, the government has once again increased its use of policy loans, which require banks to make loans according to criteria and at interest rates established by the government itself. Finally, as the major stockholder in all banks, the Ministry of Finance ensures its continuing control over bank decisions by placing its own officials in mid-level management positions throughout the banking system, as well as exercising veto rights over the selection of top bank management. Thus, after more than ten years of government privatization, South Korean banks continue to operate largely under the direction of the state.

Neither the chaebol nor the U.S. government has, of course, conceded to the state in this struggle for control over finance. In fact, the state pledged, under pressure, to further deregulate the country's financial system gradually over the decade of the 1990s. It remains to be seen, however, what kind of financial reform will, in fact, be implemented. While these developments and their significance for South Korea's economic and political future will be considered more fully in Part III, at least two comments are appropriate here.

First, this struggle over finance underscores the main point of this section: state control over the price and allocation of credit has been central to the state's ability to direct private economic activity and thus South Korea's rapid growth and economic transformation. Second, as forces internal and external to South Korea continue to weaken the ability of the state to direct economic activity, there is strong reason to believe that South Korea's past economic progress will prove difficult to sustain.

State Production

While direction of credit was the government's single most important instrument of industrial policy, it was far from the only one. As we will see in this section, the South Korean state also made extensive use of nonfinancial public enterprises to spur and direct the country's economic growth. In fact, according to Jones and Sakong, South Korea "has utilized the intervention mechanism of public ownership to an extent which parallels that of many countries advocating a socialist pattern of society."[38]

There is a long history of public enterprise in Korea, although before colonization by Japan it was largely one of state production of luxury goods (such as green celedon pottery) for elites. Under Japanese rule, the public sector in Korea was greatly expanded in both size as well as scope of activity. As a result, public enterprises generated almost one-quarter of total government revenue from 1910 to 1920 and over half of all state revenue from 1926 to 1945.[39]

Those Japanese public enterprises operating in southern Korea were seized by the U.S. military at the end of World War II and eventually given to the newly established South Korean government in 1948. But, under pressure from the United States, Syngman Rhee sold off all but thirty-six of them to South Korean businessmen before his ouster in 1960. With Park's military takeover, however, this trend toward privatization was reversed. The new government's nationalization of the banking system perhaps best symbolized Park's different understanding of the importance of state ownership as a tool for industrialization. As Byung-Nak Song explains:

> The [Park] government PE [public enterprise] policy in the 1960s and 1970s was to establish PEs in any area if they were essential in expanding Korea's export capacity and could not be properly handled by private enterprises. Thus the government established PEs to handle even such items as iron and steel, petroleum and chemicals, and tourism, that are normally considered to be traditional areas of private business.[40]

In what follows I will briefly highlight the expansion and significance of state activity in the period of its most rapid growth, 1963 to 1972. In many ways, state infrastructure activity, by rapidly creating an industrial framework within which private producers could thrive, functioned as a leading sector during South Korea's early years of industrial growth. Every year from 1961 to 1969, for example, government social overhead capital grew at a faster rate than did manufacturing or any other sector of the economy.[41]

The public sector as a whole grew more than three times in absolute size from 1963 to 1972. This increase translates into a real average annual growth rate of 14.5 percent as compared to a 9.5 percent rate of growth for the economy as a whole and a 12.2 percent rate of growth for the non-agricultural sector.[42] Moreover, most of this growth came from new enterprises established by the Park government and not from the expansion of those that existed prior to his coming to power.

Nearly half of all public enterprises added during this period (in terms of 1972 value added) were in manufacturing. As a result, even though manufacturing activity grew rapidly from 1963 to 1972, the public sector share of manufacturing output (in terms of value added) remained roughly constant at 15 percent. Thus, state manufacturing activity grew as rapidly as did that of the private sector.

In terms of strategic location, those public enterprises established by Park, especially in manufacturing, had extremely high backward and forward linkages relative to those of any other sector of the economy. Control of these firms thus gave the South Korean state considerable leverage to shape the overall direction of the economy. State firms were also among the most capital intensive in the entire economy, averaging twice the capital intensity of firms in manufacturing. South Korea's public firms were also among the country's largest. In 1972, for example, twelve of the country's sixteen largest firms were state owned. Finally, public sector operations were heavily import-substituting; without them, according to some estimates, the nation's current account deficit would have been approximately 25 percent larger.

As we can see, public sector firms operating in a variety of fields—transport and communication; electricity, water, and sanitation; mining; and manufacturing—played a leading role in South Korea's rapid economic transformation. They created the physical infrastructure needed by private producers as well as ensured timely production of those industrial products essential for the expansion and diversification of South Korean industry. To elaborate on this point, I will present two examples of public sector activity: the first illustrates how state infrastructure activity was used to promote export activity; the second illustrates how state production was used to promote South Korea's industrial restructuring.

Infrastructure and Exports

Beginning in 1967, Park had the Ministry of Construction undertake construction of a series of industrial estates to be operated by the state-owned Export Industry Public Corporation.[43] This program of estate building was an important part of the government's export promotion policies. It encouraged, by providing subsidized modern factory sites and a supporting infrastructure, rapid expansion of business activity along lines determined by the state.

By the end of the decade the government opened new estates in Seoul, Masan, and Kumi. Following implementation of the Regional Industrial Development Law in 1969, the government further committed itself to establish at least one industrial estate in every provincial capital.[44] By the end of 1981, twenty-three government-owned-and-operated industrial estates were providing facilities and services to over 2200 firms.[45]

While enhancing private profitability, these estates also functioned as a powerful instrument of government control over corporate activity. For example, firms that did not meet government-mandated export targets were often punished by the MTI with loss of those basic services provided by the estate, including electricity, water, and telephones.[46]

State Production and Industrial Deepening

The government also played a direct production role in advancing South Korea's industrial deepening, most important, perhaps, through the establishment of the Pohang Iron and Steel Company Ltd. (POSCO), one of the country's most successful public enterprises. South Korean planners attempted to launch an integrated iron- and steel-making industry as early as the mid-1960s. At that time, aid donors, including the World Bank, refused to lend the government the necessary money, arguing that because South Korea lacked iron ore, steel-making skills, and a large market, it should obtain its steel from efficient Japanese producers.

The South Korean government persisted, however, and eventually succeeded in forming POSCO in 1968. Although foreign project advisors suggested that South Korea enter the steel business with only a small and limited operation, the government ordered sixteen plants with facilities to cover the full range of integrated steel mill activity including a railway system. One indicator of the success of this venture is the fact that POSCO is now one of the lowest-cost steel producers in the world.[47]

POSCO's founding is a good example of the South Korean government's determination to maintain national control over strategic areas of production. Rather than import steel or invite a foreign corporation to undertake and control production, the government turned to foreign loans and foreign technology to establish its own state-owned enterprise. The state was forced to rely on foreign expertise for almost all phases of POSCO's creation, from preinvestment feasibility studies, personal training, and actual construction to process engineering and production control skills. POSCO itself was responsible only for the actual physical labor involved in the construction.[48] But given the South Korean government's commitment to steel as an integral part of an overall protected industrialization strategy, POSCO has since become increasingly self-reliant.

For example, in 1977 POSCO bought approximately 44 percent of its consumables from local suppliers; in 1984 it was 75 percent. The percentage of capital goods purchased locally has also risen.[49] In 1987, POSCO expanded its steel facilities from its first location at Pohong to include a second steel works at Kwangyang. This second facility is considered by many to be the most modern and fully automated steel plant in the world. While only 12 percent of spending on equipment for POSCO's first steel complex went to South Korean firms, this figure rose to approximately 50 percent in the case of the second facility.[50] POSCO is now involved in a joint venture with USX, supplying the U.S. firm with semifinished steel from its Kwangyang facility, as well as helping it modernize its Pittsburg, California, steel operations.

Although POSCO made a profit every year since it began operation in 1973, this record has only been achieved with substantial government support. Besides relatively low labor costs, the company has also benefited from government-guaranteed long-term, low-interest foreign loans and substantially discounted user rates for railroad services, port services, water supply, and gas.[51] This program of support illustrates how South Korea's efficient steel industry is the result of sustained and substantial government intervention, and not free-market forces. POSCO received this level of support because the government expected it to do far more than produce quality steel at low prices. POSCO has lived up to these expectations by playing a major role in South Korea's transition from exporter of labor-intensive manufactures to producer and exporter of capital-intensive, higher value-added products. By providing high-quality, low-cost steel, it enabled producers in automobiles, shipbuilding, construction, and electronics to successfully compete in international markets.

South Korea's present industrial success would not have been possible had the state not taken leadership to establish public sector production in a number of strategic sectors of the economy, such as steel. The establishment of POSCO, the country's largest single investment at almost $4 billion, was part of a broader pattern of direct state activity to transform the economy. For example, public enterprise investment as a share of total investment rose from 19 percent in 1970 to more than 33 percent in 1975.[52]

In fact, until the early 1970s, there were those within the military and state planning apparatus who wanted to build on the example of POSCO and continue to establish new heavy and chemical industries under direct state ownership.[53] A number of factors, however, including the need to maintain positive relations with the United States, eventually led the state to promote private ownership through the chaebol as the dominate form of enterprise. Reflecting this change in emphasis, public enterprise investment shares fell to approximately 28 percent in 1980 and 16 percent in 1986. Nevertheless, the absolute size of public sector activity, in terms of value added, investment, and employment, continued to grow over this same period.[54]

Conclusion

The point of this chapter is to highlight the role of the state as the driving force behind South Korea's rapid economic transformation. In contrast to the comments of Paul Kuznets, whose quote began this chapter, it is, I believe, no exaggeration to say that the state, through its planning and direct involvement in both finance and production, was responsible for almost all aspects of every major economic decision made over the decades of the 1960s and 1970s, the period when South Korea was designated a free-market miracle by mainstream analysts. One of the lessons we can learn from the South Korean experience, then, is that a highly aggressive and interventionist state is very capable of achieving economic "success."

Effective implementation of state plans depends, however, on more than just attention to national economic activity. Because imports and multinational corporate activity can, if unrestricted, easily overwhelm state attempts to control market entry, prices, and production, successful national planning also requires regulation of international economic activity. The South Korean experience proves the wisdom of this statement. As we will see in the next chapter, the South Korean government defended its domestic initiatives with a complex and effective system of regulation of foreign trade, foreign exchange use, and foreign direct investment.

CHAPTER 4

POLICY IMPLEMENTATION: STATE REGULATION OF INTERNATIONAL ECONOMIC ACTIVITY

We have so far examined the organization and operation of South Korea's planning network, highlighting the state's use of credit policy and public-sector activity to shape and direct national economic activity. To complete this discussion of policy implementation, we will now focus on the various strategies and procedures by which the state regulated foreign trade, foreign exchange use, and foreign direct investment.

Regulation of Trade

The South Korean government has used a number of non-price mechanisms to limit imports into South Korea. First and most direct, all importers are required to have an import license. Working through the Korea Foreign Traders' Association (KFTA), which all traders must join, the MTI sets the standards for obtaining such a licence. Eligibility is usually conditional on satisfactory export performance, which is in turn based on government-determined annual requirements. Import licenses can also be quite detailed, in some cases specifying the types of products that can be imported. By limiting the number and breath of the licenses, the government is able to maintain some control over importers and imports.

Even more significant in terms of government efforts to regulate imports are the following visible and less visible controls on the quantity of imports:

Visible restrictions. The MTI regularly lists products whose import the government wants restricted because they are considered to be luxury goods, similar to domestically produced goods, or goods considered dangerous to public health or morals. Such goods must meet special "discretionary licensing requirements" to be imported; thus even licensed traders are required to apply for special permission to import these goods. Products that have been listed as restricted include pharmaceuticals, machinery, sewing machines, watch-movement parts, alcoholic beverage base, and automobile components.

Less visible restrictions. In 1967, the government shifted its import control system from a positive to a negative list system. Under the positive list system goods listed could not be imported unless explicit government permission is granted. Under the negative list system, goods listed are supposedly approved automatically for import without the need for additional governmental permission.

South Korea's trade liberalization is usually measured by the "import liberalization ratio," the percentage of imported goods that are listed as automatically approved and thus allegedly not subject to governmental nonprice restrictions. In 1988, South Korean trade officials asserted that since their country's import liberalization ratio had reached 95 percent for manufactures, South Korea had an open market-based trading system.[1] However, the Automatic Approval (AA) list system has many exceptions which allow the South Korean government to regulate foreign trade as it deems necessary. Among the most important are special laws, import area diversification measures, and surveillance measures.

Special laws. These laws affect even those items declared AA by the MTI. Among the most important are the Petroleum Refining Industry Law, Textile Machinery Import Law, Grain Control Law, Pharmaceutical Law, and Fertilizer Control Law. In a valuable study of South Korean trade practices in 1982, Richard Luedde-Neurath found that out of $14.2 billion of AA-classified imports, imports supposedly not subject to quantitative restrictions, approximately $8.7 billion fell under one kind of special law or another. As such, they required special permission from a relevant agency before their importation could be allowed.[2]

Import area diversification measures. Since 1977 the South Korean government has used import area diversification measures to limit or restrict imports, especially by country. These measures can be used to control imports of items that are already under restriction; they can also be used to influence the quantity and origin of imports listed as AA. According to estimates made by Luedde-Neurath, an additional $2.1 billion of AA-listed imports in 1982 were also affected by this measure and thus required special permission.

Imports falling under the import area diversification law must be approved by the Korea Foreign Traders' Association. Such approval must be obtained regardless of the country from which the goods are purchased, thereby making the law product as well as area specific. Automobiles are one of several significant imports regulated by this trade measure, and its effectiveness can be illustrated by the fact that no Japanese cars produced in Japan are sold in South Korea.

Surveillance measures. Introduced in 1978, surveillance measures were originally designed to allow the government to monitor the domestic effects of a trade liberalization initiative. They are now used for general import control purposes. Products listed for surveillance are all AA items. Initially the system was one of ex-post monitoring by the KFTA and the MTI. This was changed in 1979 when the MTI announced that surveillance imports would now require prior approval by the Korea Foreign Traders' Association at its twice-monthly meetings. Each import and its domestic impact are considered on a case-by-case basis.[3]

Finally, the government has also used a number of special customs and excise duties to restrict imports. As Luedde-Neurath explains:

> To anyone familiar with the fact that tariffs in Korea do not currently exceed 150 per cent (formally 200 per cent), even on the most luxurious of import items, it must come as somewhat of a surprise to hear references to 400 per cent duties on golf clubs, 500 per cent on French wines, and 933 per cent on imported whisky.
>
> The explanation lies in an array of "other" taxes that crawl out of the woodwork when the import of nonessential items is actually attempted: education tax, defense tax, special expense tax; etc. Their effect, in combination with high tariffs, is thoroughly to discourage undesirable imports.[4]

Such restrictions have enabled the South Korean government to tightly regulate imports. As a result, according to the MTI, luxury goods, broadly defined, constitute less than 3 percent of the country's total imports.[5] These restrictions have also enabled the government to direct economic activity according to its own priorities. The automobile industry illustrates the way the state has successfully combined domestic and international policy tools to pursue its industrial objectives.

A Case Study of Industrial Policy: Automobile Production

South Korea's auto industry has gone through a number of changes in response to a series of government initiatives. Phase one (1962-66) was characterized by import-processing. Semi-knocked-down components were imported from foreign car manufacturers and assembled locally. The Industry was protected by the Motor Vehicle Industry Protection Law (1962) which made the importation of assembled vehicles or parts not related to assembly uses illegal. Phase two (1967-71) was characterized by the creation of an import-substitution industry. Local production of parts and components was emphasized under the "Basic Plan for Promotion of the Motor Vehicle Industry" (1967). Phase three (1972-79) was characterized by the development of "indigenous" models of passenger cars under the "Long-Term Plan for Motor Vehicle Industry Promotion" (1973). Phase four began in 1979 with government designation of the car industry as a strategic export center.[6]

In response to government planning, the car industry in South Korea has emerged as one of the most successful in the third world. For example, exports of cars grew 20 percent in 1983-1984; 42.6 percent in 1984-1984; and 60 percent in 1985-1986.[7] By 1988, South Korean automakers were producing over one million vehicles a year, with slightly over half of this number being sold abroad. This success, as I will show next, has little to do with free-market, free-trade policies.

Government Control over Prices

There is no price competition between South Korean passenger car producers within South Korea. All domestic prices are set by the government based on engine size.

Government Control over Market Entry

In 1981, fearing that the South Korean auto industry had expanded too rapidly and was in danger of undermining its own competitiveness, the government decided to protect the industry by limiting the number of producing firms to the existing five and freezing their particular areas of production. Initially Hyundai Motor Co., Daewoo Motor Co., and Kia Motor Co. were the only companies allowed to produce passenger cars. Kia was the only company allowed to produce lightweight trucks. These three firms as well as Ssangyong and Asia Motors were, however, all granted permission to produce nonpassenger commercial vehicles such as heavy trucks, buses, and tractors.

In 1985, Samsung, which had been frozen out of the industry, petitioned the government for permission to join a passenger car joint venture with Chrysler Corporation. The government said no, citing the industrial rationalization provisions of the Industrial Development Law, which gives it the authority to reject any new enterprise that it believes might negatively affect the nation's economy.

Finally in July 1989, the government agreed to end its closure of the industry. Samsung again sought to enter, but this time as a producer of commercial vehicles rather than passenger cars. However, to engage in production, Samsung needed to import technology and components. Unfortunately for Samsung, because the South Korean government also had the regulatory power to limit imports of technology, it needed to receive government approval before it could finalize its import agreement with Nissan Diesel Motor Company.

After a forty-day investigation period, the MTI returned Samsung's petition without approval. Permission was denied, according to the MTI, because the Nissan technology that Samsung wanted to import was similar to technology already imported by Ssangyong Motor Company. As Lee Kyong-Tae, chief of the MTI investigation team said, "Samsung's participation in the manufacture of commercial vehicles would not contribute to the industry."[8]

Government Control over Imports

The government has also carefully protected the development of the auto industry through strict import controls. For example, only recently did the government classify automobile imports as automatically approved. Cars with engines over 2000cc were classified AA in July 1987 and cars with engines smaller than 2000cc in April 1988. Before then, the government had direct authority to restrict automobile imports. The effect of such trade controls was clear: a total of 305 foreign cars were sold in South Korea in 1988, none from Japan. This compares with over 500,000 South Korean cars sold abroad in the same year.

With greater market freedom, however, car imports began to grow rapidly. Over 300 cars were sold in the first five months of 1989. Ford alone sold nearly 500 of its Mercury Sables in the fourth quarter of 1989 and more than 300 a month through March 1990.[9] The government's response was an anti-import campaign directed at both consumers and importers. The campaign was effective, producing a sharp drop in automobile imports. Ford, for example, sold only eighty-eight cars in July.

The campaign worked as follows: consumer demand for foreign cars was greatly reduced by an aggressive government tax offensive. According to a *Los Angeles Times* report:

> A government official got hold of a list of 200 South Koreans who had placed orders for a European luxury car.... One by one, the customers were contacted by telephone and told their tax filings would be investigated if they went through with the purchase.... All the orders were canceled.[10]

South Korean car buyers are also required to purchase special bonds to support subway construction when buying a new automobile. In May 1990, to further reduce sales of foreign cars, the government raised the required subway bond purchase, making the increase substantially greater for a buyer of an imported rather than a domestic automobile. For example, the bond purchase requirement for a Mercedes buyer went up over four and one-half times to approximately 14 million won ($20,000), while the requirement for a buyer of a domestic luxury car went up only 50 percent to 5.9 million won ($8,500).[11]

Importers did not escape government pressure either. Kia, a 10 percent-owned affiliate of Ford, was Ford's sales outlet for the Mercury Sable. But as the *Wall Street Journal* explained:

> Recently, Kia cut its advertising for the Sables and then its orders from Ford. Why? Because, Kia says, the Korean government told it to. Government leaders thought Korea was importing too many foreign cars.[12]

This brief case study of the auto industry illustrates two salient points. First, government intervention in this industry has been decisive at the macro level in terms of shaping overall automobile activity and at the micro level in terms of deciding such issues as firm entry, product specialization, pricing, and access to technology. Second, these government initiatives succeeded in creating an internationally competitive automobile industry, largely as a result of the government's ability to create a closed and profitable domestic market from which to support its export campaign.

It should also be noted, however, that anti-import campaigns such as the one described above are now being openly challenged by foreign companies and their governments, the United States in particular. In fact, South Korea's continuing determination to restrict access to its markets has already begun to trigger, in response, new and more far-reaching protectionist measures in the more advanced capitalist countries. The political dynamics and economic significance of the growing international struggle to force open South Korea's domestic markets will be considered in more detail in Part III.

Regulation of Foreign Exchange Use

South Korea also regulates imports through its ability to influence business use of foreign exchange. Each year, the Ministry of Finance receives a detailed assessment of import requirements from the various producer associations on behalf of their members. That information is then used to establish a foreign exchange demand and supply plan which sets general guidelines for foreign exchange use by the associations. The plan is administered by the country's foreign exchange banks, but it is the responsibility of the individual associations to inform their member firms of the guidelines and, if necessary, to organize a procedure for rationing imports among them.[13] This process is not designed or intended to rigidly fix a precise foreign exchange distribution or use. It does, however, offer the government yet another way to monitor international transactions and, when necessary, limit imports for a given group regardless of whether they were listed as AA.

Regulation of Foreign Direct Investment

South Korea's planners have also supported their initiatives with aggressive regulation of foreign direct investment. In fact, South Korea currently has one of the most restrictive foreign investment codes in the world. Before examining the various state structures and policies used by planners to direct multinational corporate activity, I will briefly review the development of South Korea's regulatory framework as well as the country's experience with foreign direct investment.

The Foreign Capital Inducement Act (FCIA), enacted in 1960, was South Korea's first attempt to establish a legal framework for foreign lending and direct investment. This act provided a number of incentives to foreign investors but, given South Korea's unstable political situation, it proved difficult to attract multinational corporate activity. The first foreign investment project did not begin until 1962.

The Park regime's early attempts to attract multinational corporations were largely unsuccessful. Conditions rapidly changed, however, beginning in 1965. Above all, relations between Japan and South Korea were formally normalized that year. Moreover, the South Korean economy was by then growing rapidly. Later, the government began offering new incentives for foreign investors, including access to the country's first free trade zone in Masan. In response, foreign firms, especially Japanese, began greatly increasing their direct investment in South Korea.

Viewing this growing foreign presence with some alarm, the South Korean government began to re-evaluate its relatively open door policy for foreign direct investment. As Bohn-young Koo, a special economic advisor to the minister of the Economic Planning Board explains:

The government began to feel that unlimited approval of foreign investment might create some adverse effects on the domestic economy, such as the control of domestic industry by foreign firms and the resultant problem of implementing development strategies, an increase in vulnerability in times of external shocks due to potential massive withdrawals, and a hindrance to the development of indigenous firms.[14]

Thus, in 1973, along with the publication of its heavy and chemical industrialization plan, the government substantially revised the FCIA. New eligibility requirements were announced by the government, denying any foreign investment that might disrupt either the supply or demand of raw materials and intermediate capital goods or undermine the position of national firms in either domestic or overseas markets. In addition, joint ventures were assigned priority over wholly-owned foreign ventures, and both export and minimum-per-project investment standards were enacted.

In short, by the early 1970s, the South Korean government was determined to promote production by nationally owned and controlled firms, even at the cost of greater foreign borrowing or import of foreign technology. Foreign direct investment would be restricted to only those projects that offered substantial foreign marketing benefits or advanced technical production skills.

The Record on Foreign Direct Investment

South Korea has been relatively successful in limiting multinational corporate investment. For example, from 1967 to 1971, the period covered by the second five-year plan, foreign direct investment equaled only 3.7 percent of net foreign capital inflows into South Korea. During that same period, the equivalent percentage was 36.6 percent in Mexico; 33.8 percent in Brazil; and 26.1 percent in Thailand. From 1972 to 1976, the period covered by the third five-year plan and the launching of the heavy and chemical industrial drive, foreign direct investment still equaled only 7.9 percent of net foreign capital inflows, as compared with 22.9 percent in Brazil, 16 percent in Mexico, and 28 percent in Thailand.[15]

From 1962 (when the first foreign project was initiated) to 1985, only $2.65 billion of foreign direct investment was approved and only $1.9 billion actually invested. Over that same period, $7 billion was invested in Singapore, $8 billion in Taiwan, $17 billion in Mexico, and $24 billion in Brazil.[16]

South Korea was also successful in limiting foreign direct investment to joint ventures. A 1977 study of sixty-six countries found South Korea to be the country with the lowest percentage of wholly owned foreign firms—approximately 17 percent. Next was Israel with 30 percent, followed by Japan with 33 percent. More recent figures show a significant decline in South Korea's percentage: between 1981 and 1985, only 10.7 percent of all foreign investment proposals approved were for wholly owned foreign firms; majority-owned foreign firms accounted for only another 28.1 percent.[17]

These aggregate figures do, however, tend to understate the impact of multinational activity in South Korea. While multinational activity accounted for less than 4 percent of South Korea's overall Gross National Product in 1977, its impact in manufacturing was substantially greater. Multinationals accounted for 16 percent of total manufacturing output and over 10 percent of manufacturing employment. They also produced almost 19 percent of South Korea's total exports.[18]

Although significant, it is also true that the South Korean state was able to confine multinational corporations to those industries and activities consistent with its own priorities. In the early days of industrialization, government policy attempted to channel foreign direct investment into development of synthetic fibers for textile production and into major import-substitution projects in petroleum refining and chemical fertilizers. By late 1960s, the government shifted its emphasis toward directing foreign investment into production of apparel, textiles, and electronics for export. Then, in the mid-1970s, priority was placed on directing multinational activity into targeted capital-intensive heavy and chemical industries such as chemicals, machinery, electronics, and metal products.

The effectiveness of government policy can be seen in the following statistics from 1978: the export/sales ratio of multinationals was especially high in targeted light manufacturing industries such as apparel (99.5 percent), textiles (72.2 percent), and electrics and electronics (65.4 percent). Multinational corporations were also major producers in targeted import-substitution industries such as petroleum (90.4 percent of local output), chemicals (44.2 percent), electrics and electronics (40.9 percent), and metal assembly and machinery (24 percent).[19]

State Structures of Regulation

South Korea's success in managing multinational activity owes much to its regulatory system as defined under the Foreign Capital Inducement Act. According to this act, all foreign direct investment must be evaluated by the Foreign Capital Deliberation Committee, initially part of the EPB, but since 1981 under the jurisdiction of the Ministry of Finance. The approval process begins with a multinational corporation submitting a detailed proposal stating the terms of its proposed project, including the monetary value of the investment, the nature of the technology to be transferred, the projected output level and export/output ratio, and design of recruitment and training programs.[20] Such information is used by the South Korean government to not only evaluate proposed foreign direct investment activity, but also monitor approved projects.

The Foreign Capital Deliberation Committee, composed of top officials from a number of government ministries (including the Ministry of Finance, the Ministry of Trade and Industry, and the Ministry of Science and Technology) has ultimate authority to approve or reject a proposal. After receiving a proposal, the Committee distributes it to each of the relevant ministries for their own individual evaluation: the Ministry of Finance looks at the proposal from the point of view of its balance of payments implications; the Ministry of Trade and Industry considers its impact on domestic producers; the Ministry of Science and Technology looks at its impact on domestic technological development.

If any one ministry opposes the proposal it is then rejected. The government has never approved an application for foreign investment for a venture designed to produce domestic consumer goods. Moreover, no foreign firm, regardless of industry, has ever been allowed to purchase or take over an existing South Korean firm.

If all of the individual ministries approve, then the committee is empowered to negotiate with the foreign company over the precise terms or conditions under which the investment will take place. These negotiations are far from pro forma, even if the investment is part of a joint venture operation and both parties have agreed upon the terms. The Foreign Capital Deliberation Committee has often demanded renegotiation of already signed contracts if economic conditions substantially change, asking for an increase in exports or greater domestic content in production. In some cases it has even used the Foreign Exchange Control Law to block payment of previously agreed upon service charges.[21]

In general, proposals for foreign direct investment in targeted capital-intensive, import-substituting industries have been supported when the government believed that it had no other alternative to obtain needed technology or raw materials. In these cases, the government offered very profitable investment incentives while negotiating very detailed agreements that specify the technology to be transferred and/or the quantity and nature of raw materials to be supplied.

In general, proposals for foreign direct investment in labor-intensive, low-technology sectors win approval only if the projects are export oriented and the government is seeking access to new foreign markets. Agreements for these kinds of investments include very high export requirements and restrictions on domestic sales.

We can see the outcome of this negotiating process in the following breakdown of contract terms for agreements signed in 1986: 38 percent of all agreements with foreign investors had specific export-level requirements; 80 percent had specific technological transfer requirements; 36 percent had specific requirements for raw material supply; and 28 percent contained agreements whereby foreign firms were required to help South Korean firms gain access to export markets. At least one of the above requirements was present in over 92 percent of the investment agreements; at least two or more were specified in over 68 percent.[22]

Such agreements are also closely monitored by specialized agencies in the relevant ministries. For example, the Ministry of Trade and Industry has a Foreign Investment Control Bureau whose job it is to oversee the operational activities of foreign firms. These firms must submit monthly reports which include such sensitive information as output levels, imports and exports, profit rates, domestic content, taxes paid, and numbers and nationality of employed personnel. This information is used to not only ensure that foreign firms follow existing agreements, but also strengthen the government's position in future contract renewal negotiations.

The Bureau of Customs, part of the Ministry of Finance, keeps watch over imports and exports to see that foreign firms follow

South Korean trade laws, do not import more than they are allowed based on agreements, and that charges for equipment as part of intrafirm trade are not overstated. The Ministry of Finance inspects foreign exchange transactions to ensure that multinational corporations finance their activities with foreign rather than domestic funds. Combined with the above-mentioned restriction on foreign takeovers, this policy helps to ensure that multinational corporate investment will contribute to, rather than replace, domestic activity.

Disinvestment Policy

As noted above, the South Korean state has a strong preference for joint ventures in which majority ownership is held by domestic firms. When ventures with foreign ownership levels exceeding 50 percent are approved, it is usually because they produce exclusively for export markets or transfer a key technology that cannot otherwise be purchased. However, even in these cases, it is state policy to seek eventual foreign disinvestment, leading to South Korean majority control.

This disinvestment is pursued in a number of ways. During negotiations with foreign firms the government will attempt to limit foreign representation on the board of directors to the percentage of stock owned by the foreign firm. Similarly, the government will seek contract terms that provide for significant technical and managerial training for South Korean personnel. Most important, the government will try to convince the foreign firm to accept a contract containing a divestiture agreement. This agreement would normally become operational after a given period of time (ten years) or after a certain level of profits have been earned (150 percent of original investment). South Korean firms would then typically be given the opportunity to purchase a sufficient percentage of shares (15 percent) to give them operational and financial control of the joint venture.

Because such restrictions tend to reduce South Korea's attractiveness to foreign firms, the South Korean government has had to entice foreign producers with generous financial and tax incentives or monopoly rights. Most multinationals have been willing to accept South Korean terms, agreeing to eventually yield control over the joint venture in exchange for extremely attractive short-term business conditions. To illustrate this process, I will present two case studies of foreign disinvestment.[23]

A Case Study: Foreign Disinvestment in Electronics and Textiles

In the late 1960s and early 1970s, several Japanese consumer electronic and textile producers established facilities in South Korea to take advantage of the country's low-cost labor force. To attract them, the South Korean government was forced to provide tax breaks and low utility costs as well as allow them financial and operational control of their operations. In exchange, the Japanese firms had to enter into joint venture agreements and accept disinvestment stipulations.

These stipulations, requiring the Japanese firms to sell sufficient stock to give their South Korean partners majority control, came into effect beginning in the mid-1970s. The Japanese initially resisted, but South Korean state pressure eventually forced them to comply. To ensure a smooth and rapid transfer of management control, the government also offered the affected South Korean firms low-cost financing for the stock purchase.

The result: most Japanese electronics producers, including Mashushita, Toshiba, and Sony, sold all of their shares to their South Korean partners. The South Korean firms continued operations as nationally owned enterprises. Most Japanese textile producers decided to remain and accept minority status. For example, one Japanese firm ended up reducing its equity holdings from 50 percent to 33.5 percent, and turning over financial and operational control over the joint-venture to its South Korean partner.

A Case Study: Foreign Disinvestment in Oil Refining

In 1962, South Korean planners designated oil refining as a strategic import-substitution area. But, with no national firms having the necessary technological capability, the government was forced to seek foreign direct investment. Offering substantial financial incentives, the government succeeded in attracting Gulf Oil into a joint-venture agreement which created the Korea Oil Company. Gulf Oil was allowed total operational and financial control over the enterprise.

In 1965, the government decided to further expand the production capacity of the sector and deliberately sought out a new foreign partner for the venture. This time a joint venture was formed between Caltex and the government-selected Gold Star Corporation. The government was forced to offer Caltex a number of incentives, including price supports, tax breaks, and financial and operational control of the joint venture.

Further industry growth led to a 1968 joint venture between Union Oil Corporation and the Korean Explosives Corporation and a 1976 joint venture between the National Iran Oil Corporation and Ssangyong Corporation. However, in contrast to Gulf and Caltex, which enjoyed total operational and financial control over their joint ventures, Union Oil was able to negotiate total operational control but only 50 percent financial control. The National Iran Oil Corporation held an even weaker position, with only 50 percent financial control and no operational control.

By the late 1970s, sufficient national expertise had been developed to allow the government to begin a process of "nationalizing" the oil industry. After the overthrow of the Shah of Iran, the South Korean government loaned money to Ssangyong to buy out the Iranian National Oil Corporation. It then negotiated buy-outs with both Gulf and Union. By 1983, only Caltex was left, and it was forced by the government to renegotiate its contract, giving Gold Star operational and financial control over the joint venture.

South Korea's continuing progress in developing its own oil refining capabilities is reflected in the terms of a 1986 joint venture agreement between British Petroleum and Kukdong Corporation. British Petroleum holds 40 percent of equity and supplies raw materials; Kukdong has financial and operational control of the enterprise. Thus, as a result of state policy, South Korea now has significant control over an industry that was once dominated by foreign firms. It purchases its own oil on a contractual basis or on the spot market, transports the great majority of it in its own ships, and does all of its own refining in firms under South Korean financial and operation control.

Through such policies and actions as described in this chapter, the South Korean state is able to protect national firms and markets from foreign corporate control. This behavior reflects the government's strong commitment to maintain an economic environment responsive to nationally centered initiatives. In short, by combining planning and state direction of domestic economic activity with aggressive regulation of international economic activity, South Korea has been able to build a relatively diverse industrial base in a very short period of time.

Evaluating the Role of the State in South Korea Industrialization

I have so far accepted mainstream praise for South Korea's achievements without challenge and focused my efforts on refuting the conventional wisdom that attributes the country's economic success to its reliance on free-market, free-trade policies. I have done so through a detailed examination of the logic and operation of South Korean state planning and policy implementation. However, in using the South Korean state and its industrial policies as my point of entry into a larger study of the South Korean experience, I have sought only to affirm the effectiveness of social regulation of economic activity, not South Korea's specific approach to economic development.

It would be a serious mistake to conclude this work here, satisfied at having demonstrated the "superiority" of state intervention over market forces. Refutation of free-market mythology as it concerns South Korea is an important accomplishment. But it addresses only one aspect of South Korea's rapid growth. Left unaddressed are issues related to the quality, sustainability, and social consequences of this growth, issues that lead to the question of whether the South Korean economic strategy, now more accurately understood, continues to be deserving of promotion. It is this question that I will attempt to address next.

As we will see in Part II, while South Korea has indeed grown rapidly, it did so in a manner designed to enrich the few at the expense of the many. The South Korean approach to development, based on brutal dictatorship and inequality, does not deserve our support. In fact, growing numbers of South Koreans, in response to the contradictions and class conflict inherent in their country's state capitalist development, are now rapidly organizing in an effort to radically transform their own system.

Thus, while the South Korean experience underscores the importance of the state, it also makes clear that we cannot ignore the social relations that define and shape its policies. South Korea, not surprisingly, has both positive and negative lessons to teach us. Recognizing this reality means that we must do more than simply inform those who hope to emulate the South Korean "economic miracle" that it was produced by aggressive state planning and intervention, not market forces. Rather, we have the more difficult task of helping working people everywhere understand the repressive and exploitative nature of the South Korean experience while simultaneously drawing upon it to illuminate the possibilities it suggests for new and more progressive forms of social organization.

PART II

THE SOUTH KOREAN EXPERIENCE: THE STATE AND CLASS STRUGGLE

CHAPTER 5

JAPANESE IMPERIALISM, THE STATE, AND CLASS STRUGGLE

In Part I, I examined the structure and dynamics of South Korean state planning, refuting the conventional wisdom that attributes South Korea's economic success to market forces. In Part II, I will explore the forces that shaped South Korea's state-led development strategy and analyze the consequences of the resulting growth. In doing so, I also will attempt to refute those who promote South Korea's state capitalist strategy as a model for other countries.

The political significance of this task is highlighted by the small but growing number of scholars who both reject free-market explanations for South Korea's growth *and* celebrate South Korea as an example of successful development. In fact, these scholars now constitute an impressive intellectual force, giving legitimacy to what I call the new conventional wisdom, a position that advocates state capitalism along South Korean lines as the most promising strategy for third world development.

For example, Alice H. Amsden, one of the more influential of these economists, strongly believes that South Korea's growth strategy, based on state direction of economic activity and chaebol organized production for export, represents "a new way of industrializing that challenges long-held assumptions of a generation of economic thinkers."[1] Byung-Nak Song makes the same point, arguing that South Korea's economic strategy "appears to be the only right development strategy, not only for Korea, but perhaps also for any developing country that wants to sustain economic development for a long period of time."[2]

While I heartily agree that the South Korean experience has much to teach us, including the importance of the state in promoting economic growth, I strongly disagree with those who advocate this new conventional wisdom. Their conclusions are seriously flawed largely because their studies of South Korean state capitalism incorrectly equate industrialization with development as well as ignore the reality of contradictions and class conflict.[3]

Development is concerned with more than just state power and growth. Only by recognizing contradictions and class conflict as an essential part of the South Korean state capitalist experience can we hope to understand the origins and nature of the economic and political contradictions that now push the country toward a crisis; as well as the roots and vision of the growing progressive movement that seeks to overcome these contradictions through radical transformation of the country's existing political economy. In sum, any serious evaluation of the South Korean experience requires that we move beyond issues of state industrial policy to investigate the historical and political conditions that allowed for the creation of a strong state; the class interests and contradictions that shaped and directed its policies; and the social, political, and economic consequences of these policies for the South Korean people. Such an investigation is the goal of Part II.

This chapter begins this investigation with an examination of the impact of Japanese imperialism on Korea. As we will see, Japanese imperialism had been primarily responsible for the replacement of Korea's traditional economic and political structures with state capitalist forms of social organization. Also Japanese imperialism set in motion the growth of a working-class-led political movement committed to building a democratic, unified socialist Korea.

The Collapse of the Yi Dynasty and the Colonization of Korea

On August 22, 1910, after more than a thousand years of history as an independent and distinct geographic unit, Korea lost its independence and became a province of the Japanese empire. The Yi dynasty, which had ruled Korea since 1392, was unable to defend the country against sustained efforts by the Japanese to colonize it.

Although appearing to control a powerful, centrally organized government bureaucracy, the Yi state was in fact a relatively weak institution. In theory, all lands were owned by the king, and the aristocracy depended upon a designated share of the surplus output from assigned estates to sustain itself. Such control over the land and its surplus should have given the king the power to mobilize resources and thus initiate whatever changes in political and economic activity might have been necessary to protect the independence of the country. In actuality, however, it was the aristocracy and not the king who dominated the centralized state bureaucracy. As a result, the state operated primarily as a revenue-raising institution for the elite, rather than as a source of power for the king.

By balancing power in this fashion, the Korean system proved remarkably resistant to significant transformation. The lords organized the estates assigned to them, but had no real ownership rights. The king, on the other hand, formally owned most lands, but had responsibility only for revenue collection, not management. Thus, while both sides engaged in frequent struggle over the distribution of the collected surplus, neither side had a clear interest in pursuing greater wealth through investment or innovation.[4]

This arrangement, while relatively stable, still generated serious social tensions. During periods when the aristocracy grew in number or power, the king was often forced to buy peace by offering them a larger share of the existing agricultural output. Such a strategy commonly left the government without sufficient revenue to support its own activities, including payment to the military and lower-level officials. This constant struggle over a relatively fixed agricultural output was usually resolved by raising taxes, tribute, and labor demands on the peasants who worked the land. This, in turn, led to peasant rebellions.

The Yi state faced more than periodic internal challenges to its power, however. Beginning in the early nineteenth century, Western powers became increasingly interested in Korea. Seeking access to Korean markets and raw materials, the British sent warships in 1832 and 1845, the French in 1846, the Russians in 1854, the Germans and Americans in 1866, and the Americans again in 1871.

Having observed the tremendous harm Western contact brought to China, Korea fought fiercely to maintain itself as the "Hermit Kingdom"; all attempts by foreign warships to secure access to Korean ports were rebuffed in military battle. Korea's success was due not only to its own efforts, but also to the fact that none of the Western powers was prepared to send an occupying army or large fleet to crush the Korean resistance. Each had hoped that intimidation alone would be sufficient; when it proved otherwise, they turned their attention to other more lucrative and strategic areas.

Japan, however, facing its own external threat, was not so easily put off. Japan had been forced by the United States to sign a commercial treaty in 1854 and, not long afterward, other Western countries demanded and were granted similar rights of trade. Recognizing that the world was quickly being divided into colonizers and colonies, a significant sector of the Japanese elite committed itself to action, hoping to prevent Japan from falling into the latter category. Their response was the Meiji Restoration of 1868, which eventually succeeded in transforming Japan into an aggressive industrializing nation.

With Western attention focused on China, Japan was afforded a period of time, free from direct foreign intervention, to strengthen itself. Aware of the need for raw materials and foreign markets to support industrialization, Japan sought to solve its own problems at Korea's expense. However, while geography made Korea a natural target for Japanese expansion, China remained an obstacle to Japanese plans.

Although formally an independent nation, Korea had long been under Chinese suzerainty. Thus, in exchange for Korean tribute and deference, China had, in the past, provided the Korean kingdom with military protection. It had, for example, sent troops in the late sixteenth century in support of Korean resistance to an earlier Japanese invasion.

Korea and China were far weaker now, however, and Japan confidently confronted them both. After deliberately creating an incident in which one of its warships was attacked in Korean waters, the Japanese demanded that Korea make restitution by entering into treaty negotiations. To press its case, it simultaneously sent several warships to Korea and a diplomatic mission to China.

Faced with Japanese determination to make war against Korea, China advised the Korean government to negotiate trade concessions with Japan. The result was the 1876 Treaty of Kanghwa which proclaimed Korea independent from China and gave Japan access to Korean ports and markets. Seeking to minimize the advantage of this concession to Japan, the Korean government, again with Chinese support, signed similar treaties with other countries including the United States in 1882, Britain in 1883, and Russia in 1884.

This strategy, which sought to preserve national independence by playing one foreign power off against another, was a losing one, however. By obligating the Korean government to make financial payments and undertake port modernization, these treaties forced the state to increase the tax burden on the peasantry at the same time that foreign imports were destroying the village economy. One of the most significant internal repercussions was the Tonghak Uprising in 1894.

Tonghak was a religiously based social movement whose founder, Ch'oe Che-u, had preached the unity of human beings and God. According to his ideas, serving God meant serving the people. A true believer was obligated to actively participate in the struggle to make Korea a more just and equal society. Fearful of Ch'oe's activist message, growing peasant support, and prediction that 1864 would be a year of massive social change, the Korean government arrested him in 1863 and executed him the following year.

While the Tonghak movement was greatly weakened by the death of its founder, his ideas continued to gain popularity among a peasantry that faced ever greater hardships. By 1894, after years of patient organizing, the Tonghak movement was once again a major political force. Angry at the decline in peasant living conditions, the corruption of the aristocracy, and the growing domination of Korea by foreigners, especially the Japanese, the Tonghak movement determined to take action. A large army was formed among the peasants under the banner "Sustain the Nation and Provide for the People," and it set out to force the king to end slavery and discrimination; distribute land to those who worked it; cancel all debts; punish those who had abused their office; and expel all foreigners.[5]

The king dispatched an army to suppress the revolt, but it was defeated in battle by the Tonghak. Frightened by the strength of this popular uprising, the King simultaneously called upon the Chinese to send troops and offered to negotiate with the Tonghak. Hopeful that the king's offer for talks would result in a satisfactory agreement, the Tonghak halted their military actions and demobilized most of their army. This proved to be a serious mistake.

In response to the king's request, Chinese troops soon arrived in Korea. Moving quickly to take advantage of the situation, the Japanese government sent an even bigger force to Korea, claiming that it was needed to protect Japanese property and lives. With the Tonghak no longer an armed threat, the Korean government now recognized the Japanese military as posing the biggest danger to its rule. Hoping to deny Japan any excuse for action, the Korean and Chinese governments announced the pending withdrawal of Chinese troops. The Japanese, determined to eliminate Chinese influence and establish their own unchallenged dominance over Korea, were unmoved.

Ignoring repeated Chinese attempts to negotiate a mutual withdrawal, the Japanese force in Korea launched a surprise attack on the palace, seizing the Korean king and forcing him to sign an agreement that would allow Japan free movement of troops in Korea. Soon after, Japan launched another surprise attack, this time on Chinese forces. The Tonghak took up arms again, this time to fight the Japanese, but were quickly defeated. The Chinese were also easily beaten in a war that lasted only eight months. The 1894-1895 Sino-Japanese War ended with China accepting the "full and complete independence of Korea," agreeing to pay indemnity to Japan, and giving up control of Taiwan to Japan.

Just as Japan was on the verge of achieving control over Korea, a new challenger suddenly appeared to frustrate its plans: Russia. Desperate to block Japan's growing foothold in Korea, the Korean government eagerly courted the Russians. The Japanese, however, were not to be stopped. On February 10, 1904, Japan launched a surprise attack on Russian forces in the region. The Korean government immediately announced its neutrality, but Japanese forces ignored the declaration and occupied the country. The Japanese scored an overwhelming victory in the fighting and the Russians were soon forced to sue for peace. The Russian-Japanese war formally ended on September 5, 1905, with U.S. President Theodore Roosevelt acting as mediator in the negotiations. In the final treaty, Russia acknowledged the right of Japan to guide, control, and protect Korea.

Korea could find no more foreign protectors. In fact, both England and the United States, the only two countries powerful enough to block Japan's advance in Korea, favored Japanese colonization of Korea in order to protect their own imperialism. In January 1902, for example, England and Japan signed the Anglo-Japanese Alliance whereby Japan pledged to recognize England's "rights and interests" in China, and England promised to respect Japan's dominance in Korea. Similarly, U.S. Secretary of War William Taft signed a secret agreement in July 1905, known as the Taft-Katsura Agreement, in which the United States recognized Japanese rights to Korea in exchange for Japanese recognition of U.S. dominance in the Philippines and Hawaii.

With such international support, Japan had little trouble forcing the Korean government to sign a treaty, ten weeks after the end of the Russo-Japanese War, making Korea a protectorate of Japan. Through the office of the resident-general, newly established by this treaty, the Japanese came to exercise broad control over Korea's domestic policies and international relations. Japanese domination was finally complete on August 22, 1910, when the prime minister of Korea signed a treaty of annexation with Japan.

In contrast to the Korean government's complete capitulation to Japan, popular resistance to Japanese colonialism remained strong throughout this period. For example, when Japan dissolved the Korean army in 1907, many soldiers refused to turn in their weapons and formed "righteous armies" to engage in armed guerrilla struggle against Japanese troops from bases within and outside the country. Over 18,000 Koreans were killed resisting the Japanese in the period between the Protectorate Treaty of 1905 and the Annexation Treaty of 1910.[6]

In summary, Korea's loss of independence had much to do with the nature of the Yi state. Not only did it prove unable to mobilize the resources necessary for renewal, it was also unwilling to draw upon the strength of the Korean people to defend the nation. The state response to the Tonghak Uprising illustrates clearly that the Korean ruling class feared losing privilege to the peasants far more than it did dependence on foreign powers. With the international balance of power unfavorable to Korea, foreign treaties and agreements proved insufficient even to save the Korean ruling class, much less the independence of the nation.

Japanese Colonialism and the Economic Transformation of Korea

Korea was now to be transformed in response to Japanese needs by a powerful colonial state organized around the newly created office of the Government-General. The governor-general, always a Japanese military leader, enjoyed total control over Korean affairs. All Koreans who refused to obey his dictates were subject to arrest by the newly created police force. This was no idle threat: in 1918 alone, more than 140,000 Koreans were arrested by the police.[7]

Agriculture and Raw Materials

Japan was initially interested in Korea as a source of foodstuffs and raw materials. This interest was expressed through the earliest policies of the new colonial state, which were directed toward establishing Japanese control over Korean lands. From 1910 to 1918 the Government-General carried out a comprehensive survey of all land to determine its ownership and quality. The process was designed to ensure a massive export of foodstuffs to Japan and resulted in outright transfer of land to the Japanese as well as the overall concentration of land in the hands of a few owners, Korean as well as Japanese.

Many Koreans lost ownership of their land to the Government-General because they were not aware of the registration requirements or did not understand how the procedure worked. More important, all lands formerly owned by the Yi state were automatically declared the property of the Government-General. As a result, the Government-General became the largest landowner in Korea. A similar procedure also transferred all formerly state-owned forest lands to the colonial government. Statistics from 1930 show that the Government-General owned approximately 40 percent of the combined total of Korea's agricultural and forest lands.[8] Some of the best lands were eventually sold at greatly reduced prices to select Japanese development companies as well as to individual Japanese who came to Korea to farm.

Not all Koreans were disenfranchised by this land program. In fact, the governor-general was more than willing to allow a small number of former Korean landholders, primarily those aristocrats who demonstrated their willingness to collaborate with the Japanese, to use the registration process to establish title to their lands as well as expand their holdings. Japanese policy thus deliberately supported the development of a highly dependent but wealthy Korean landowning class.

These land policies also led to the impoverishment of the Korean farm population, the great majority of whom were forced into tenant farming. In the south, for example, approximately 90 percent of all farmers worked as tenants, with most paying rents equal to between 80 and 90 percent of their harvest.[9] Under such conditions, most Korean peasants struggled just to survive.

The Japanese did not judge their agricultural policies by the well-being of Korean peasants, however. What counted was the size of the rice surplus that could be exported to Japan. And, if evaluated on this basis, the land program must be judged a success. While Korean rice production grew only 38 percent from 1912 to 1936, exports grew by over 700 percent. From 1932 to 1936, Korea was exporting more than half of its total production of rice. This massive flow of rice to Japan exceeded even the levels set by Japanese planners and was of enormous help to the Japanese government, allowing it to stabilize food consumption and wages in Japan at acceptable levels. This "success" was possible only because Koreans were forced to reduce their own rice consumption in both absolute as well as per capita terms.[10]

Korea also proved to be an important source of minerals for Japan. Shortly after annexation, the Government-General surveyed Korean mineral holdings and, in coordination with a select few giant Japanese conglomerates, undertook the exploration and mining of raw materials such as gold, silver, iron, led, tungsten, and coal. Such mining activity greatly increased during World War I, allowing Japan to earn considerable foreign exchange through sales to the Allies. Japanese exploitation of Korean minerals increased once again as a result of World War II, although this time it was to support its own military offensive against China in 1937 and the United States in 1941.

Manufacturing

Between 1900 and 1929 the Japanese economy enjoyed extremely rapid economic growth, far out-performing the other developed industrial countries. As the Japanese economy became increasingly industrialized, Japanese interest in Korea also began to change. Beginning in 1920, in response to the growing needs of Japanese industry, the Government-General implemented new policies designed to encourage and support Japanese investment and production of manufactures in Korea. The result was that Korea itself began to experience industrialization.

Japanese industrial investment in Korea greatly accelerated with the 1931 Japanese attack and conquest of Manchuria. The worldwide depression then underway had convinced the Japanese government of the need to aggressively establish its own imperialist system in order to ensure control over the raw materials and markets necessary to sustain the country's economic growth. The newly established puppet state of Manchukuo (formerly Manchuria) was a rich source of raw materials, and Korea was targeted to become a strategic base for Japan's continuing military and economic exploitation of the region, including north China.

With Japan's giant zaibatsu (family-owned conglomerates) leading the way with new investments, especial in munitions and related heavy and chemical industries, the share of manufactures in Korea's total production of commodities rose from 17.7 percent in 1925, to 31.3 percent in 1936, and to 39 percent in 1939. Within the manufacturing sector itself, the share of heavy and chemical industries rose from 16.5 percent in 1930 to 47 percent in 1939.[11]

Korea's growing integration into a Japanese organized and dominated international division of labor is also reflected in Japanese-Korean trade patterns. By 1931, 95 percent of all Korean exports were sold to Japan and 80 percent of all Korean imports came from Japan. In turn, Korea was Japan's main export market, accounting for approximately 34 percent of all Japanese exports in 1939.[12] More significantly, the composition of Korea's trade with Japan was dramatically transformed by Japanese investment activities in Korea. While raw materials accounted for over 80 percent of Korean exports to Japan in 1929, this fell to less than 50 percent by 1939. Over the same period, manufactures as a percentage of Korean exports to Japan rose from approximately 13 percent to approximately 46 percent.[13]

The overall economic impact of Japanese policy on Korea was enormous. For example, from 1910 to 1940, Korea's GNP grew at an average annual rate of over 4 percent, while its manufacturing sector grew at an even faster 10 percent rate. Between 1911 and 1938, Korea even recorded a higher average annual rate of GNP growth than did Japan.[14]

Japanese officials often pointed to these figures to argue the benefits of their colonial rule. But this industrialization neither responded to Korean needs nor was directed by Koreans. According to 1938 data, Japanese companies owned almost 90 percent of all manufacturing capital in Korea. The same was true for mining. In 1945, Japanese companies accounted for almost 95 percent of all investments in coal mining and their share of investment and facilities in other mining industries was even higher.[15]

This rapid industrialization, although under Japanese control, did have a major impact on Korea's class structure. Pushed off their land by colonial land policies as well as by labor mobilizations, displaced peasants were transformed into wage workers. In 1931, there were only 106,781 factory workers and 35,895 mine workers employed in Korea. By 1937, the year that Japan invaded China, those numbers had grown to 207,000 and 162,000 respectively. Finally, in 1944, approximately 600,000 Koreans were employed in factories and 350,000 in mines. If we add to these figures all those workers employed in transportation, construction, forestry, and marine products, the Korean wage labor force in Korea topped two million.[16] And these figures do not include the great many Koreans who worked in factories and mines in Manchuria and Japan.

Perhaps not surprisingly, this Japanese-directed industrialization was achieved with very little regard for the well-being of Korean wage workers. Wages in 1935 were 50 percent less than they had been in 1927. The normal industrial work day was lengthened over the same period from twelve to sixteen hours. Moreover, health and safety conditions were nonexistent, resulting in a very high rate of industrial accidents, diseases, and deaths.[17]

Japanese Colonialism
and the Political Economy of Exploitation

The Korean economy was, as described above, transformed in response to Japanese needs. Equally significant, the geographic closeness of the two countries allowed the Japanese to shape and direct this process of transformation by using their own institutions and the logic of their own industrial system. One important legacy of this period of Japanese colonialism, then, was an imposed social organization.

The basic structure of the modern Japanese political economy was formed in the 1930s. Over that decade, national industrial planning was extended to include most major industries in Japan. New state institutions of planning and management were also developed to regulate, among other things, the purchase and use of foreign technology, to control market entry through a system of licensing, and to allocate foreign exchange according to state planning priories. State policies also encouraged the development and integration of big banks and large family-owned conglomerates known as zaibatsu; by the end of the 1930s, the largest of these zaibatsu, especially the big four—Mitsui, Mitsubishi, Sumitomo, and Yasuda, dominated the Japanese economy. A new, highly regimented and repressive system of labor control was also introduced.

While this economic structure proved to be a powerful engine of growth, other factors contributed decisively to Japan's rapid industrial development. Among the most important was the country's aggressive colonization and exploitation of other countries, especially Korea. The fact that Korea was geographically so close to Japan meant that economic activity in Korea could be tightly integrated into the core activities of the Japanese economy.

This integration was achieved not only through substantial Japanese investments in railroads, ports, communications, and heavy industry in Korea, but, more important, through the establishment of a massive colonial state under direct Japanese control. Comparing the French administrative presence in Vietnam with that of the Japanese in Korea underscores this point. France ruled Vietnam, which in 1937 had a population of 17 million people, with approximately 3,000 French administrators, 11,000 regular French troops, and about 38,000 Vietnamese who served either in the administration or the militia.

The Japanese, in contrast, ruled approximately 21 million Koreans with a colonial administration employing 246,000 Japanese and an additional 63,000 Koreans. Nearly 42 percent of all Japanese in Korea in 1937 were in government service.[18]

This combination of geographic proximity and commanding colonial presence meant that Japanese domination over Korean economic activity could be carried out largely by direct extension of existing Japanese state and corporate institutions and strategies. Thus, although the colonial state exercised far greater economic power in Korea than did the Japanese state in Japan, and labor policies were far more brutal in Korea than in Japan, the economic organization imposed on Korea was in broad outline similar to the Japanese system described above. For example, the dominant institutions in Korea were the colonial state and the leading Japanese zaibatsu, with the state playing the key role of planner, financier, and manager of colonial activity.[19]

While we will discuss the influence of Japanese imperialism on the development of the contemporary South Korean state in detail in Chapter 7, a few general comments are in order here. Because economic growth in Korea was primarily directed by the colonial state and economic activity was dominated by a few large Japanese firms, the Japanese-initiated process of industrialization did little to strengthen the power or position of Korean capitalists. Japanese colonialism thus left Korea with a strong centralized state apparatus and weak capitalist class. This history helps explain the later dominance of the state in South Korea.

But Japanese colonialism did more than create the conditions for a dominant state to arise in Korea, it also directly transmitted a development model based on military power, state direction of economic activity, production by large family-owned conglomerates, and extreme exploitation of workers, especially women. The historical link between the Japanese colonial experience and the South Korean political economy was Park Chung Hee himself. Park had been a lieutenant in the Japanese military during the colonial period and served with distinction defending Japanese interests in Manchuria. As a great admirer of Japanese development, he eagerly sought to recreate the Japanese political economy as he understood it. As we will see later, Park's efforts produced a state structure and growth strategy that had more in common with

Japanese colonial state practices in Korea than it did with the actual Japanese political economy.

The Korean Independence Movement and Class Struggle

Japanese colonialism also heavily influenced the dynamics of class struggle in Korea. As mentioned earlier, Koreans actively resisted Japanese expansionism. From 1905 to 1910 the most active military opposition was led by the "righteous armies." Originally organized by members of the Korean aristocracy and made up primarily of peasants, they became most effective after 1907, when they were joined by members of the disbanded Korean army. These armed units were active throughout the country, attacking Japanese garrisons as well as rail lines and telegraph facilities. According to Japanese estimates, these righteous armies had almost 70,000 fighters in 1908 and engaged Japanese forces in almost 1,500 separate incidents.[20] When Korea's annexation in 1910 made it impossible to maintain bases in Korea, most of these armed units reassembled in Manchuria or the Russian maritime territory, from where they continued to wage guerrilla warfare against the Japanese.

With the end of organized military resistance in Korea, leadership of the independence movement within the country soon passed to those members of the Korean elite who advocated peaceful and diplomatic means to force the Japanese out of Korea. This approach, energized by U.S. President Woodrow Wilson's highly publicized support for the self-determination of nations, reached its highest expression with the 1919 March First Movement. On that day, thirty-three leading Korean citizens read aloud a Declaration of Independence which proclaimed Korea to be once again an independent nation. And, under the slogan "Long Live Korean Independence!" millions of students, workers, farmers, and shopkeepers took to the streets to peacefully express their opposition to Japanese rule. The demonstrations even spread to Manchuria and the Russian maritime territory.

This nonviolent strategy failed; not one Western country was moved to speak out against Japanese colonialism much less Japan's brutal suppression of the movement. A youthful Korean participant described the Japanese response as follows:

> The Japanese were very confused. They didn't know what to do. Such a movement puzzled them by its intensity no less than by its peaceableness. But they quickly decided. On the second day they arrested the leaders and up to May 21, when the movement stopped, arrested altogether three hundred thousand people. All the hospitals and schools were turned into prison camps. Two-thirds of those arrested were freed after a short detention, after having been beaten. The other one hundred thousand were "legally" arrested and sent to court. About fifty thousand of these were sentenced to imprisonment. Not one was executed—there was no legal excuse for this. Korean civil law forbade this, as the demonstrators had openly and insistently announced, "We struggle only for Korean independence and not against Japan." Execution was legal only for murder, so the Japanese killed the people on the streets instead of arresting them—a nice technicality.[21]

The destruction of the March First Movement marked another major turning point in the Korean independence struggle. The Korean elite now split into two camps. The members of one group decided to leave the country, eventually joining with other Korean leaders in April 1919 to form a government-in-exile, the Korean Provisional Government (KPG). Although the KPG initially represented many different political tendencies, it was soon dominated by conservatives who continued to insist that independence required winning Western support for an international campaign to pressure Japan to withdraw from Korea. However, unable to gain Western interest and increasingly isolated from developments within Korea, the KPG ceased to function as an active organization after 1921. Although it eventually resumed limited activities after the attack on Pearl Harbor, even fielding a small military force, it played no significant role in the Korean independence struggle.

The elite that remained in Korea were also affected by the collapse of the March First Movement. After it became apparent that no international support for Korean independence would be forthcoming, most ended their open opposition to the Japanese, hoping in this way to ensure the survival of Korean culture and leadership until some future day when the struggle might reasonably be resumed. This strategy, based on what its advocates called "nationalist reformation principles," was made easier by a simultaneous change in what the Japanese called their "cultural policy."

The Japanese, deciding that the March First Movement was the result of an overly repressive governor-general, appointed a new official who introduced reforms granting Koreans expanded economic and cultural opportunities, including the right to open factories, newspapers, and schools. Many Korean elite took advantage of this opening. Data for 1928 show, for example, that while Japanese firms owned the overwhelming majority of all manufacturing assets, Koreans owned more factories than did the Japanese and employed 30 percent of the manufacturing work force.[22] The decade of the 1920s thus saw the beginning of an alliance between the Japanese and the small but influential Korean bourgeoisie.

But the gradual end of direct elite opposition to Japanese colonialism did not mean the end of the independence struggle. Instead, it became radically transformed under the increasingly effective leadership of leftists, especially communists. As noted above, many Korean resistance fighters moved to Manchuria and the Russian maritime provinces where they continued armed struggle against the Japanese. Influenced by the revolutionary developments in both China and Russia, these activists organized socialist and communist formations in 1918 and 1919. In early 1921, a number of these formations came together, still outside of Korea, to form the first Korean Communist Party. Its platform included the following demands: nationalization of all industries; free and compulsory education for all; compulsory labor for men and women; the emancipation of women; and the confiscation of all capitalist property.[23] In 1925, a new Korean Communist Party (KCP) was established, this time in Korea itself.

Although the KCP was under constant surveillance by the Japanese colonial police force, suffering almost total destruction many times, it succeeded in organizing an active popular resistance to Japanese rule. Dae-Sook Suh, a widely respected Korean political scientist, described the determined efforts of communist organizers who "planted a deep core of communist influence among the Korean people, particularly the students, youth groups, laborers, and peasants. . . . The haggard appearance of the communists suffering from torture, their stern and disciplined attitude toward the common enemy of all Koreans, had a far-reaching effect on the people."[24]

Communists and the Labor Movement

Industrialization in Korea began in the 1920s. Employment conditions were brutal, and workers had to overcome active police and army interventions to defend their rights. Women in particular played a key role in the Korean labor movement. As a case in point, in July 1923 more than one hundred women workers from four rubber factories located in northern Korea went on strike to protest reduced wages and harsh treatment by management. Two days later, women workers in another rubber factory in the same area struck in solidarity. The strike, known as the Kyungseong rubber factory women workers' strike, helped launch the Kyungseong Rubber Factory Women Workers' Union which, in turn, played an important role in the 1925 formation of the Korean Labor Federation (KLF).

While the communist movement within Korea was initially led by left-wing intellectuals, Japanese police repression and the industrialization of Korea soon led to the rise of working-class party leadership and a growing solidarity between the Korean communist and labor movements. This solidarity was reflected in the politics of the KLF which brought together approximately 150 Korean labor and trade union organizations around a statement of mission that proclaimed:

Our purpose is to liberate the working class and to build a completely new society.

We will fight with the capitalist class with the collective power of the workers until a final victory is won.

We will fight for better welfare and economic improvement of the present working class.[25]

The KLF called for working-class unity and led numerous struggles for the eight-hour day and a minimum wage system. It was active at not only the enterprise level but the regional and industrial levels as well. As part of its broader program, it also "emphasized solidarity relationships between labor organizations and other social and political organizations."[26]

Strike activity greatly increased throughout the 1920s, reaching a peak in 1929-1930 when labor disputes took place in almost every major city. There was, for example, a major solidarity strike in

Pusan of five rubber factories during which time the women workers physically attacked the facilities of one of the companies and then marched to the police station to free one of their leaders. In South Hamkyung Province, graphite miners went out on strike for higher wages and a shorter work week. Workers at all the companies in the area, including those who worked at the printing shop, brewery, and brassware factory joined them, creating a regional general strike.

One of the most important labor actions of the period was the 1929 Wonsan labor strike. Called by the dock and transport workers of the Federation of Labor Unions of Wonsan to protest low wages and poor working conditions, the strike lasted approximately three months. Union workers throughout Korea sent aid and transport workers throughout the region went on a solidarity strike. The Japanese refused to yield, however, and in the end the strike leaders were arrested, the union destroyed, and the strike lost.

The Japanese occupation of Manchuria in 1931 brought a further intensification of class struggle within Korea. With Korea becoming an important regional base for Japanese economic and military operations, union activities of any kind became unacceptable to the colonial government. The police also greatly increased their anti-communist operations, successfully destroying the ability of the Korean Communist Party to organize national programs. While the arrest or forced exile of the party's leadership made central direction of party work impossible, it did not stop communist organizing activity. Activists responded by intensifying their regional work, providing leadership and support for numerous labor strikes and rural tenant struggles throughout the country.

While anti-Japanese activities in Korea were important, the most effective resistance to Japanese imperialism during the 1930s was led by communists who engaged the Japanese in armed struggle in Manchuria. Their efforts also had an important impact on the political development of workers in Korea, drawing left and labor activists closer together into a unified national liberation movement. The growing politicalization of the labor movement in Korea through the 1930s is illustrated by the following popular labor slogans:

Japanese police, don't get involved in labor strikes!

Guarantee the rights to strike and to form or participate in a revolutionary organization!

Guarantee the right of freedom of speech and of public assembly! Release immediately all political prisoners!

Withdraw immediately Japanese Army from Korea and Manchuria![27]

The integration of economic and political demands by Korean workers was a natural outgrowth of Japanese imperialism. Japan did not only colonize Korea but did so through the introduction of capitalism. Workers therefore came to identify imperialism and capitalism as an organic whole and supported those movements that opposed both. This class understanding of the nature of their oppression was further strengthened by Japan's occupation policies. As Bruce Cumings, a scholar who has done pioneering work on the Korean politics of the period, explains:

> It was really in the post-1931 period of industrialization that the coincidence of ethnicity and position waned; as class antagonisms and socialist ideology spread, the Japanese, like other colonial powers, recognized the uses of divide-and-rule techniques. As the colonial regime penetrated and mobilized more Koreans, the artifice of pitting Koreans against Koreans spread. The extension of the bureaucracy, as offices proliferated, opened more of it to Koreans. Koreans could no longer simply blame the foreign race for the misfortunes that befell them, since the regime often presented itself in the person of a Korean official.[28]

As Japan launched its war against China in 1937, new sacrifices were demanded of the Koreans. Thus, beginning in 1938, some 100,000 to 200,000 Korean young women were forcibly recruited by the Japanese military to serve as prostitutes for Japanese soldiers in brothels known as "battlefield comfort stations." Even those prominent Koreans who had been allowed a measure of independence in the 1920s were now ordered to actively show their support for Japanese rule and war policies. All existing Korean cultural, political and social groups were dissolved and replaced by new organizations such as the Korean League for the General Mobilization of the National Spirit which had branches in provinces, counties, townships and the workplace.

After bombing Pearl Harbor, the Japanese demanded still greater sacrifices from the Korean people in support of the Japanese war effort. Estimates are that over four million Koreans were drafted for labor activities in Korea. Approximately one million Koreans were also sent to Japan to work in the factories and mines. By January 1945, Koreans accounted for over 30 percent of the entire Japanese labor force.[29]

These labor mobilization measures were coupled with new social measures designed to break Korean resistance. In 1943, the governor-general declared Japanese the official language of Korea; Korean could no longer be taught in any school or used at public meetings. All Korean newspapers were closed and only Japanese periodicals allowed to circulate. Emperor worship and Shinto shrine visitations were also required. Finally, Koreans were ordered to change their family names to Japanese.

Resistance, of course, did exist, and was led, as noted above, by communists. As living and working conditions for Koreans worsened through the 1930s, resistance increased, forcing the Japanese to organize a number of new compulsory anticommunist organizations for purposes of social control. The Korean Anti-Communist Association, for example, was established in 1938, with local groups operating at the village level. As Bruce Cumings notes, the establishment of such organizations was "a measure of the degree to which socialism had become attractive. . . . "[30]

Such an attraction should not be surprising. Japanese identification of all who opposed the colonial government as communists certainly increased popular support for socialism among working people. But this support was based on more than admiration for those who struggled against the Japanese. Only socialism offered the working class of Korea a vision that transcended both the imperialist and class nature of their oppression. The harsher the mobilization and resulting industrial experience, the more intense working class support became for social revolution. In short, Japanese imperialism unintentionally created what it most feared: a communist-led, working-class movement committed to building a socialist Korea. As we will see in the next chapter, only the intervention of U.S. imperialism frustrated its realization.

CHAPTER 6

U.S. IMPERIALISM, THE STATE, AND CLASS STRUGGLE

In the last chapter we examined the way Japanese imperialism directed a brutal capitalist transformation of Korea, producing in turn a working-class-led socialist movement. In this chapter we will examine the role U.S. imperialism played in the defeat of this socialism movement, the division of Korea, and the rise to power of a capitalist-oriented, military dictatorship in the south.

The Surrender of Japan and the Occupation of Korea

Although many conservative Korean leaders had spent years trying to enlist the United States and other Western powers in an international campaign to force Japan to grant Korea its independence, they received little response. The first formal international statement in support of Korean independence was not made until December 1943, when the United States, Great Britain, and China issued the Cairo Declaration, one part of which read:

> The aforesaid three powers, mindful of the enslavement of the people of Korea, are determined that in due course Korea shall become free and independent.[1]

The significance of the phrase "due course" became clear at the Yalta Conference in February 1945, when U.S. President Roosevelt suggested to Stalin that Korea should spend twenty to thirty years under the joint trusteeship of the United States, USSR, Great Britain, and China before being granted its independence. Stalin is quoted as having replied, "the shorter the period the better."[2]

In general terms, the U.S. offer of trusteeship reflected both U.S. desires to maintain a dominant position in Asian affairs and U.S. recognition that Soviet involvement in the war against Japan would make it impossible to exclude it from playing some role in a postwar Korean settlement. The United States was, in fact, very pleased when Stalin finally agreed, at Yalta, to Roosevelt's request that the Soviet Union declare war against Japan and directly engage the Japanese army in Manchuria and Korea. U.S. military planners believed these troops to be among Japan's best, and that more lives might be lost fighting in Korea than in an invasion of Japan itself.[3]

U.S. plans for unhurried international negotiations over the future of Korea were frustrated, however, by the unpredicted rapid disintegration of Japanese resistance. The United States dropped atomic bombs on Japan on August 6 and August 9, and the Soviet Union declared war on Japan on August 8, immediately sending troops into northern Korea. Within days, the Japanese war effort collapsed and Emperor Hirohito prepared to announce his country's unconditional surrender. Suddenly, Soviet entry into the war against Japan, especially its offensive in Korea, had become a serious threat to U.S. foreign policy objectives. The Soviet army was moving rapidly down the Korean peninsula and, facing only minimal Japanese resistance, would soon be in command of the entire country.

Responding to this growing foreign policy disaster, Truman's special ambassador, Edwin Pauley, sent an urgent message to the U.S. President from Moscow, recommending that the United States "occupy quickly as much as possible of the industrial areas of Korea (the north) and Manchuria."[4] Unable to mobilize U.S. troops quickly enough for such an operation, yet determined to block the Soviet advance, the U.S. War Department sent two colonels into a room on August 11 and gave them thirty minutes to decide upon a dividing line in Korea, one which would allow U.S. troops to accept Japan's surrender as far north as was possible given United States logistical limitations and the Russian troop advance. The recommendation of the colonels was the 38th parallel, a division that placed approximately two-thirds of the country's population and the capital city, Seoul, in the United States zone.

This recommendation was accepted by the U.S. War Department

and became part of General Order No. 1, the U.S. plan for receiving the surrender of Japanese forces. General Order No. 1 was announced without prior consultation with other countries, including the Soviet Union, and no one in the U.S. military was sure how the Soviets would respond to this proposed limit on their advance in Korea. Much to their surprise, the Soviet Union accepted the U.S. plan without comment or challenge even though some of its troops had already moved south of the declared dividing line. Although U.S. troops would not actually arrive in Korea until September 8, 1945, the division of Korea had begun.

The Promise of a Socialist Korea

While U.S. officials met in war rooms in Washington, D.C., to map out Korea's future political orientation, Koreans in Korea were actively working to shape the political economy of their own independent country. Unfortunately for the Korean people, their plans turned out to be incompatible with those of the U.S. government.

The Japanese in Korea reacted with alarm to the reports they received concerning Japan's decision to surrender. They greatly feared that the Korean people would seek revenge for the harsh treatment they had received under colonial rule. Hoping to save themselves, Japanese officials in Korea approached several Koreans before the actual surrender was announced, in an attempt to establish a Korean-run "administrative committee" whose one purpose would be to maintain order and preserve Japanese property and lives after the surrender. The Koreans, however, would accept nothing less than the immediate establishment of new structures of self-governance.

The Committee for the Preparation of Korean Independence (CPKI) was formed in Seoul on liberation day, August 15, 1945, and within a few days all thirteen provinces had provincial-level branches. By the end of August there were approximately 145 CPKI branches operating throughout the country. These regional and local committees functioned to ensure the peace. But they also organized punishment of those who had collaborated with the Japanese as well as factory production and food distribution. Above all these largely independent committees were instruments of popular power; they were most often led by communists and other leftists who had won the respect and trust of their community because of their role in the anti-Japanese resistance.

The strength and determination of the Korean independence movement in this period gave rise to a rapid and widespread grassroots mobilization and organization of the people. Workers were especially active, often taking control over their workplaces and forming unions. In many cases, workers took responsibility for managing the enterprises themselves. Sometimes workers solicited bids from potential managers, then selected the one they thought would best serve the collective interest.[5] Peasant unions also sprang to life, organizing land takeovers and rice collection, storage, and distribution. This explosion of union activity was made possible largely because of the past organizing efforts of communists during the 1920s and 1930s.

While regional and local activities were often carried out independently of any national center, the Seoul-based CKPI had begun a process that was leading quickly and surely to the establishment of a national Korean government. The CPKI was, in fact, already in control of a national press and radio network. When it became known that U.S. forces were to arrive in Korea on September 8, 1945, the Seoul leadership of the CKPI decided to take action to consolidate the gains of the movement so as to make clear to the United States that Korea was ready and able to run its own affairs.

On September 6, 1945, the Committee for the Preparation of Korean Independence called a national congress in Seoul which was attended by approximately one thousand delegates from both the north and south of Korea. The congress established the Korean People's Republic (KPR), elected an executive committee, and authorized it to form a broad-based coalition government. The congress also passed an action program which was to be carried out by the new government. The program pledged the new government to do the following:

- Establish an independent and democratic state.
- Repeal all Japanese laws, decrees, and regulations.
- Nationalize all Japanese and pro-Japanese Korean-owned lands and properties and give them without charge to those who worked them.

- Nationalize all basic heavy industries, natural resources, means of communication, and transportation.
- Establish an eight-hour work day.
- Improve the living standards of working people.
- Introduce compulsory primary education.
- Guarantee basic human rights and freedoms including those of speech, press, assembly, and religion.
- Guarantee universal suffrage to all males and females above the age of eighteen.
- Cooperate with other countries to advance the cause of world peace.[6]

This was a powerful program, reflecting the desires of most Koreans to create a new political economy responsive to the needs of working people. As such it symbolized the powerful popular sentiment for the rejection of both capitalism and colonialism.[7]

With the establishment of the KPR, existing branches of the CKPI changed their name to people's committees and transferred their organizational allegiance to the KPR. Spontaneous local organizing continued, and within a few months people's committees were functioning as local organs of government in nearly every city and village throughout Korea. Almost all local committees had sections for organizing, propaganda, peacekeeping, food provisions, and finances. In many areas, they also had sections for welfare relief, consumer affairs, labor relations, and tenant rights. Some people's committees even took ownership of Japanese-owned homes and factories.[8]

The work of the KPR and its affiliated people's committees was carried out in close cooperation with an increasingly organized and highly politicized population. In early November, for example, representatives of the recently formed labor unions met in Seoul to create one unified central labor organization called the National Council of Korean Labor Unions (NCKLU). One of the NCKLU's first acts was to announce its affiliation with the KPR. Given the fact that workers were in direct control of Korea's railroads, public utilities, and major industries after their abandonment by the Japanese, this decision had great significance. In fact, it was recognition of the importance of this alliance between the Korean working class and the left-led KPR that caused President Truman's special advisor, Edwin Pauley, to warn that "Communism in Korea could get off to a better start than practically anywhere else in the world."[9]

Following the example of labor, representatives of provincial peasant unions from all over Korea came to Seoul in early December to form their own national organization, the National League of Peasant Unions, and declare their support for the KPR. Three days later young Koreans held a national meeting that led to the establishment of the Korean Democratic Youth League. Not long after, women's groups met in Seoul to form their own organization, the Women's League. Both of these national organizations also declared their support for the KPR and its program.

While there were Koreans who opposed the KPR and its program, primarily large landowners and Japanese collaborators, they were clearly in the minority. In fact, the mood of the country was such that in the period immediately following liberation no one dared to openly challenge those who spoke for land reform, workers rights, or people's democracy. Without outside intervention, it would have been only a matter of months before the KPR and its sponsoring organizations succeeded in creating a functioning, popular national government. Unfortunately for the majority of Korean people, there was outside intervention, specifically massive U.S. intervention, which resulted in the destruction of these organizations and their movement for self-governance.

Significantly, this history, forgotten in the South for decades because of government suppression, has recently been rediscovered by many who are now active in the labor, farmer's, women's, and student movements in South Korea. The struggles and hopes of the past thus remain very much alive, playing an important and positive role in shaping the political understandings and vision of those who currently seek to transform the South Korean political economy.

U.S. Intervention and the
Restoration of the Right

The political developments described above were frightening to those Koreans who had accumulated significant land or wealth or had previously served in the colonial government. These people, many of whom had recently arrived from the north to avoid the advancing Soviet troops and newly formed CPKI committees, were greatly cheered by the news that it would be the U.S. military that would accept the Japanese surrender in the south. In fact, in accord with General Order No. 1, the existing Japanese governmental structure had remained in limited operation in southern Korea until the arrival of U.S. troops on September 8. On the following day, General Hodge, commander of the U.S. military in Korea, announced that he wanted the Government-General, with all its existing personnel, Korean and Japanese, to continue to carry out its responsibilities.

Gaining confidence from U.S. policy, a number of those Koreans who had grown wealthy through collaboration with the Japanese established their own political party, the Korean Democratic Party (KDP), on September 16, 1945. Largely compromised by their past actions, yet anxious to offer an alternative to the Korean People's Republic, KDP leaders issued a call for recognition of the Korean Provisional Government (at the time headquartered in Chungking, China) as the official government of Korea. The United States refused, having no clear plan yet in mind for Korea.

One thing was immediately clear to U.S. military forces however: political organizing led by the KPR represented a direct challenge to United States authority in southern Korea. The fact that people's committees had been allowed to function in the north made them even more dangerous in the eyes of U.S. officials, strengthening the KPR's claim to represent the entire Korean nation. After a brief period of hesitation, the U.S. military decided on its strategy: destroy the KPR and its associated organizations in the south and create, in their place, a new Korean political movement friendly to the United States.

To carry out this strategy, U.S. policymakers found it useful to breathe new life into the old institutions of Japanese colonial rule and promote leading members of the KDP into positions of political power. For example, the U.S. military government restored the Japanese colonial police force, recruiting for duty the very same Koreans. As under Japanese rule, the Korean National Police (KNP) was to operate as a highly centralized, national force, with local and provincial police responsible only to national police headquarters, and not local political officials. This command structure enabled the U.S. government, as it did the Japanese colonial government before it, to move troops rapidly and maintain tight discipline when confronting a hostile population. The KNP trained at the same police academy the Japanese had established, wore the same uniforms, and used the same rifles. But now the police drove U.S. rather than Japanese army vehicles. The national police were to become an important weapon in the U.S. military government's offensive against the KPR and the National Council of Korean Labor Unions. Leadership positions in the KNP hierarchy were given to KDP officials.

This strategy was seriously flawed, however, in that few people were likely to abandon the KPR in favor of a movement led by collaborators and identified with Japanese colonial institutions. To overcome this problem, both U.S. and KDP leaders turned to Syngman Rhee. Rhee's advantage to both groups was obvious: he had spent the period of Japanese colonialism living in the United States and working to win U.S. support for Korean independence, he was strongly anti-Japanese as well as anti-communist, and he had been a leading figure in the KPG. Returning to Korea on October 16, in one of General Douglas MacArthur's private planes, he lent legitimacy to U.S.-KDP efforts to construct an alternative to the KPR.

After his return, Rhee formed his own political organization, the Central Council of the Society for the Promotion of Korean Independence, of which the most important member organization was the KDP. Rhee was no one's puppet, however. He had his own political agenda and, as we will see, successfully out-maneuvered all other rivals to dominate the anti-communist movement in the south and win the support of the United States to become South Korea's first president. He ruled the country until driven from office in 1960.

U.S. Intervention and the Destruction of the Left

The U.S. offensive against the KPR and the NCKLU began in earnest in November 1945. That month Syngman Rhee denounced the KPR for its claim to represent the government of Korea. At the same time, the U.S. military government took the control of Japanese properties away from Korean workers and appointed new Korean managers. It then outlawed all strikes and ordered that all disputes be settled by newly formed mediation boards which were staffed by politically conservative Korean businessmen. In December, U.S. military authorities declared the KPR and its activities illegal.

In concert with its attack on the KPR and NCKLU, the United States created new alternative political structures. In February 1946, the United States formed the Representative Democratic Council led by Syngman Rhee. Later that year, it established the South Korean Interim Government. Half of the ninety seats on the Interim Government were appointed by the U.S. military government while the other half were elected under procedures established by the Japanese which limited the vote to landlords, taxpayers, and village headmen. Rhee and his supporters were in charge of organizing the election. In many places voting schedules were not publicly announced, which further narrowed participation.

All of these developments had one logic: the division of Korea and the establishment of a separate pro-U.S. government in the south. U.S. and Soviet negotiations over the future of Korea stressed the need to maintain and strengthen existing common national Korean organizations—there were, however, the people's committees and associated mass organizations, precisely the organizations that the United States was destroying.

Unable to exercise control over all of Korea because of the Soviet presence in the north, and fearful that Koreans would themselves choose to follow the socialist-oriented program of the KPR, the United States rapidly came to the conclusion that to secure its position of regional influence it had no choice but to create a separate South Korean state under its own control. In Syngman Rhee, the United States had the only major anti-Japanese Korean leader who supported division. Recognizing that his own political future depended upon the defeat of the KPR, Rhee was, by mid-1946, openly advocating the division of Korea and the establishment of a separate government in the south.

The objectives of the U.S.-Rhee alliance were widely understood and rejected by the great majority of southern Koreans. The conflict finally came to a head with a railway strike in Pusan in September

1946. Rail workers in Seoul and then workers in other industries and cities quickly declared strikes of their own, producing a national general strike with over 250,000 participants. Worker demands were political as well as economic: workers wanted higher wages and better working conditions, labor laws similar to those approved in northern Korea, the release of political prisoners, and transfer of power back to people's committees.

The U.S. military command in southern Korea immediately recognized this general strike for what it was—a direct challenge to its authority and policies. The Korean National Police and right-wing thugs were sent to break the railway strike and the union in Seoul, and many workers were beaten and arrested. Simply said, the U.S. military government had declared war on the Korean labor movement.

Demonstrations against this U.S.-directed attack on rail workers in Seoul took place in a number of southern cities, the most serious in Taegu. In early October, thousands of people rioted there in response to the police killing of a demonstrator; they killed a number of police, attacked police stations, and destroyed the homes of Korean officials. What started as a strike wave was now rapidly becoming an insurrection against U.S. rule. In response, the United States declared martial law and sent tanks and troops to enforce order. U.S. soldiers fired on any Koreans who gathered in groups on the streets.

In spite of this show of force, the United States could not contain the demonstrations. From October to December, popular uprisings spread rapidly to cities and villages throughout the Kyongsang provinces and then to South Ch'ungch'ong, Kyonggi, Kangwon, and South Cholla provinces. One of the most popular slogans of this rebellion was "Return the Korean Government to the People's Committees!" Other slogans called for an end to the U.S. military government and the adoption of land reform and labor laws similar to those in northern Korea. As the struggle spread westward into the agricultural heartland of southern Korea, the leadership of the movement passed from workers to farmers, making it the most significant peasant rebellion in Korea since the Tonghak Uprising. But like its predecessor, it also failed.

U.S. military strength proved too great and the organizational capabilities of the left too weak. The uprising had proceeded from one area to another in a largely spontaneous fashion without any national leadership or coordination. As a result, the United States and Korean National Police had the freedom to use their superior communication and firepower to confront each regional uprising separately, arresting or killing the leaders and thus ending open opposition in one area, before having to confront a new challenge in another location. More than one thousand Koreans died and 30,000 were arrested in the three-month rebellion. When it was over, the United States had succeeded in extending its control down to the provincial level. Regional and local leaders of the people's committees and peasant and labor unions were now either arrested, dead, or underground; their organizations no longer functioned.

U.S. Intervention and the Division of Korea

With U.S.-Soviet trusteeship negotiations at a standstill in late 1947, the United States took advantage of its newly won political dominance in southern Korea to unilaterally request United Nations involvement in the formation of a Korean government. More specifically, the United States asked for the establishment of a United Nations Temporary Commission on Korea and the holding of elections under its authority to select a Korean National Assembly which would, in turn, elect the president of the country.

The U.S. plan called for elections to be organized separately in the north and south, a "win-win" situation for the United States. If the USSR refused to cooperate, a vote would still be held in the south, thereby ensuring the United States of a friendly regime on the Korean peninsula. If the USSR agreed, then the U.S.-controlled vote in the far larger south would guarantee a U.S.-dominated Korean government regardless of the outcome of the vote in the north. Moreover, with the United Nations involved in the election process, the United States would be able to present itself as a neutral party.

The Soviet Union and its allies vigorously opposed this plan, which violated all earlier U.S.-Soviet agreements on Korea. As an alternative to the U.S. plan, the Soviet Union proposed the withdrawal of all foreign forces from Korea, the end of trusteeship, and the right of the Korean people to come to the United Nations and present their position on national election procedures. The

United States held firm to its own position that a United Nations-sponsored vote must precede either withdrawal of foreign forces or a United Nations presentation by Korean political forces. Domination of the United Nations ensured ultimate victory for the United States in this political struggle.

In November 1947 the United Nations Temporary Commission on Korea (UNTCOK) was established and ordered to begin preparations for Korean elections. The Commission's first meeting in Korea was held in Seoul in January 1948 but, having been denied access to the north by the Soviet Union, even the UNTCOK chairman voiced grave misgivings about the wisdom of proceeding with an election in the south alone.[10] However, under heavy U.S. pressure, the United Nations ordered the commission to proceed and observe the election "in such parts of Korea as are accessible to the Commission."

It was clear to the great majority of Koreans that an election held in the south alone would mean division of the country; they therefore vigorously opposed it. Officials from northern Korea invited the leadership of more than forty different groups in southern Korea, excluding only Syngman Rhee and the leadership of the KDP, to a North-South Korean Political Leaders Coalition Conference in the hopes of organizing a united Korean opposition to the elections. Although the U.S. military and Syngman Rhee condemned the conference, the great majority of south Koreans, regardless of political persuasion, supported it. Almost all those invited attended, and the conference issued a joint communique which called for immediate and simultaneous withdrawal of all foreign troops; peaceful unification of Korea without foreign interference; opposition to separate elections in the south; and opposition to monopoly capitalism.[11] But the United States would allow nothing to stop the elections in the south or the victory of Syngman Rhee.

National Assembly elections took place in southern Korea on May 10, 1948, and was organized by the Korean National Police and its right-wing auxiliaries. Every major political party in the south, except Syngman Rhee's own political formation and the KDP, refused to participate. The UNTCOK again expressed its doubts that there was a suitably free atmosphere for the election results to be taken as representative of the wishes of the Korean people in the south.[12]

The election results were a great victory for those who supported the KDP and Syngman Rhee. The National Assembly convened on May 31, 1948, adopted a constitution on July 12, and elected Syngman Rhee president on July 20. On August 15, 1948, the Republic of Korea—also known as South Korea—officially came into being. In response, a separate government, the Democratic People's Republic of Korea—also known as North Korea—was established in the north on September 9, 1948. Korea was now split into two halves. As we will see next, while the United States had the power to divide the country and engineer the election victory of Syngman Rhee in the south, it could not so easily ensure the legitimacy of his government.

U.S. Intervention and the Korean War

South Korean resistance to the U.S.-Syngman Rhee alliance and political program did not end with the suppression of the autumn uprising in 1946. With limited freedom to operate at the provincial level, opposition during 1947 was forced down to the village level and increasingly expressed through guerrilla struggle. With no other alternative to stop the division of the country, armed resistance to the U.S.-backed regime of Syngman Rhee finally broke out in 1948, first at Cheju Island.

Led by former leaders of the disbanded people's committees, South Korean guerrillas successfully re-established popular control over most villages on the island by June 1948. What followed was a terribly bloody and violent offensive by the South Korean military against the people of Cheju. After almost a year of intense fighting and the death of approximately 12 percent of the island's population as well as the forced migration of one-third of the population into designated government-controlled villages, the South Korean military succeeded in crushing the uprising.

During the campaign against Cheju, another rebellion broke out in the port city of Yosu. On October 19, 1948, members of several regiments of the South Korean army refused orders to join the government offensive against the Cheju guerrillas. About two thousand of these Korean soldiers took control of Yosu and sent some of their number to organize takeovers in other nearby towns.

This development was considered so serious that American officers were put in charge of the military campaign to suppress the rebellion. After U.S.-directed forces regained control over a contested area, the South Korean military normally secured it by organizing executions of those prisoners as well as civilians thought to be sympathetic to the left. The only rebels spared were those that agreed to help hunt down their comrades. According to U.S. records, one of those who participated in this rebellion was Park Chung Hee. It is alleged that he escaped death by helping the military track down his former associates, including his brother.[13]

More than a thousand Yosu rebels escaped capture and fled to the mountains where they joined existing bands of guerrillas. Although a constant threat to South Korean authorities in the region, the guerrillas were unable to hold any towns or create base areas outside of the mountains. Over time, U.S.-led military campaigns left them increasingly isolated and ineffective. By March 1950, organized guerrilla activity in South Korea, for the most part, came to an end.

Koreans in the north looked on throughout this entire period of struggle first with alarm and then with horror. Their hopes for an independent, unified Korea had been crushed by the intervention of U.S. forces. Those who had collaborated with the Japanese during Korea's darkest days had once again been placed in positions of leadership by a foreign power. Moreover, these very same people were now calling on the United States to support military efforts to gain control of the north. Tensions between the two countries were thus understandably high, especially late 1949 and early 1950 when constant fighting took place around the 38th parallel, sometimes involving between one to two thousand soldiers.

It is this history that provides the context for the June 25, 1950, beginning of the Korean War. The triggering events of that day are still unclear. The South claims the North launched an unprovoked attack while the North claims the same about the South. Both agree that fighting began on the Ongjin Peninsula and that once the fighting began North Korean troops quickly moved south across the parallel, eastward and westward. Unfortunately, the continuing debate over which side fired the "first shot" has drawn attention away from the more relevant question for understanding Korea's political development: what was this war about?

Bruce Cumings has probably done more than any other scholar

to answer just this question. As he and Jon Halliday make clear in their powerful book, *Korea: The Unknown War*, the Korean War was a civil war over two competing visions for Korean society. If it had not been for U.S. intervention, the issue would have been settled relatively quickly in the immediate post-World War II period in favor of those who supported a revolutionary transformation of Korean society. As a result of U.S. actions, the issue was settled only after the long and bloody Korean War and in favor of the minority who opposed such changes.

Political as well as military actions in the first period of fighting lend support to this understanding of the Korean War as a civil war. Northern forces quickly swept down the peninsula, pushing South Korean and U.S. troops continually southward until August, when U.S. forces were able to secure a stable base around Pusan in the southeastern coast. As Halliday and Cumings explain:

> In the midst of the massive push towards Pusan thousands of Korean cadres, from North and South, set about restoring the people's committees disbanded in 1945-1946 and pushing through land redistribution on a revolutionary basis. Through it all they beat the drum of Korean unification and independence. The North Korean occupation of the South is thus an essential ingredient in determining this war's origins and what manner of war it was.[14]

Perhaps somewhat ironically, it was this revolutionary land reform that finally broke the power of the large South Korean landowners and made possible Syngman Rhee's own more modest post-Korean war land redistribution program. Before the outbreak of war and the efforts of the left, the landlord class successfully used its control of the National Assembly to block any reform attempts. If nothing else, this history shows how difficult it is to apply the lessons of South Korea (e.g., the need for a thorough land reform) to other countries.

The military success of northern forces in liberating most of South Korea did not last long. The United States had reclaimed Seoul and restored Syngman Rhee to power by September 1950. According to U.S. embassy reports, Rhee took maximum advantage of U.S. victories to have more than 100,000 people killed in the immediate period of his return to power. This figure is larger than the total number of people the United States claims were murdered by northern and southern communists during the entire war.[15]

U.S. forces continued to fight against the guerrillas throughout South Korea until well into 1952. However, the combination of military actions by U.S. troops and political executions by Rhee's officials took their toll on left political forces in South Korea, ensuring at war's end no organized left to influence the country's political agenda. It would be years before a credible labor and farmers movement would once again be able to defend the interests of working people.

An armistice was finally signed on July 27, 1953, thereby ending the fighting. The cost of the war in human lives was staggering: more than 3 million Korean civilians died, over 2 million North Koreans and 1 million South Koreans. Hundreds of thousands of North Korean soldiers also died as did tens of thousands of South Korean and U.S. soldiers. The Peoples Republic of China, which came to the aid of North Korea during the war, lost perhaps 1 million soldiers.[16]

A non-UN-organized peace conference was held in Geneva, from April to June 1954, to determine the future of Korea. The North Koreans proposed a simultaneous and proportional withdrawal of all foreign forces from Korea followed by nationwide elections to be organized by a Korean electoral commission and supervised by delegates from a group of neutral nations. The United States and South Korea supported elections only in the North and under the supervision of the United Nations. The North Koreans understandably rejected this proposal and refused to accept any role for the United Nations because of its participation in the fighting on the side of the United States and South Korea.

A number of Western diplomats present at the conference stated their belief that the United States did not want the conference to succeed for fear of losing in nationwide elections what it had won in battle. It had, after all, already achieved its basic goal: South Korea remained a separate nation and the government of Syngman Rhee remained in power.[17] The South Korean government never signed the armistice agreement and no peace treaty was ever signed by North Korea on the one side and the United States or South Korea on the other to formally end the Korean War.

The Collapse of the Rhee Government

The United States had, for reasons discussed above, cast its lot with Syngman Rhee, supporting his rise to power and election as South Korea's first president. But Rhee, ruthless and corrupt, proved unable to secure what the United States wanted most: a popularly supported South Korean government.

Rhee's approach to politics is well illustrated by his response to the Yosu rebellion of October 1948. After U.S.-led South Korean troops restored order, Rhee pushed a National Security Law through the National Assembly which made "disturbing the tranquility of the nation" a crime against the state. Using this ambiguously worded law against any who opposed his rule, Rhee had over 90,000 people arrested.

Even members of the National Assembly were not safe. When, in 1949, the National Assembly began to pass resolutions that threatened his power, Rhee arrested over a dozen lawmakers. Actions such as these eventually turned the majority of South Korean voters against him; Rhee and his supporters suffered a devastating defeat in the May 1950 National Assembly elections. On the verge of being driven from political power, Rhee was saved only by the start of the Korean War.

Using the wartime emergency to strengthen his hold on power, Rhee had tens of thousands of opponents, mostly leftists, murdered on charges of being North Korean agents. The army soon became his most effective instrument of social control. By the end of the war he commanded a combined force of over 700,000 armed men. The seeds had been planted for a powerful military, soon to rule in its own name.

Rhee also took advantage of war conditions to resume his attack on his conservative opponents in the National Assembly. In 1952, Rhee wanted an amendment passed authorizing the direct election of the president. To overcome National Assembly opposition, he organized youth gangs to engage in demonstrations in the city of Pusan, the wartime capital, and then used the demonstrations as an excuse to declare martial law. When the National Assembly met to revoke the declaration of martial law, Rhee used the police and threats of violence to ensure passage of the legislation he desired. A quick election was called, and with the opposition unable to mount a viable challenge, Rhee was easily re-elected president. Rhee flouted the law once again in 1954 when he forced the National Assembly to lift the two-term presidential limitation, thereby allowing him to run for a third term.

In spite of his power, voter opposition to Rhee was growing. Although Rhee was successful in winning re-election in 1956, the mainstream opposition did succeed in electing its own candidate, Chang Myon, to the vice-presidency. When the ruling Liberal Party did poorly in the 1958 National Assembly elections, Rhee responded, as in the past, by aggressively attacking all who opposed him.

Even though the left in South Korea had been destroyed as an organized mass force, many of its principles continued to enjoy public support and were expressed politically by the Progressive Party and its leader Cho Pong-am, who ran for president in 1952 and 1956. Cho received 2 million votes in 1956, advocating what one scholar of Korean politics has described as "a program of socialist democracy, a planned economy, and peaceful unification."[18]

Fearing resurgence of organized activity from the political left, Rhee had Cho arrested in 1958 on charges of collaboration with North Korea. Cho was executed by the government. The Progressive Party was ordered to disband the following year. As in the past, Rhee used his attack on the left to support a broader offensive against his more moderate political opponents. Raising fears of a new North Korean offensive, Rhee demanded revision of the National Security Law as well as the passage of a new local self-governance law which would give him the power to appoint all local officials. To overcome National Assembly resistance, Rhee had police trained in martial arts arrest and remove opposition legislators from the National Assembly building. The remaining legislators, all from Rhee's Liberal Party, then passed twenty-two bills without opposition, including the revised National Security Law.

Rhee entered the 1960 elections confident of his own personal victory. Determined to ensure the election of one of his supporters to the office of vice president, Rhee used ballot box stuffing and terrorism to defeat Chang Myon. Students immediately responded to the government's announcement of Chang Myon's defeat with protest demonstrations calling for the resignation of Rhee. Police fired on the students, killing over one hundred. Yet, rather than intimidate the students, police brutality only increased their anger. Demonstrations spread to other cities and back again to Seoul. The government hired gangs to attack student demonstrators, but this only brought other anti-Rhee forces out into the streets.

Although the demonstrations were touched off by election fraud, they represented far more than just pro-Chang Myon sympathy on the part of the students who were fed up with Rhee and the entire political-economic system that he had created. This mood was reflected in one of the most popular student slogans of the time: "Democracy in Politics, and Equality in the Economy."

Finally, in a last desperate act to save himself, Rhee declared martial law and ordered the military to impose order by whatever means necessary. By this time, however, even the U.S. government recognized that Rhee had become a political liability. The Korean army refused to fire on the students, and the U.S. military withheld ammunition from the martial law command. Rhee had no choice but to resign and accept a United States offer to go into exile in Hawaii.

The Necessity of Military Dictatorship

At issue for the United States and South Korean elite was whether the new government, led by Chang Myon, could do any better than Rhee in creating a stable South Korean political economy. Unfortunately for Chang Myon, he had inherited a bad economic situation. Unhappy with Rhee's policies and worried about growing international pressures on the dollar, the U.S. government began to cut back its financial aid to South Korea in 1958. Given the economy's dependence on U.S. support, this decision triggered a fall in production, employment, and per capita income as well as a rise in the rate of inflation.

In spite of the popular protests his election defeat inspired, Chang Myon nevertheless faced a growing political movement beyond his control. Students, for example, were determined to continue their political activity. To advance their agenda of popular democracy and unification they staged numerous demonstrations, threatened to organize general strikes, and at one point took control of the National Assembly building.

Chang Myon and his Democratic Party, for the most part dependent on U.S. support, faced this situation with no real economic or political program of their own. The United States opposed meaningful economic reform as well as unification. The opposition demanded nothing less. Fearful of angering either the United States or the student-led political movement, Chang took no action, which had the effect of allowing the growing mass movement to set the terms of a national debate.

Approximately two thousand street demonstrations, involving about one million people, took place during the ten months of Chang's rule. The South Korean military estimated that approximately 3,900 people protested each day in the streets of Seoul alone.[19] The most popular demand was for direct negotiations with North Korea for reunification of the country. There was also strong opposition to U.S. initiatives designed to restore ties between Japan and Korea; a Japanese economic mission to Korea had to be cancelled because of public outcry.

Taking advantage of Chang's political paralysis, the left began to regroup. Former members of the Progressive Party reorganized as the Socialist Mass Party and called for removal of all foreign armed forces. The Socialist Mass Party also joined with student organizations, labor unions, and other newly formed progressive organizations to form the Council for Independence and National Reunification. The Council advocated a reunification process based on establishing trade, cultural, and educational ties between South and North Korea, followed by a general election to reunify the country.

Students, led by the National Student League for Unification, passed a resolution on May 5, 1961, calling for a North-South Student Conference in Panmunjom on May 20, to be attended by student delegates from both North and South Korea. This was to be the largest Korean unification meeting since the April 1948 North-South Korean Political Leaders Coalition Conference. The North Korea government welcomed all these developments. In particular, students in North Korea eagerly accepted the invitation from the South Korean students for the May meeting.

This political mobilization of the population frightened the South Korean elite, especially those in the military. The South Korean military had been the main instrument of political repression in the

South and had recently fought a war to keep the country divided. Quite naturally, then, many in the military strongly opposed all efforts by the progressive movement to reunify the country. This opposition was translated into action on May 16, 1961, four days before the North-South Korean student meeting was to take place. A small group of army officers led by Major General Park Chung Hee carried out a *coup d'état*. Military dictatorship, the determining feature of South Korean political life from that moment until the present, had begun.

Conclusion

The history presented in this and the previous chapter brings us back to the starting point of this book, the coming to power of Park Chung Hee. However, these two chapters provide us with valuable insight into the origins and nature of his regime. First, rule by military dictatorship was a logical consequence of the illegitimacy of the entire U.S. project to create a separate South Korea; it could be saved in no other way. Second, the relative strength and independence of the state under Park was largely the result of prior colonial state-directed industrialization, which spread capitalist relations of production without creating a significant Korean capitalist class. As we can see, strong dominating states are not simply willed into being, but rather develop out of specific historically defined conditions. Finally, this history also provides an essential context for our later investigation into the character and political consequences of South Korea's rapid economic growth.

CHAPTER 7

U.S. AND JAPANESE INFLUENCE ON THE ORGANIZATION AND PERFORMANCE OF THE SOUTH KOREAN ECONOMY

The establishment of military dictatorship in South Korea did not end the considerable influence of the United States and Japan on South Korea's political and economic development. As we will see in this chapter, the policies of these countries were instrumental in shaping both the structure of South Korea's planning system and Park Chung Hee's choice of development strategy. Moreover, South Korea's rapid economic growth and industrial transformation would not have been possible had it not been for United States and Japanese willingness to grant South Korea access to financial aid, technology, and markets on especially generous terms.

The Organizational Structure
of the South Korean State

When Park Chung Hee took power in 1961 his most important task was reversing South Korea's economic decline—only in this way could he hope to gain legitimacy for his coup and solidify his hold on power. With so much at stake, Park turned to Japan, the country he most admired, for a development model he believed capable of delivering the economic success he so desperately needed.

Park had been a favorite of the Japanese during the Second World War. He attended the Japanese military academy in Manchukuo where, chosen to give the graduation address, he pledged to "fall like cherry blossoms in the holy war for the establishment of the Greater East Asia Co-prosperity Sphere and in defence of the odo rakudo [realms of righteousness]."[1] He then received special training at the Cadet Academy in Tokyo, eventually rising to the rank of lieutenant in the Japanese Imperial Air Force under his Japanese name Okamoto Minoru.

Through such experiences, Park became both a student and admirer of the Meiji Restoration and Japanese modernization long before he came to power in South Korea. For Park, the most important lesson of the Japanese experience was that modernization required a dominating state committed to economic advancement. Moreover, with the Japanese colonial state his most personal reference point, it is also likely that he viewed military dictatorship as necessary for advancing what he called the "Korean revolution."

The legacy of Japanese imperialism was far more specific than this, however. South Korean state planning institutions and policies were largely recreations of those used by Japan during the 1930s and 1940s.[2] For example, the South Korean ministerial structure was closely modeled on that of the Japanese. More specifically, the South Korean Ministry of Trade and Industry (MTI) followed the same organizational logic as the Japanese Ministry of Trade and Industry, which was itself reconstituted after World War II as the Japanese Ministry of International Trade and Industry (MITI). Park's Ministry of Agriculture and Fisheries was a copy of the Japanese Ministry of Agriculture and Fisheries. The South Korean Ministries of Transportation, Communication, and Home Affairs were also given similar responsibilities to those they had had when first created by the Japanese colonial state in Korea. Finally, the legislation establishing the South Korean Ministry of Construction was a direct translation of the Japanese legislation which had earlier established the Japanese Ministry of Construction.

The South Korean financial system was also closely modeled on the financial system created by Japan during the colonial period. The contemporary South Korean central bank, for example, is the direct descendent of the Bank of Chosen which the Japanese established in Korea in 1910. The heavy South Korean government reliance on control of credit to direct industrial activity also replicates the earlier policies of the Japanese state. This

is especially true in terms of the role played by special development banks. These were first used by the Japanese in the Meiji
period and introduced in Korea after 1906.

Park also followed Japanese tradition when he forced all South
Korean corporations into producer associations in 1961. These
associations were patterned on the Japanese "self-control associations" which were introduced in Japan during World War II.
Similarly, the Korean Trade Promotion Corporation (KOTRA),
which was designed to boost exports, was modeled after the
Japan External Trade Organization (JETRO). Even Park's decision
to support the growth of large family-owned conglomerates, the
chaebol, followed the earlier policies of the Japanese state which
encouraged the monopolization of economic activity by large
family-owned conglomerates, the zaibatsu. Thus, while Park
reshaped the South Korean political economy, it is obvious that
he drew his inspiration from the wartime structures and policies
of the Japanese state.

Choice of Development Strategy

Although today South Korea is widely celebrated for its export-
led orientation, the government of Park Chung Hee did not originally embrace such a development strategy. In fact, Park's initial
economic policies were directed at creating a "self-reliant economy."
As we will see, it was largely foreign pressure that forced Park to
abandon this goal and implement a new growth strategy based on
export promotion.

The country's first five-year plan spoke of using "guided
capitalism" to build a heavy industrial base; primary commodity
exports were to be promoted in order to finance this industrial
transformation. To stimulate national production, the military junta
immediately increased government spending on infrastructure,
raised public-sector wages, and guaranteed high grain prices.

State support for agriculture was especially significant in promoting growth during the first years of the military regime. U.S. policy
during the 1950s had stressed the importance of price stability, especially in food and agricultural products, for creating the conditions
necessary for successful free-market policies. In fact, massive United

States PL-480 grain shipments to South Korea succeeded in driving South Korean grain prices far below their domestic production cost. These shipments naturally devastated the rural economy and, in a largely agricultural nation, undermined overall purchasing power and investment.

Park's agricultural policy—which initially included abolition of farm debts, creation of new rural credit institutions, and an increase in the availability of credit for farmers—reversed this decline and led to a rapid increase in agricultural production. Farm profits were in turn spent domestically, stimulating production in the manufacturing sector. Thus, in describing South Korea's early growth, the Economic Planning Board explains that:

> the high growth rate registered, with a relatively small investment ratio, was attributable to the remarkable expansion of agricultural production . . . and also to the fact that hitherto idle capacity and surplus labor were more effectively utilized.[3]

While agriculture may have stimulated growth, manufacturing soon came to dominate the growth process and, consistent with the state's domestic focus, until 1966 was largely directed toward the domestic market. Exports of manufactures did grow rapidly but, as we can see from Table 7.1, it was not until the mid-1960s that they became quantitatively significant. South Korea's early economic policies and patterns of growth were thus far different from those we currently identify with the South Korean experience.

External pressures, especially changes in U.S. aid policy, were probably the single most important reason for South Korea's change in economic strategy. The United States government was not pleased with Park's early economic policies. Facing its own international economic problems, the United States wanted to reduce its aid commitment to South Korea. But, with Park's expansionary, domestic-oriented growth strategy generating large international trade deficits, the U.S. government feared that any substantial reduction in aid might lead to a foreign debt crisis and collapse of the South Korean economy. Determined to avoid this outcome if at all possible, the U.S. government began pressuring the South Korean government to actively promote exports as well as seek an alternative source of foreign aid. And from the U.S. point of view, there was only one simple and quick way for South Korea to accomplish both

TABLE 7.1
Trade and Growth

Year	Exports (in billion U.S. dollars)	GNP (in billion U.S. dollars)	Exports/ GNP (in percent)
1960	.03	1.9	2
1961	.04	2.1	2
1962	.05	2.3	3
1963	.09	2.7	3
1964	.12	2.9	4
1965	.18	3.0	6
1966	.25	3.7	7
1967	.32	4.3	7
1968	.46	5.2	9
1969	.62	6.6	9
1970	.84	7.8	11
1971	1.07	9.4	11
1972	1.62	10.6	15
1973	3.23	13.5	24
1974	4.46	18.6	24
1975	5.08	20.9	24
1976	7.70	28.7	27
1977	10.05	37.4	27
1978	12.71	52.0	24
1979	15.06	62.4	24
1980	17.51	60.3	29
1981	21.25	66.2	32
1982	21.85	69.3	32
1983	24.45	79.5	31
1984	29.25	87.0	34
1985	30.28	89.7	34
1986	34.72	102.7	34
1987	47.28	128.4	37
1988	60.70	169.2	36
1989	62.38	211.2	30
1990	65.02	237.9	27
1991	71.87	272.7	26

Source: Economic Planning Board.

of these tasks: normalize relations with Japan. Japan could then become South Korea's new sponsor, providing both aid and export markets for South Korea.

Japan had its own economic reasons for wanting to resume formal diplomatic ties with South Korea. The Japanese wanted to use South Korean labor and raw material to further their own export-led development. They wanted to produce in South Korea for export as well as sell to South Korea. To the extent that South Korea remained domestically oriented in policy and short of foreign exchange, this would not be possible. Thus, although for different reasons, both the United States and Japan favored a new economic strategy for South Korea as well as normalization of relations between South Korea and Japan.

The United States began its campaign to force a change in South Korean policy as early as 1962. U.S. aid financed almost 70 percent of South Korea's total imports between 1953 and 1962, thereby giving the United States government a powerful weapon to influence the South Korean government. Taking advantage of a severe food shortage caused by a bad harvest in 1962-63, the U.S. government began to use its weapon: aid fell from $225 million in 1960, to $165 million in 1962, $119 million in 1963, $88 million in 1964, and finally to $71 million in 1965.[4]

Desperate for an alternative source of foreign exchange, the South Korean government sought to obtain commercial bank loans. Unable to secure acceptable terms or sufficient credit, it finally entered into serious negotiations with U.S. officials over economic reform in 1964. The South Korean government pledged to take action to stabilize prices and promote greater international trade and investment activity and, over the next several years, responded to U.S. demands by raising interest rates, devaluing the currency, reducing import barriers, and increasing export incentives.

While Park did indeed shift from an economic strategy based on import-substitution to one based on exports, he did not do so by surrendering state power to market forces. For the United States, unconditional government support for free-trade, free-market policies is normally a non-negotiable demand. In this case, however, South Korea's increasingly favorable economic performance compared to North Korea, as well as Park's willingness to re-establish relations with Japan and support the U.S. military in Vietnam, appears to have led the United States to overlook what may normally have been considered an unacceptable ideological deviation.

Park's general willingness to comply with U.S. and Japanese demands for a change in South Korea's economic and political orientation was greatly encouraged by the fact that these demands did not threaten his political survival. In a very real sense, one economic strategy had no more significance for him than another if it could produce regime-sustaining growth. There was no established capitalist or landowning class to oppose or resist a change in policy. Nor did Park have an ideological objection to closer relations with Japan—far from it. Thus, from Park's perspective, if the United States and Japan favored a certain set of policies, and if following them would ensure the financial and political support he needed, there was little reason for him to resist.

Foreign Financial Support

Although Park adopted an export-led growth strategy in response to balance of payments difficulties, Table 7.2 shows that South Korea's rapid export growth did not solve the country's trade or foreign debt problems. In fact, while South Korea is well known for its export prowess, the country did not achieve its first overall trade surplus until 1986. Thus, without new and substantial financial support, South Korea's export-led growth strategy would also have proven to be unsustainable.

South Korea did obtain the funds it needed to cover its trade deficits, pay its debt obligations, and thus maintain its growth. As we will see in this section, these funds came largely from Japanese and U.S. sources and were made available for very specific political reasons. South Korea's economic success was not simply the result of the government adopting "correct economic policies."

The South Korean state was able to secure funds it needed largely because it was willing to normalize relations with Japan and support the U.S. war effort in Vietnam. Ironically, while both foreign policy decisions were essential for the success of South Korea's economic strategy, neither was supported by the majority of the South Korean population. The ruling party had to rely on parliamentary tricks to ensure approval of these policies by the National Assembly.

As part of the 1965 Japan-R.O.K. Normalization Treaty, Japan agreed to give South Korea $200 million in public loans, $300 million in grants, and at least $300 million in commercial credits, to be paid over a ten-year period beginning in 1966. Between 1966 and 1967, South Korea received approximately $90 million in Japanese grants and credits and over $100 million in private commercial loans from Japanese banks. This immediate infusion of money more than replaced shrinking U.S. aid.

After the 1965 treaty was signed, Japan and South Korea created a number of committees to coordinate economic relations, including the Japan-R.O.K. Ministerial Conference, Japan-R.O.K. Economic Committee, and Japan-R.O.K. Cooperative Committee. The Ministerial Conferences were especially important. At the first conference in 1967, the Japanese government agreed to arrange $200 million in private loans for South Korea. At the second, in 1968, the Japanese government offered South Korea another $90 million. At the third meeting, in 1969, the Japanese government agreed to help South Korea finance and build the Pohang Integrated Steel Works. Both the World Bank and a consortium of European firms had rejected South Korean requests to finance the steel complex, and the entire project was saved only because of substantial Japanese financial assistance, including a $124 million grant and loan agreement. Japanese companies also played a leading role in the actual design and plant construction. At the fourth Ministerial Conference, in 1970, Japan offered new loans totaling $160 million to help South Korea finance construction of four heavy industry plants and develop several light manufacturing export industries.

Japanese funding was thus enormously important to South Korea, enabling it to finance its trade deficit and launch its heavy and chemical industrialization drive. The Japanese government did not offer this financial support for altruistic reasons however. Rather, it hoped to shape South Korean industrial development along lines that would be beneficial to the Japanese economy. As we will see later, it largely succeeded. South Korean growth is, as a result, heavily dependent on Japanese equipment and technology.

Generous U.S. financial aid also played an important role in South Korea's economic success. Overall U.S. economic aid to South Korea from 1946 to 1978 totaled some $6 billion. To place this amount in perspective, over the same years, the total amount of U.S. economic

TABLE 7.2
Trade and Debt

Year	Increase in exports (in percent)	Trade balance (in billion U.S. dollars)	Foreign debt (in billion U.S. dollars)
1960	65.0	-.31	—
1961	24.2	-.24	—
1962	34.1	-.34	—
1963	58.2	-.41	.16
1964	36.8	-.25	.18
1965	47.1	-.24	.21
1966	42.9	-.43	.39
1967	28.0	-.57	.65
1968	42.2	-.84	1.20
1969	36.7	-.99	1.80
1970	34.2	-.92	2.25
1971	27.9	-1.05	2.92
1972	52.1	-.57	3.59
1973	98.6	-.57	4.26
1974	38.3	-1.94	5.94
1975	13.9	-1.67	8.46
1976	51.8	-.59	10.53
1977	30.2	-.48	12.65
1978	26.5	-1.78	14.87
1979	18.4	-4.40	20.29
1980	16.3	-4 38	27.17
1981	21.4	-3.63	32.43
1982	2.8	-2.59	37.08
1983	11.9	-1.76	40.38
1984	19.6	-1.04	43.05
1985	3.5	-.02	46.76
1986	14.6	4.21	44.51
1987	36.2	7.66	35.57
1988	28.4	11.44	31.15
1989	2.8	4.60	29.37
1990	4.2	-2.00	31.70
1991	10.5	-7.90	39.20

Source: Economic Planning Board; Bank of Korea.

aid to all of Africa was only $6.89 billion, all of Latin America received $14.8 billion. And India, with a population seventeen times greater than South Korea, received only $9.6 billion.[5]

While the normalization treaty unlocked Japanese funds for Park, it was Park's willingness to send South Korean troops to fight in Vietnam which was the key to winning U.S. financial support. Beginning in late 1964, Lyndon Johnson launched his "Many Flags" campaign which involved trying to recruit other countries to send soldiers to Vietnam in order to convince the U.S. public that the U.S. war effort had wide international backing. He was, in general, rather unsuccessful. Park, however, understood that South Korean participation in the war could secure substantial U.S. backing for his regime. Thus, from 1965 to 1973, in response to repeated U.S. requests for troops, Park sent over 300,000 South Korean soldiers to fight in Vietnam and was rewarded generously by the United States for doing so.

The South Korean military force in Vietnam was a mercenary force and as such it was paid a special bonus by the U.S. government, a fact kept secret from both the U.S. Congress and other countries such as Thailand and the Philippines which also sent troops. One example of the size of the bonus: in 1969 the normal monthly salary of a South Korean private was $1.60; with special U.S. payments for fighting in Vietnam it came to $37.50. From 1965 to 1973, $185.3 million was remitted to South Korea by South Korean military forces in Vietnam.[6]

In terms of foreign exchange earnings, U.S. commercial support for South Korean business was even more significant, totaling almost $540 million from 1966 to 1972. The major forms of support were U.S. procurement of war supplies in South Korea and construction and service contracts for South Korean firms in Vietnam. Frank Baldwin, a well-respected Asia scholar, details this activity as follows:

> Among the major South Korean exports to Vietnam were military uniforms, jungle boots, corrugated metal roofing and cement. In the construction and service field, at one point more than eighty South Korean companies held contracts with the U.S. government in Vietnam. Their activities included construction and engineering, transportation of goods, and operating service facilities such as laundry shops and entertainment clubs. South Korean civilian workers in Vietnam were especially well rewarded.[7]

All together, from 1965 to 1973, South Korea earned almost $1 billion from the combination of military and civilian activities carried out in Vietnam and increased exports to Vietnam. South Korea made an additional $1.1 billion from U.S. military activities in South Korea itself, including local spending, the provision of goods and services, and construction contracts. This total of more than $2 billion represented approximately 19 percent of South Korea's total foreign exchange earnings over the period. During the key transition years of 1966 to 1969, approximately 30 percent of South Korea's foreign exchange earnings came from Vietnam-related operations.[8]

These payments were formally agreed to as part of the Brown Memorandum which was signed by American Ambassador Winthrop Brown in 1966, but not made public in the United States until Senate hearings in 1970. The Brown Memorandum also committed the United States to further promotion of South Korean exports and modernization of both the South Korean army and U.S. forces in South Korea. The income earned as a result of these commitments is not included in the figures presented above.

Finally, as the Korean scholar Joungwon A. Kim explains: "The decision to send troops to Vietnam in 1965 and 1966 bolstered confidence abroad in the American willingness to defend South Korea and helped to induce commercial loans from other nations."[9] Between 1966 and 1967, for example, South Korea got a total of $256 million worth of private commercial loans from banks in the United States, West Germany, Italy, France, and Great Britain as well as from several other countries not including Japan.[10]

Such extraordinary financial assistance did not end with President Park's death in 1979. As Table 7.2 shows, South Korea's trade deficit and foreign debt exploded in 1979 and 1980, forcing the economy into recession. South Korea, desperate for a new long-term aid package, asked Japan for a $6 billion development assistance loan. What it received was a sizable $4 billion loan under exceptionally generous terms. Thorkil Casse, in a research report for the Danish Center for Development Research, offered the following comment on this loan agreement: "There is hardly any other NIC country in the world facing these soft loan conditions. To comprehend the magnitude of the loan, it should be noted that Japan from 1965 to 1982 provided altogether $4.1 billion in public and commercial loans to Korea."[11]

There should be no doubt about the fact that South Korea's import-dependent export growth could not have been sustained without such timely and generous financial support. As essential as the amount of financial support was the fact that most funds were channeled directly to the South Korean government with minimal restrictions on their use. This experience presents a clear contrast with aid programs currently being offered to the countries of Eastern Europe. Not only are total amounts quite small, they are normally targeted to advance and strengthen private-sector activity at the expense of state authority.

Foreign Support for
South Korean Industrialization

The strong financial support described above represents a central explanation for South Korea's rapid export growth and industrial transformation. Additional reasons for South Korea's economic success were the extraordinary direct involvement of Japanese firms in the South Korean economy and the openness of the U.S. market to South Korean exports.

Japanese Economic Involvement in South Korea

To understand Japan's important post-World War II role in the South Korean economy, one needs to understand the dynamics underlying Japan's own postwar economic reconstruction. Not long after the war, the United States reversed its initial efforts to dismantle Japan's industrial base, deciding instead that the country was needed as a bulwark against Asian communism. This decision was reinforced by Japan's role as an important military base during the Korean War. In fact, the Korean War proved to be an economic bonanza for Japan. As a result of U.S. military-related spending from 1950 to 1955, Japan earned approximately $1.7 billion in valuable foreign exchange.[12]

With this external boost in demand, Japan was able to attain its prewar peaks in mining and manufacturing as early as 1953. But, when the Korean War ended, the Japanese economy quickly fell back into recession. The connection was rather direct: the country's heavy and chemical industries, revived during the Korean War, were heavily dependent upon imported materials and equipment. The end of the war meant a decline in dollar earnings, leaving the Japanese government with no way to support continued growth. For Japanese planners the message was clear: long-term growth required secure export markets to finance necessary imports.

Although textiles and other light manufactures made up the majority of Japan's exports in this period, the heart of the Japanese export promotion drive was the development of an export capacity in heavy and chemical industry. Initially, such products were sold mostly to Asian third world countries, but, by the mid-1960s, the Japanese were having considerable success selling cars, steel, ships, electrical appliances, and precision machines to the United States and Europe as well. However, while Japanese export efforts produced a healthy trade surplus, the country's overall economic situation was far from stable.

Japan's super growth was beginning to undermine itself. The country's expanding industrial sector was beginning to face a growing labor shortage and sharply escalating labor costs. Ever increasing industrial production was also leading to a shortage of affordable industrial sites as well as serious environmental problems. By the end of the decade, the Japanese government and corporate elite had come to the conclusion that continued economic growth required a new economic strategy, one that supported internationalization of the more labor-intensive and environmentally destructive parts of Japanese heavy and chemical industry production.

This outline of Japanese interests and actions provides the framework necessary for understanding the motivation behind Japanese involvement in the South Korean economy. Committed to export expansion, Japan moved quickly to take advantage of Park's rise to power in South Korea. Thus, from 1962 to 1964, Japan recorded a trade surplus of almost $300 million with South Korea, an amount greater than South Korea's total exports over that same period.[13] This one-sided trade relationship helps to explain Japan's willingness to extend financial assistance to South Korea. As Park Choong Hoon, a former minister of the South Korean Economic Planning Board, explains:

> The Korean trade deficit with Japan in the 10 years prior to 1975 was a surprising U.S. $6.28 billion, reaching U.S. $1.2 billion in 1974 alone. This is nearly $4 billion more than the capital assistance (loan and

investment) of this period. From this perspective, whereas Japan assisted South Korea with its large surplus, South Korea contributed to the Japanese economy at the cost of an immense deficit.[14]

Japan's ability to expand its trade and investment opportunities with South Korea was initially limited by the lack of official relations between the two countries. It was for this reason that the Japanese welcomed U.S. support for the signing of the Japan-South Korea normalization treaty. Almost immediately after its ratification, the Japan Economic Research Council and the Korean Productivity Organization published a joint report supporting policies which by their logic encouraged South Korean incorporation into a Japanese-dominated international division of labor.[15]

Among other things, the report called for expansion of the system of bonded processing, within which Japanese businesses operating in South Korea were able to combine cheap South Korean labor and land with duty-free imports of Japanese capital equipment and supplies for the production of exports. The proposal was agreed to by both countries; Table 7.3 shows the rapid increase in this trade, especially beginning in 1965. This Japanese-dominated system, which accounted for over 20 percent of South Korean exports in 1969, is one reason why South Korea was able to rapidly expand its exports of manufactures yet simultaneously suffer from a growing trade deficit.

Japanese interests were again significant in the launching of South Korea's heavy and chemical industrialization drive. In April 1970, Yatsugi Kazuo (a longtime Japanese friend of Park Chung Hee) prepared a report for the second general meeting of the Japan-R.O.K. Cooperative Committee. His "Draft Plan for Japan-Korea Long-Term Economic Cooperation," called for closer cooperation between the two countries in two specific areas. The first involved the further expansion of South Korea's bonded processing program. The report proposed the establishment of new "bonded land areas" or "free trade zones," especially along the south-east coast of South Korea. The creation of the MAFEZ Free Trade Zone in Masan was one concrete response to this Japanese initiative. Japanese business leaders made many trips to Masan to work with the South Korean government in the actual development of this zone.

The second area singled out for action was the development of "specialization and co-operative industry." The report called for Japan to transfer to South Korea "the labor-intensive and processing

TABLE 7.3
Bonded Processing Trade

Year	Total exports (in million U.S. dollars)	Bonded processing exports (in million U.S. dollars)	Bonded exports/ total exports (in percent)
1962	54.8	1.2	2.2
1963	86.8	4.9	5.6
1964	119.1	5.6	4.7
1965	175.1	19.7	11.3
1966	250.3	28.0	11.2
1967	320.2	57.8	18.1
1968	455.4	87.0	19.1
1969	622.5	130.7	21.0
1970	835.2	152.3	18.2
1971	1067.6	208.8	19.6
1972	1624.1	285.3	17.6
1973	3225.0	703.1	21.8
1974	4460.4	1064.8	23.9

Source: Tsuchiya Takeo, "Masan: An Epitome of the Japan-ROK Relationship," *AMPO: Japan-Asia Quarterly Review* 8, no. 4, and 9, nos. 1-2 (1977): 60.

sectors of such main Japanese industries as steel, aluminum, oil and zinc refining, chemicals, plastics, electronics and even ship-building."[16] Japanese corporations supported such a transfer, hoping that cheaper South Korean labor and land would enable them to remain internationally viable competitors in these industries, either as overall organizers of an internationally integrated production process or as key suppliers of advanced technology. They certainly had no intention of yielding organizational or technological control over the relevant production processes to South Korean firms.

It was, in fact, just these industries that Park later targeted for development in his 1973 Heavy and Chemical Industrialization Plan. The Japanese were actually given a direct role in the formulation and shaping of South Korea's industrialization process. Japanese representatives sat in on the drafting of the third five-year plan in 1972 and were also involved in establishing the priorities of the fourth five-year plan which began in 1977 as well.[17]

In sum, we can see that South Korea's economic success was

due not only to the aggressive direction of economic activity by the South Korean state but also to the fact that this activity coincided with Japanese policy interests. The importance of this coincidence of interests in making possible South Korea's rapid export growth and industrial transformation is often overlooked by those who advocate the South Korean approach to development and its adoption by other countries.

South Korean Economic Dependence on Japan

However, Japanese involvement in the shaping of the South Korean economy proved to be a two-edged sword. While Park was adapt at using it for his own purposes, as in the case of South Korea's heavy and chemical industrialization drive, it did leave the South Korean economy heavily dependent on Japanese industry for capital goods, components, and technology. For many years this dependence posed no threat to South Korean growth. That no longer is true.

South Korea began the 1980s facing a number of serious economic problems, including a deep recession in 1979-1980, a large trade deficit, and a rapidly increasing foreign debt. Nevertheless, the economy proved able to overcome these difficulties. For example, GNP grew by 12.9 percent in 1986, 12.8 percent in 1987, and 12.4 percent in 1988, the best three-year record in the country's history. Similarly, South Korea posted its first ever trade surplus in 1986, and new trade records were set in each of the following two years. As a result, the country succeeded in rapidly and significantly reducing its overall foreign debt.

As Table 7.1 showed, this economic revitalization was largely the result of increasingly successful export activity: exports rose from 29 percent of GNP in 1980 to 37 percent in 1987. As we can see from Table 7.4, these trade gains were largely the result of export success in the U.S. market. This table also reveals, however, that South Korea's positive trade balances with the United States were to a considerable degree counterbalanced by trade deficits with Japan. In fact, because of South Korea's economic dependence on Japan, there is a direct connection between South Korea's exports (to the United States) and imports (from Japan).

For example, in 1986, almost 90 percent of South Korea's imports from Japan went to export industries.[18] More specifically, approximately 35 percent of the money South Korea earns from selling a VCR or building a ship goes to Japan for parts and components.[19] Every time South Korea exports a computerized lathe or other machine tool, approximately 40 percent of the money earned goes to Japanese manufactures of computer-guidance equipment. In the case of many key electronics exports there is even greater dependence on Japan; Japanese parts make up 85 percent of the value of a South Korean color TV.[20]

Kim Tae Yon, a former official at the Economic Planning Board, explains the roots of South Korea's economic dependence on Japan as follows:

> We have traditionally been assemblers—using materials and machines from the outside and exporting the final product. . . . This has left us with a structural weakness in our parts and machinery industries which the Japanese have always filled.[21]

Thus, during the 1980s, South Korea depended upon Japan for 40 percent to 60 percent of its machines and approximately 60 percent of its parts.[22] Japan was also the source of about one-half of all South Korea's licensed technology.[23] This dependence was of great economic value to Japanese firms, enabling them to specialize in higher value-added production while leaving environmental and labor problems to South Korean firms. It was also an indirect way for the Japanese to maximize export sales to the United States market. South Korean firms also benefited, of course, to the extent that this trade relationship with Japan allowed them to concentrate on production rather than product development, thereby increasing exports more rapidly than would otherwise have been possible.

However, as South Korean export growth soared in the second half of the 1980s, it brought South Korean firms into competition with Japanese firms in a number of important product areas, including cars, color televisions, steel, shipbuilding, and electronics. And much to the displeasure of Japan, South Korean firms succeeded in cutting into Japanese market share, especially in the United States market. Concerned by this development, Japanese firms have become unwilling to sell South Korean exporters the latest components or technology that they need to remain internationally competitive. As a result, the South Korean growth strategy faces a potentially fatal crisis.

The current difficulties of South Korean automobile producers highlight the more general problems faced by South Korean ex-

TABLE 7.4
Trade Balance
(in billion U.S. dollars)

Year	Trade balance with United States	Trade balance with Japan	Overall trade balance
1970	-0.2	-0.6	-0.9
1975	-0.3	-1.1	-1.7
1980	-0.3	-2.8	-4.4
1981	-0.4	-2.9	-3.6
1982	0.3	-1.9	-2.6
1983	2.0	-2.8	-1.8
1984	3.6	-2.3	-1.0
1985	4.3	-3.0	-0.02
1986	7.3	-5.4	4.2
1987	9.6	-5.2	7.7
1988	8.6	-3.9	11.4
1989	4.5	-4.0	4.6
1990	2.4	-5.9	-2.0
1991	-0.6	-8.7	-7.9

Source: Economic Planning Board.

porters. As Table 7.5 illustrates in the case of Hyundai, South Korea's leading auto exporter, South Korean automakers have seen sales abroad stagnate since the peak export year of 1988. One important reason is that they have been unable to upgrade the engine design of their vehicles. The Japanese have sold individual engine plans to South Korean auto producers, but not the design technology necessary for independent engine development.[24] Hyundai Motors is still using the same basic engine that Mitsubishi Motors designed for it some years ago. Hyundai is now trying to design its own engine but officials admit that even if successfully produced, it will be only as good as one that Mitsubishi introduced in Japan several years ago.[25]

Similar problems plague South Korean producers of other fast-growing export products such as fax machines. Japanese firms are no longer selling South Korean firms the latest technology, forcing the South Koreans to invest in their own research and development. The South Koreans hope to introduce their own locally produced plain-paper facsimile machine sometime in the mid-1990s. But given

TABLE 7.5
Hyundai Automobile Sales
in the United States

Year	Number of cars sold
1986	168,882
1987	263,610
1988	264,282
1989	183,261
1990	137,448
1991 (Jan.-June)	57,090

Source: Henrik Hansen, "Fierce Competition and Tighter Regulations," *Business Korea* (August 1991): 22.

the country's technology gap, it will only be competitive with fax machines that the Japanese have been selling since the mid-1980s.[26]

In fact, the Japanese have often actively undermined South Korean development efforts by dumping or starting local production of a contested product in South Korea itself. For example, when Samsung began production in 1990 of a thermal printer head, a key component of fax machines, the Japanese firm, Rohn, first slashed prices to undercut Samsung's efforts and then attempted to set up a local subsidiary, Rohn Korea, to directly compete against Samsung in South Korea.

Rohn's behavior is not uncommon. According to industry sources in South Korea, "Japanese firms . . . pushed Korean firms to the brink of bankruptcy several years ago with dumping offensives when the Korean firms succeeded in developing convergence technology and connectors, a crucial component in color television."[27] South Korean firms have been unwilling to publicize these actions or press charges, however, for fear of endangering future access to needed Japanese-produced components, equipment, and technology.

The problem for South Korean exporters is clear: without the latest technology they either compete by offering the lowest prices on standard models, which means minimal profits at best, or they are forced out of markets altogether. The *Los Angeles Times* describes the significance of South Korea's technology gap as follows:

After initially welcoming Korean products to the market, consumers have been disappointed by their quality and lack of important features. . . . Japanese manufacturers sneer that Korean sales are limited to the low-profit end of every product line. In televisions, Japanese makers contend that Korean companies are competitive only at the 13-inch level and have been virtually cut out on the more profitable market for big-screen televisions.[28]

The case of Goldstar, one of South Korea's leading electronics exporters, offers another good example of the negative ramifications for Korea of Japan's new technology policy. Before the mid-1980s, Goldstar successfully bought the components and technology it needed to produce products such as VCRs and microwave ovens from the Japanese firm Hitachi. Hitachi, in a reversal of its past policy, now refuses to share technology on a timely basis. Unable to offer the latest features on its products, Goldstar recently lost its exclusive contract with Sears to provide microwave ovens.[29]

Further adding to South Korea's economic problems, foreign firms, especially those from Japan, are beginning to re-evaluate the benefits of South Korea as a location for production. Largely in response to militant labor activity and wage increases of 9.2 percent in 1986, 11.6 percent in 1987, 19.6 percent in 1988, and 25.3 percent in 1989, twenty-eight foreign manufacturing firms closed down their South Korean operations in 1989. Most reopened in other lower-cost Southeast Asian countries. Moreover, there were only eighteen new Japanese investments throughout South Korea in 1989, down from twenty-seven in 1988, and thirty-seven in 1987.[30] From 1988 to 1990, ten Japanese firms left the free-trade zones in Masan and Iri and most of those that remain are automating production. Employment in the Masan free trade zone was, at the end of 1990, almost 44 percent below what it had been at the beginning of 1989.[31]

In short, while Japanese interests helped launch and sustain South Korea's export-led growth and industrial transformation, they also left the South Korean economy highly dependent upon Japanese parts, machines, and technology. This weakness was exposed by the recent change in Japanese corporate policy toward South Korea. To overcome this weakness and maintain the country's export-led growth, the state's long-term strategy is to encourage greater research and development spending by the chaebol. For reasons to be discussed in Chapter 10, progress in this area will be slow if at all.

For the short run, the South Korean state has sought to breathe new life into the country's export-driven economy through anti-labor actions designed to force down wages and boost productivity and by depreciating the value of the South Korean currency relative to the dollar. Both of these strategies will likely prove unworkable. New attacks on the labor movement, as we will see in Chapter 11, can only be expected to further radicalize the South Korean working class and lead to more militant efforts to oppose the policies of the state. Depreciation of the South Korean currency risks provoking U.S. retaliation and protectionism. As we see next, U.S. economic problems have produced a shift in U.S. economic policy toward South Korea. No longer is the United States willing to allow South Korea to solve its economic problems at the cost of a larger U.S. trade deficit. Thus, while new Japanese policies now threaten South Korean export production, new U.S. policies now threaten South Korean export sales.

South Korean Economic Dependence on the United States

South Korea's export-led growth strategy obviously required access to a large and profitable market and, given the nature of Japanese interests that helped structure this strategy, the United States was selected as the market of preference. Until recently, South Korean exports to the United States were small enough compared with overall trade flows that they were not a major political or economic issue within the United States. Moreover, anticommunist foreign policy objectives, as discussed earlier, made South Korea's economic success a high priority for U.S. government leaders. As a result, the U.S. share of South Korean exports rose rapidly along with South Korean growth.

In 1961, the United States accounted for approximately 16 percent of all South Korean exports. This percentage rose steadily over the decade, before peaking at 52 percent in 1968. For the next four years the U.S. share of South Korean exports fluctuated in a fairly narrow range, from approximately 47 percent to 51 percent. Between 1973 and 1980, the U.S. share of South Korea's export trade fell significantly, even though the absolute dollar value of South Korean exports to the United States rose yearly. The U.S. share fell largely because South Korea was able to take advantage of growing Middle East oil wealth to diversify its international activities. However, when this market collapsed along with oil prices, the United States once again became South Korea's export savior. The U.S. share of South Korean exports rose steadily from approximately 26 percent in 1980 to 40 percent in 1986.

Changing international conditions have forced U.S. officials to rethink their traditional trade policies toward South Korea. South Korea's recent export success in the U.S. market came at a time of ever worsening U.S. trade deficits. Faced with the need to halt its trade decline, the U.S. government has begun to take steps to reduce imports and boost exports. Toward this end, reducing South Korea's trade surplus with the United States has now become an important goal of U.S. policy. This shift in U.S. policy is illustrated by the changing number and nature of trade disputes initiated by the United States. According to a survey of trade conflicts, there were a total of thirteen significant conflicts between South Korea and the United States between the years 1961 and 1981. By contrast, there were eighty-seven significant conflicts during the next five years alone, 1982-1986. Moreover, while all of the trade conflicts from 1961 to 1981 were limited to disputes over South Korean access to U.S. markets, the more recent conflicts involved a broader range of issues, including U.S. demands for greater access to South Korean markets and an end to exchange rate manipulation.[32]

These demands represent a serious threat to South Korea's future export growth. For example, the South Korean government has repeatedly and successfully used currency devaluations to promote exports and growth. In 1980, the government devalued the South Korean won by 17 percent in an effort to boost exports and lift the country out of recession. At the same time, it introduced a new system of currency determination designed to give it maximum discretionary power over the value of the won. *Business Korea* describes the workings of this system as follows:

> The composite basket exchange rate system, uniquely Korean, measures the won's value against the currencies of Korea's five major trading partners and the Special Drawing Rights of the World Bank. The greatest weight, however, is given to the so-called "alpha" (political) factor. When then Assistant Finance Minister and Former Deputy Prime Minister Chong In-Yong and other government officials "invented" the current system in 1980, even currency experts at the International Monetary Fund could not understand how it worked.[33]

The steady decline in the won relative to the dollar in 1980 did stimulate Korean exports. But, with currency rates relatively constant over 1981 and 1982, exports once again began to stagnate. Devaluation in 1983 reversed this slump, helping South Korean exports grow by almost 20 percent in 1984. However, with the South Korean won pegged to the U.S. dollar, and the U.S. dollar soaring in value relative to such currencies as the Japanese yen, German mark, and Mexican peso, South Korean exporters found it difficult to maintain their international price competitiveness. As a result, South Korean exports to the United States fell 26 percent over the first seven months of 1985 and overall growth suffered accordingly.

The South Korean government responded to this export slowdown as it had before, devaluating the won in late 1985. This time South Korean exporters also benefited from the dollar's movement. The major developed capitalist countries had agreed to take steps to reverse the rise of the dollar and their coordinated interventions succeeded: from September 1985 to September 1986, the yen rose 50 percent and the mark 40 percent relative to the dollar. Over the same period, the won fell by 4 percent relative to the dollar. These currency movements more than restored South Korea's international price advantage and were a major reason for the country's 1986-1988 export success in the U.S. market.

However, as noted above, this export offensive, coming at a time of growing trade problems in the United States, triggered a hostile U.S. response. In October 1988, the U.S. Treasury reported to Congress that South Korea (and Taiwan) had used trade restrictions to gain unfair advantage in trade with the United States and had "manipulate[d] the rate of exchange between their currency and the U.S. dollar for purposes of preventing effective balance of payments adjustments or gaining unfair competitive advantage in international trade."[34] The U.S. government demanded that South Korea revalue upward the value of the won and open South Korean markets to U.S. products and investment.

We can see the fragility of South Korea's export competitiveness by what happened next. The South Korean government allowed the won to rise in value by 16 percent in 1988 and another 3 percent in the first half of 1989. This policy decision, coupled with the above-mentioned change in Japanese technology policy and sharp rise in manufacturing wages, proved disastrous for South Korean exports.

Export growth slowed from 36.2 percent in 1987, to 28.4 percent in 1988, 5.7 percent in 1989, and 3 percent in 1990. Equally significant, profit margins for South Korean exporters also fell. For example: VCRs surpassed color TVs in 1988 as South Korea's leading electronics export. Yet, because of the upward movement in labor costs and the won, South Korean producers of VCRs lost money on every VCR they sold in the United States. For Samsung, the loss was as high as 6-7 percent of cost.[35] More generally, South Korean exporters (those who export more than 50 percent of their annual turnover) reported *declines* in their net profit rate of 2 percent in 1987, 1.5 percent in 1988, .8 percent in 1989, and a further .6 percent in 1990. The percentage of all export-oriented manufacturing firms that lost money rose from 5.3 percent in 1987 to 16 percent in 1990.[36]

Faced with growing economic problems, the South Korean government decided to reverse course in 1990. Risking U.S. anger, it devalued the won and launched a new anti-import campaign. So far the U.S. government has yet to back up its calls for an end to these policies with retaliatory actions, but if South Korea's growing economic difficulties continue to force the government to follow policies that anger the United States, the threat of such actions is very real.

In fact, there are two important reasons for believing that even if South Korea succeeds in avoiding U.S. retaliation for its currency and trade policies, the country's export-driven economy may be in serious trouble as far as sales to the United States are concerned. The first reason has to do with South Korea's economic dependence on Japan. Unless South Korean firms can overcome their technological backwardness and deliver competitive products, they will lose market share regardless of price. For example, poor quality has played an important role in South Korea's declining automobile exports. A *Los Angeles Times* article makes the point as follows:

> Hyundai has been plagued by poor ratings on frequency-of-repair ratios, and the resale values of Korean cars have been far lower than that of Japanese models. . . .
>
> "Unless they develop a very high-quality car, they aren't going to sell very many," said Hitoshi Nishiyama, analyst at Nomura Research Institute in Japan. "It's a zero-sum game; they are competing in mature markets with entrenched companies."[37]

The second and perhaps more important reason is that the U.S. government is itself exploring new strategies to boost U.S. corporate profits and power, including a North American free trade agreement. A North American free trade agreement, in particular, has the potential to seriously reduce South Korean exports to the United States. *Business Week*, for example, tells the story of Stanley M. Cohen and his Los Angeles pipe-fixture company which was being driven out of business by foreign competition. In 1987, Mr. Cohen moved part of his operation to Tijuana where workers earn about one-eighth of Los Angeles wages. "Last spring [1990], Cohen went the whole route. He shipped his $11 million company down the coast and replaced his South Korean steel source with a Mexican one."[38]

The threat to South Korea's export competitiveness from Mexican-based U.S. production is obvious: in 1989, average hourly wages plus benefits for a worker in a maquiladora manufacturing plant in Mexico were only $1.63 as compared with $2.94 for a worker in South Korea's manufacturing sector. Recognizing the significance of such a wage spread, Kodak Mexicana President Donald F. Spieler spoke for many U.S. corporate leaders when he commented that, "By 2000, I see Mexico as being a Korea but with an even wider industrial base."[39]

Conclusion

This chapter completes a three-chapter block designed to highlight the enormous influence U.S. and Japanese policies have had on South Korea's economic strategy and industrial transformation. As we have seen, these policies helped to shape and sustain South Korea's export-led growth. They also left the South Korean economy highly vulnerable to changes in the international environment. And now that South Korea's continuing growth has begun to challenge the economic interests of the United States and Japan, both countries have responded in ways that seriously threaten South Korea's future economic progress.

This internationally framed perspective on South Korea's economic experience shows why it is misleading and dangerous to promote South Korea's specific export-led industrialization strategy as a generalizable approach to development. Beyond problems associated with creating states able to dominate national economic activity, third world countries are unlikely to enjoy the same international financial, technological, and market support given to South Korea. Moreover, there is strong reason to believe that the South Korean economic strategy is no longer capable of furthering South Korea's own industrial development. With this perspective providing essential background, we are now ready to consider the consequences of South Korea's rapid economic growth on the lives of the South Korean people, the essential perspective for evaluating the South Korean experience.

CHAPTER 8

THE POLITICAL ECONOMY OF GROWTH AND CRISIS: 1961 TO 1972

Having explored the domestic and international forces shaping South Korea's export-led growth, we are now ready to examine the political and economic consequences of the resulting industrial transformation. This chapter and the next consider developments from 1961 to 1981, a period which includes the rise and fall of the Park regime as well as the renewal of military dictatorship under General Chun Doo Hwan.

As these two chapters will reveal, South Korean industrialization was far more difficult and problematic, from both an economic and political standpoint, than those who celebrate it are willing to admit. More specifically, in addition to rapid growth, Park's economic strategy also produced an unbalanced and unstable economy. Moreover, because of the oppressive nature of the growth process, Park's strategy generated its own political opposition. Growth itself thus created the need for ever greater state repression. In short, contradictions and class struggle were as central to the South Korean experience as was rapid economic growth.

The Military in Control: The Nature of the Regime

The May 16, 1961, military coup led by Major General Park Chung Hee brought to an end a brief period of democratic revival. Park quickly established his control over the country's political life. He declared martial law and dissolved the National Assembly and all political parties. Demonstrations were made illegal. The press was censored. New anticommunist laws, which gave the state greater power to arrest and convict opponents, were also passed. And, within one month of the coup, a new organization was established which was to play a major role in the political and economic life of South Korea: the Korean Central Intelligence Agency (KCIA). Its charge was broad: "to supervise and coordinate both international and domestic intelligence activities and criminal investigation by all government intelligence agencies, including that of the military." Reflecting its importance to the new military regime, it grew quickly in size, from 3,000 at its founding in 1961 to 370,000 by 1964.[1]

Park also moved quickly to establish his control over the economy. As previously discussed, he created new planning agencies such as the Economic Planning Board and new business organizations such as the various producer associations. Labor also did not escape untouched. Park first dissolved the existing labor federation, the Federation of Korean Trade Unions (FKTU), and then re-established it under terms which better ensured its obedience to state dictates.

We have already seen how Park used the country's political and economic institutions to direct economic activity. This same power also allowed him, as well as other government officials, to enrich themselves at the public expense. Park initially justified his coup by claiming that it was necessary to end corruption in the government and society at large. In fact, over 4,000 people were arrested within the first week of the coup, charged with being hoodlums and made to parade through the streets with signs proclaiming "I Was a Hoodlum." Forty-one thousand members of the bureaucracy were dismissed by the KCIA for allegedly having obtained their jobs illegally.[2] Even the wealthy were targeted for punishment; fifty-one of South Korea's largest business owners were arrested and charged with having made their fortunes through illegal and corrupt business practices. Finally, the military took steps to reduce conspicuous consumption and end "immoral social behavior": restaurants were denied rice; bars, cafés, and dance halls were closed; and movies were censored.

This anti-corruption campaign did not last long, however, especially with regard to the wealthy. All of the fifty-one business owners were quickly released after pledging their loyalty to Park and agreeing to pay fines; with the exception of commerical bank shares, none of their existing assets were confiscated. In fact, Park was quick to exploit his own power for illegal gain. A U.S. House of Representatives report on South Korean–American relations makes this point clearly:

> Commenting on the overall situation [in late October 1961], the [U.S.] Embassy reported to Washington that the junta was displaying leniency toward those arrested for corruption after the coup; that signs of corruption and graft were reemerging at the highest levels of the Government.[3]

Park desperately needed funds to solidify his own base of support. Having been forced to promise the U.S. government that there would be a prompt end to military rule, Park had the KCIA establish a new political party, the Democratic Republican Party (DRP), to serve as his own personal political vehicle. To raise funds for party activities, the KCIA also became involved in a number of illegal schemes, including the construction of the Walker Hill Resort which was designed for use by U.S. military personnel; the duty-free importation and profitable resale of pinball machines and Japanese cars; and the covert manipulation of the South Korean stock market.[4] Additional funds were also obtained from Japanese government and corporate leaders who were eager to keep Park in power. These funds were the fruit of secret talks held between the Japanese foreign minister and the head of the KCIA in late 1962 over terms for normalizing relations between the two countries.

By the end of 1962, Park felt confident enough of his position to announce his resignation from the military and desire to run for president. Almost immediately, however, Park's campaign was put on the defensive by press reports which publicized both the KCIA's secret dealings with Japan as well as the "Three Flours Scandal" in which government manipulations had allowed a few wealthy South Korean businessmen in the sugar, flour, and cement industries to grow even wealthier in exchange for kickbacks to Park's political party. Arguments also broke out within the DRP as different factions struggled for power.

In response to these developments, Park first announced that he would not run for president, and then not long afterward announced that elections would be called off in favor of four more years of military rule. When the U.S. government expressed its displeasure with this decision by withholding aid, Park reversed himself again and agreed to hold elections. To maximize his chances for victory, he announced an election timetable that gave opposition parties only one month to register and one additional month to campaign.

In spite of all his financial, logistical, and political advantages, Park barely defeated his main opponent, 42.61 percent to 41.19 percent. The rest of the votes went to two other anti-Park candidates. Had the opposition been united, Park would have been defeated. Official statistics showed Park's campaign responsible for approximately 80 percent of total campaign spending during the election. Park's massive financial advantage over his competition, largely the result of state corruption during the period of martial law, played an important role in his victory.

Park's election did not bring an end to corruption, but rather its institutionalization. Japanese corporations offered Park his earliest and most important new source of political funds. In fact, according to a secret United States CIA report, "Japanese firms reportedly provided two-thirds of the (DRP) party's 1961-1965 budget, six firms having paid the $66 million total, with individual contributions ranging from $1 million to $20 million."[5] Key to the survival of this new system of political funding was the normalization of relations with Japan.

Park resumed normalization talks with Japan almost immediately after the 1963 election, and in March 1964, the South Korean government announced that normalization terms had been agreed upon and a treaty would soon be signed. Unhappy with the terms and trusting neither Park nor the Japanese, most South Koreans responded to the announcement with outrage. Approximately 80,000 students took to the streets in protests which lasted for five days. In early June, 15,000 students attacked government buildings in Seoul, demanding the resignation of Park. After students overpowered police in an attack on the presidential mansion, Park declared martial law, closed schools, and placed the press under censorship.

These protests forced a delay in the signing of the treaty. But with the U.S. government pressing for its ratification and the South Korean government short of foreign exchange, Park tried again in

June 1965. In response, students again led demonstrations against the treaty in every major city. In spite of this opposition, the treaty was finally signed in Tokyo on June 22, 1965.

The struggle over the treaty shifted to South Korea where it now had to be ratified by the National Assembly. Because opposition legislators did not command sufficient votes to kill the treaty outright, they hoped to defeat it through continuous filibustering. Their strategy was foiled, however, when late in the evening on August 11, the ruling party rushed the treaty through committee in a one-minute maneuver known as "the snatch." Furious, all members of the opposition handed in their resignations. The speaker of the National Assembly refused to accept them, however, and on August 14, with only members of the ruling party present, the National Assembly approved the treaty. Four days later, with opposition party members still absent, the ruling party also approved Park's decision to send South Korean troops to Vietnam.

Mounting protests over both policies, but especially the normalization of relations with Japan, forced the government to declare garrison law—modified martial law—in Seoul. At stake in this struggle was more than simple South Korean hatred of Japan. As one South Korean scholar explained:

> The primary issue throughout the political crisis in Korea was not opposition to Japan, but opposition to the Korean government, which it was feared would use financial resources from Japan to further consolidate its internal control, and in so doing would create an economic dependence on Japan in order to stay in power.[6]

The South Korean people were right to be concerned. The money that flowed from Japan and the United States was used not only to support industrial growth but also Park's political power. Park's system of illegal political funding worked as follows: to win the required government approval for foreign borrowing, South Korean firms had to agree to pay the ruling DRP a percentage of the value of the loan. The required kickback generally varied in size from 10 percent to 20 percent of the value of the loan.[7] Kickbacks were also usually required before permission for foreign direct investment would be granted. These illegal funds were especially useful to Park during election periods.

Park's re-election in 1967 was, for example, made possible by massive campaign spending. According to official government records, Park's campaign accounted for more than two-thirds of all money spent during the presidential election. This figure does not include the funds given to the KCIA and local officials who were ordered to deliver the rural vote through whatever means necessary. The 1967 National Assembly election was even worse, possibly the most corrupt election in South Korean history. The extent of the corruption was a reflection of the importance of the outcome to Park. The South Korean constitution limited a president to two terms in office, but Park wanted more. To change the constitution, he had to ensure that his party won overwhelming control over the National Assembly.

Such an election strategy required access to large sums of money and foreign multinationals, especially U.S. firms, proved to be most accommodating. Gulf Oil, for example, gave more than $1 million in secret payments to the DRP in 1966. Many firms, such as Douglas Aircraft, were approached by the head of the EPB and asked to give money to ensure governmental approval for sales to South Korean firms. Douglas Aircraft also paid money to other officials to help gain contracts.[8] These funds enabled Park to engage in massive voting irregularities and achieve what he so badly wanted: a ruling party victory and revision of the constitution.

Having discovered a winning strategy, Park again made important use of U.S. corporate funds to ensure his 1971 election victory. According to U.S. congressional investigations:

> Around the time of the 1971 Presidential election in Korea, $8.5 million was paid by U.S. firms for the benefit of the DRP, either directly or through their Korean agents or business partners. . . . While it is impossible to assess the degree to which DRP funding from U.S. sources affected the vote spread in this or any other Korean election, nonetheless the possibility exists that the $8.5 million, when comingled with funds from other sources, accounted for [Park's victory over Kim Dae Jung]. Furthermore, the figure of $8.5 million only includes payments known to the subcommittee and does not take into account, for example, other indirect payments to the DRP made by joint-venture partners of American firms unknown to their U.S. partners, the executive branch, and the subcommittee.[9]

Park's desire for money to fund his political operations also influenced his choice of economic strategy. His support of the chaebol was in part a response to the fact that an economy dominated by a few large conglomerates meant a more manageable and profitable money-making operation. Similarly, as it became clear that foreign economic activity was an ideal source of political funds, Park actively sought to increase both foreign borrowing as well as foreign direct investment.

So kickbacks, bribes, and commissions paid by those seeking loans, import and investment licenses, and government contracts—whether from the United States, Japan, or South Korea—were an important part of the workings of the South Korean state system. The chaebol and foreign firms did not seriously object to this aspect of the system because their payments were more than compensated for by access to low-cost loans or protected markets. In addition, Park made sure that funds collected in this fashion directly circulated among the South Korean elite. In the early 1970s, for example, it was reported that key military leaders as well as opposition members of the National Assembly were receiving payments from Park.[10]

I do not wish to argue that the South Korean state was unique in being corrupt or that corruption was the most serious problem facing the South Korean people. Neither is true. Moreover, in contrast to many third world countries, planning priorities generally set the framework within which the South Korean state operated its illegal fundraising schemes rather than the other way around. Nevertheless, this brief examination of corruption in the period of Park's consolidation of power does help to illuminate the important fact that while the South Korean economic strategy did produce rapid economic growth, its design and operation ensured that the benefits of that growth would be disproportionately enjoyed by a chosen few in the government, military, and business world.

The Dynamics of Export-Led Growth

As previously discussed, beginning in 1964 and continuing over the next several years, the South Korean state encouraged exports through a number of policies: currency devaluation; tax exemptions

TABLE 8.1
Real Growth in Manufacturing
(in percent)

Year	Growth in manufacturing
1962	11.6
1963	16.1
1964	9.9
1965	20.5
1966	17.2
1967	21.7
1968	27.3
1969	21.6
1970	20.0
1971	18.8
1972	14.0

Source: International Monetary Fund.

for exporters; tariff exemptions for imports used in the production of exports; subsidized interest rates for exporters; and state infrastructure support for export production. Often overlooked, however, is one of the most important state initiatives of the period: the use of agricultural policy to create a low-cost industrial labor force for the benefit of export producers.

The main instrument of state agricultural policy was a nationally organized and state-controlled system of agricultural cooperatives. Farmers were forced into membership because local cooperatives had the largest storage facilities, were the only outlet for fertilizer (a government monopoly), and were the main source of rural credit. Only members could use cooperative services and all accounts were settled in grain at prices set by the government.

Beginning in 1966, the government used its control over grain and financial markets to lower prices of such key products as rice and barley and to deny farmers sufficient credit to modernize production. As a result, average farm household income fell rapidly from close parity with urban worker households in 1965 to approximately 65 percent of average urban worker household income by 1969.[11]

TABLE 8.2
Real Growth in Exports
(in percent)

Year	Growth in exports
1962	13.1
1963	9.1
1964	23.5
1965	35.6
1966	42.5
1967	32.7
1968	39.5
1969	36.2
1970	17.6
1971	20.3
1972	36.9

Source: International Monetary Fund.

An examination of rice consumption, the country's primary food, offers one of the best indicators of the hardship these agricultural policies caused the farming population. Average family consumption fell from 29 bushels of rice in 1964, to 23.2 bushels in 1970. In fact, family consumption of all staples dropped over the same period from fifty to forty-three bushels. Farmers produced approximately the same amount of grain in 1970 as they did in 1964, but they consumed less because lower prices forced them to sell approximately 25 percent more to survive.[12]

In response to such conditions, millions of people left the farms and headed for the cities, hoping to find employment in the newly growing export industries. In one decade, 1967 to 1976, approximately 6.7 million people were forced to leave their land; the rural population declined from 54.4 percent of the total population to 35.7 percent.[13] As people left for the cities, farm labor was not replaced by machine, and the total amount of land under cultivation actually fell. These agricultural policies proved workable only because U.S. government loans allowed the South Korean government to import grains on a long-term deferred payment basis. Food

TABLE 8.3
Ratio of Exports to Imports

Year	Ratio
1962	.13
1963	.16
1964	.29
1965	.38
1966	.35
1967	.32
1968	.31
1969	.34
1970	.42
1971	.45
1972	.64

Source: International Monetary Fund.

TABLE 8.4
Trade and Debt
(in billion U.S. dollars)

Year	Trade balance	Foreign debt
1962	-.34	—
1963	-.41	.16
1964	-.25	.18
1965	-.24	.21
1966	-.43	.39
1967	-.57	.65
1968	-.84	1.20
1969	-.99	1.80
1970	-.92	2.25
1971	-1.05	2.92
1972	-.57	3.59

Sources: Economic Planning Board; Bank of Korea.

shortages and high domestic prices were avoided, but South Korea's grain self-sufficiency fell steadily from 94 percent in 1965, to 80 percent in 1970, and to 75 percent in 1976.[14]

While the government's rural policies were hard on the country's farmers and agricultural base, they did succeed in creating what the government wanted and the country's high-speed export strategy required: a low-cost industrial labor force. Taken together, the state's highly focused and integrated industrial, agricultural, financial, and labor policies were a powerful force for growth. The result, as Table 8.1 and Table 8.2 illustrate, was a rapid increase in manufacturing production and exports. The South Korean "economic miracle" had begun. But as we will see below, the economic and social dynamics of the country's economic growth were far from stable.

Economic Instability

South Korea's switch from an import-substitution to an export-led growth strategy was driven by balance of payments considerations. However, South Korea's economic strategy suffered from a serious internal weakness that caused imports to grow faster than exports beginning in 1966 (see Table 8.3). The weakness which caused this problem is not hard to find. Park's export promotion policies had created a dual economy: a dynamic import-dependent export sector fueled by cheap funds and imported capital goods and a stagnant domestic economy weakened by a depressed agricultural sector, lack of capital, and a poorly paid working class. This imbalance, reinforced by the nature of Japan's bonded processing system, meant that growth, rather than solving the balance of payments problem, made it worse (see Table 8.4).

This problem could initially be ignored because, as discussed earlier, substantial borrowing and foreign aid made it easy to finance the country's growing trade gap. This was not a viable long-term strategy, however. For example, the rapidly growing foreign debt was itself becoming a drag on the economy. South Korea had a total foreign debt of less than $200 million in 1964 and a debt service to export ratio of only 4.1 percent. By 1969, South Korea's foreign debt had grown to $1.8 billion and its debt service ratio to 13.68

percent. In 1970 and 1971 the country's total debt rose still further to $2.245 billion and then $2.922 billion, respectively. Moreover, the debt service ratio grew to over 28 percent.[15]

International developments further undermined South Korea's economic position. In 1969, President Nixon announced a major reformulation of U.S. policy regarding Asia. According to the Nixon doctrine, the United States would no longer take primary military responsibility for defending Asian countries from "communist-led or inspired aggression." In short, while the United States would continue to provide allies with military and economic assistance, U.S. troops would not be part of the package. Acting on the basis of this new policy, the United States began to reduce its direct involvement in Vietnam as well as withdraw U.S. troops from South Korea. Both moves had serious negative foreign exchange consequences for South Korea.

World economic growth had also begun to slow, triggering an increase in protectionism. In 1971, for example, the U.S. forced South Korea to sign a bilateral trade-restraint agreement on textiles. This action represented a serious threat to South Korea's economy. Textiles were South Korea's leading export item, with planners projecting a continued increase in sales. In 1970, textiles accounted for 33 percent of total manufacturing output, 32 percent of manufacturing employment, and 38 percent of total exports. Textile exports to the United States alone accounted for 15 percent of all South Korean exports.[16]

An additional concern for South Korea was the fact that several other low-wage third world countries were also attempting to increase exports of manufactures. And, with South Korea's exports heavily weighted toward such standardized, labor intensive products as textiles, apparel, plywood, and wigs, existing export markets could hardly be considered safe.

South Korea's import-dependent export strategy was fast becoming unworkable. With foreign aid, credits, and export markets shrinking, it was becoming increasingly difficult for South Korean firms to service their international debt. More than 2,000 were forced into bankruptcy by 1971.[17] Repayment problems also posed a serious challenge to state policies. It was the government's favorite firms which were deepest in debt and thus most vulnerable to default. And because of its system of loan guarantees the government was ultimately responsible for the foreign debt.

Under pressure to restore lender confidence, South Korea turned to the International Monetary Fund (IMF) for help. The IMF's stabilization program called upon South Korea to limit new private borrowing, devalue its currency, reduce fiscal deficits, slow monetary growth, and end export subsidies and import restrictions. The United States strongly endorsed the program. In spite of its refusal to end its export subsidies and import restrictions, the South Korean government was able to negotiate an agreement with the IMF. The agreed-upon austerity policies, not surprisingly, led to a slow-down in investment and growth.

The IMF stabilization program only further intensified chaebol economic problems. Burdened with heavy debt, they relied on relatively cheap foreign funds to sustain their operations. Now, as a result of the IMF agreement, they were being denied access to new foreign loans at the same time that domestic credit markets were being tightened by government policy. Perhaps even more threatening, the devaluations of 1971 and 1972, also in response to IMF demands, greatly raised the won cost of their foreign debt repayment. Desperate for funds, the chaebol had no choice but to borrow in the unregulated curb financial market where they were forced to pay extremely high interest rates for short-term loans. The following real interest rate differentials illustrate how costly this decision was for the chaebol: the real cost of capital from 1966 to 1970 averaged 39.6 percent for curb market loans, 9.8 percent for domestic loans, and -3.1 percent for foreign loans.[18]

The Federation of Korean Industrialists, an interest group representing the chaebol, demanded a change in government policy. In 1971, the organization presented its own program which called upon Park to freeze curb market repayments, transfer outstanding curb loans to the official financial market, slash interest rates, and reduce corporate taxes. Park's first response was to ignore these demands. His own strategy was to keep growth slow in order to reduce imports and to encourage greater foreign direct investment in order to reduce South Korea's dependence on foreign borrowing. It was in this context that Park responded favorably to Japanese initiatives for the establishment of the Masan Free Trade Zone. However, while such measures kept South Korea's international accounts from further deterioration, they offered no long-term solution to South Korea's economic problems.

Finally, on August 3, 1972, Park decided to accept the advice of the chaebol. His "8/3 decree" did all that business wanted: all interest rates were slashed as were corporate taxes. Moreover, an immediate moratorium was ordered on all curb market loan repayments by licensed businesses. The moratorium was to last for three years after which time the curb loans had to be turned into regular five-year loans with a maximum interest rate of 18 percent. The chaebol celebrated Park's action:

> One executive of a chaebol who was meeting with the company's board of directors, when President Park's decision was announced, stated, "We had no other solution except to declare bankruptcy. Everyone was in despair. Suddenly we received news about the decree. Everyone screamed 'Hurrah! We are saved!' and we all cried with tears."[19]

From this period forward, the relationship between the government and the chaebol would grow closer. It was now clear that each needed the other for survival and that the President would take whatever actions necessary to defend the system he had created. Nevertheless, his actions did not change the basic fact that after years of record economic growth, the South Korean economy was in serious trouble. One cannot fully appreciate the weakness in South Korea's economic strategy, however, without also examining the social tensions generated by the country's export-led economic growth.

The Social Costs of Growth

The successful transformation of South Korea's rural population into an urban labor force was, as described above, one of the keys to South Korea's rapid export-led industrialization. Most of those leaving the countryside headed directly for Seoul in search of employment. As a result, Seoul's population grew from under 2.5 million in the early 1960s, to 4.7 million in 1969, and to 7.5 million in 1977. This population explosion was too great for the social infrastructure of Seoul to accommodate. While manufacturing employers benefited from the ever expanding labor pool, South Korea's development strategy was also creating a great mass of urban poor.

Housing was usually the most immediate problem facing those arriving in Seoul. In 1972, it was estimated that there were more

TABLE 8.5
Population Growth and
Labor Market Conditions

Year	Population growth rate	Labor force growth rate	Unemployment rate	Non-farm unemployment rate
1964	2.65	1.27	7.7	14.4
1965	2.58	4.85	7.4	13.5
1966	2.55	2.39	7.1	12.8
1967	2.36	2.47	6.2	11.1
1968	2.35	3.79	5.1	9.0
1969	2.29	2.50	4.8	7.8
1970	2.21	3.15	4.5	7.4
1971	1.99	3.36	4.5	7.4
1972	1.89	4.85	4.5	7.5
1973	1.78	4.95	4.0	6.8
1974	1.73	4.14	4.1	6.8
1975	1.70	2.15	4.1	6.6
1976	1.61	5.84	3.9	6.3
1977	1.57	2.91	3.8	5.8
1978	1.53	3.66	3.2	4.7
1979	1.53	1.97	3.8	5.6
1980	1.57	1.75	5.2	7.5
1981	1.57	1.77	4.5	6.5
1982	1.56	2.52	4.4	6.0
1983	1.53	0.32	4.1	5.4
1984	1.46	-0.95	3.8	4.9
1985	1.34	3.80	4.0	4.9
1986	1.25	3.38	3.8	4.7
1987	1.23	4.70	3.1	3.8

Source: Choongsoo Kim, Labor Market Developments of Korea in Macroeconomic Perspectives, KDI Working Paper No. 8909 (Seoul, South Korea: Korea Development Institute, April 1989), p. 12.

than one million slum dwellers, living two and three families per temporary shack, out of a total Seoul population of about 5.3 million.[20] The number of slum dwellers was estimated to have grown to approximately 3 million by 1977.[21]

The government made periodic attempts to destroy these slums

TABLE 8.6
The Structure of Employment

Year	Self-employed	Family workers	Daily workers	Permanent employees
1963	37.2	31.3	12.7	18.8
1964	37.0	32.4	11.1	19.5
1965	36.8	31.1	10.4	21.7
1966	36.2	30.5	10.9	22.4
1967	36.2	28.6	10.9	24.3
1968	35.1	27.4	11.4	26.1
1969	34.9	27.0	10.9	27.2
1970	34.1	27.0	10.6	28.3
1971	34.2	26.5	10.5	28.8
1972	34.3	27.3	11.2	28.2
1973	34.5	27.7	10.6	27.2
1974	34.6	26.5	9.6	29.3
1975	33.9	25.5	9.6	31.0
1976	34.0	24.7	9.1	32.2
1977	33.2	22.2	11.1	33.5
1978	33.0	20.4	10.8	35.8
1979	33.5	18.8	10.4	37.3
1980	33.9	18.8	9.5	37.8
1981	33.7	19.1	8.8	37.4
1982	34.1	18.3	8.7	38.9
1983	33.7	16.8	8.0	41.5
1984	31.7	15.4	9.0	43.9
1985	31.3	14.5	9.3	44.9
1986	31.4	14.2	9.4	45.0
1987	30.5	13.4	9.3	46.8

Source: Choongsoo Kim, *Labor Market Developments of Korea in Macroeconomic Perspectives,* KDI Working Paper No. 8909 (Seoul: Korea Development Institute, April 1989), p. 53.

by tearing down shacks and moving people. But, no sooner were people moved out of an area than new squatters moved in. In 1970, for example, the government moved thousands of slum dwellers to Kwangju City, a newly created satellite city of Seoul. And, almost immediately, new squatters settled in the original area.

TABLE 8.7
Gender Composition of
Manufacturing Employment

Industry	1966		1973	
	Employment	Percent female	Employment	Percent female
Food and beverage	146,530	22.6	82,605	40.1
Textiles and clothing	364,220	64.8	328,930	71.3
Chemicals, including ceramics and glass	143,340	15.7	146,010	33.3
(Rubber footwear)	(20,950)	(37.5)	(36,989)	(53.1)
Metal and machinery	161,350	5.2	228,160	30.7
(Electrical and electronics components)	(18,400)	(17.6)	(92,446)	(59.6)
Other manufacturing	142,590	15.1	168,577	43.4
OVERALL	958,030	33.6	954,282	48.2

Source: Choi Jang Jip, *Labor and the Authoritarian State: Labor Unions in South Korean Manufacturing Industries* (Seoul: Korean University Press, 1989), p. 53.

Conditions were no better in the new city. In August 1971, some thirty thousand of those who had been moved to Kwangju City rioted over a lack of jobs and housing. Government buildings were destroyed and eighty-two policemen injured. When the city was finally developed, "land speculators rushed in and bought up housing sites from the slum people, forcing them to move again so that new slums mushroomed on the outskirts of Kwangju."[22]

The central problem for the urban poor was income and thus employment. Industrialization was proceeding, but it was difficult for the economy to create new industrial jobs rapidly enough to absorb the millions of people coming to the cities in search of work. Both the strengths and weaknesses in South Korea's employment picture can be seen in Table 8.5 and Table 8.6. As is typical of rapidly expanding economies, South Korea's labor force grew faster than its population. Yet, as Table 8.5 also shows, South Korea's economic growth still enabled the country to achieve a steady decline in unemployment rates. Unfortunately, as Table 8.6 also makes clear, only a minority of those employed could be classified as "permanently employed." For many of those forced to work as daily, self-employed, or unpaid family workers, earnings were insufficient to enable them and their families to escape a life of poverty.

The experiences of young women probably best capture the social dynamics of this period. Women made up the majority of those who traveled from the country to the cities: 53 percent from 1961 to 1965; 51 percent from 1965 to 1970; and 54 percent from 1970 to 1975. They were also overwhelmingly young: over 60 percent were ten to twenty-nine years old.[23] It was these young women who became the backbone of South Korea's light manufacturing labor force, making possible the country's early export growth.

Approximately 30 percent of all wage workers during the 1960s were young women aged fourteen to twenty-four. By 1973, almost half of all manufacturing workers were women. In fact, over 70 percent of all female wage workers were employed in manufacturing.[24] Most lived in company-owned dormitories and, as we can see from Table 8.7, worked in the main export industries producing textiles, clothing, rubber footwear, and electronics. These industries, known in South Korea as "female manufacturing industries," accounted for almost two-thirds of South Korea's exports during the early years of the 1970s.

Work conditions for these women were brutal. The following description of conditions at the Peace Market, a one-block-long building where some 20,000 workers, mostly young women, labored to produce clothes in over 1,000 small garment shops, offers a representative picture:

> Young girls 14 to 16 years of age had to work kneeling on the floor for an average of 15 hours a day from 8 a.m. to 11 p.m. The workers were entitled to two days off per month, the first and third Sunday. When there was a great deal of work to do, they were forced to work throughout the night. This meant that often the workers would have to work for several consecutive days and nights. In order to stay awake for such long periods of time they had to take stimulants. . . .
>
> To add to this misery was the notorious 'upper room.' The factory

owners, in order to use the limited space to the fullest, divided each room into two levels by putting in an extra floor. The distance between the floor of the second level and the ceiling measured only 3 feet. Thus the laborers were unable to stand upright throughout the whole day.[25]

Work conditions were much the same at large firms. For example, at Bando Trading Company, a large textile knitting factory:

The dormitory had no heat, so during the winter of 1974, four hundred women workers suffered frostbite. Its roof leaked in the rain ... Formerly there had been a lot of overtime work, work that began at 8:30 and frequently continued until ten o'clock or even until four o'clock the next morning, with a brief break at 5:30 for the evening meal at which two loaves of bread were supplied. A woman worker getting consumption was immediately fired without any care. Workers were afraid to hardly complain due to threats of dismissal.[26]

Women workers were not the only workers to suffer from oppressive working conditions. Most workers had no choice but to labor ten to twelve hours a day, six or seven days a week. In 1969, in exchange for such long hours, the average worker was paid a monthly wage of only $50 to $70. Those who had temporary positions made only $35 to $50 a month. Most workers had no savings and survived emergencies only by borrowing from friends and relatives.[27]

Resistance

By the last years of the 1960s, workers, especially women workers, were beginning to engage in workplace struggles to improve their earnings and working conditions. Two early and critical strikes took place in 1968 at U.S.-owned electronics firms, Oak Electronics and Signetics.

Oak Electronics employed about three hundred women who recently arrived from the countryside and were paid an average wage of approximately $17 a month. To increase their wages and improve working conditions, the women formed a union. The company refused to recognize it, however, and the workers prepared to strike. Finally, at the last moment, a top official from the U.S. home office was sent to South Korea to meet with the workers. Discussions followed, and both sides appeared to agree on a compromise settlement. But one day later, the U.S. official announced a change of mind. Oaks Electronics, he now declared, was to be closed because of the unreasonable demands and actions of the union. The workers objected, but true to his word, the plant was closed. The official's anti-union charges were widely quoted in the international press, raising fears among South Korean planners that foreign businesses would no longer see South Korea as an attractive production location.

Other noteworthy labor actions followed. In 1969, there was a large-scale strike by textile workers at sixteen cotton textile firms as well as a strike by metal workers at Chosun Shipbuilding Company. Next came a 1970 hunger strike by chemical workers at Korea Pfizer Company, a subsidiary of American Pfizer, followed by an auto workers strike against Shaehan Motor Company, a joint venture with General Motors.

Perhaps the most important labor action of the period, however, was the November 13, 1970, self-immolation of Chun Tae-il, a worker at the Seoul Peace Market. Chun had struggled to improve working conditions at the Peace Market, even appealing to the Office of Labor Affairs for enforcement of South Korean labor laws. Rebuffed and beaten by police and employers, but determined to call attention to the plight of the workers, Chun set himself on fire. He died shouting: "Obey the Labor Standards Act! Don't mistreat young girls!" Chun's death did, in fact, focus attention on labor conditions, spurring many South Koreans, especially student and Christian activists, to commit themselves to work for labor reform.

These acts of resistance, especially strikes at firms with foreign investments, were frighting to Park. As noted earlier, South Korea was, by the end of the 1960s, facing a serious balance of payments problem which Park hoped to lessen by encouraging greater foreign direct investment. Since labor struggles such as the one at Oak Electronics threatened to undermine this strategy, the government introduced new labor legislation in January 1970. Article 18 of the law establishing free trade zones made labor organizing in those zones almost impossible and labor strikes illegal. All disputes had to be settled through a compulsory arbitration procedure under the control of the government and foreign corporations. The "Special Law on Trade Unions and Mediation of Labor Disputes in Enterprises Invested by Foreigners" basically extended the same labor restrictions to all firms with foreign investments regardless of whether they were located in a free trade zone.

Popular dissatisfaction with living and working conditions continued to grow rapidly, especially as the economy slowed in 1971. Workers were finding it almost impossible to survive on what they were paid: the average manufacturing wage in the early 1970s was $40 a month, while the Bank of Korea estimated that an urban family of four needed $90 a month for its expenses. In textiles, one of South Korea's major export industries, young women commonly earned only $12 to $25 a month working ten hours a day and six days a week.[28] Not surprisingly, workplace actions increased in number and significance. Farmers and the urban poor also began to protest against their situation. According to the 1972 *Far Eastern Economic Review Yearbook*, 1971 was noted for "the increase in violence and group protests as frustration mounted among people passed over by the fruits of spectacular economic development."[29]

At the same time that workers, farmers, and the urban poor were engaged in their struggle for survival, South Korea's rapid growth was enriching those at the top. People's awareness of this development greatly worried the government. In May 1970, for example, the Ministry of Health and Social Affairs issued a report saying that the inequitable distribution of income was creating serious social problems. According to Joungwon A. Kim: "Most troublesome was the conspicuous consumption of the new elite, who began building luxurious homes and riding through Seoul in expensive imported Cadillacs and Mercedes-Benzes (a used Mercedes sold for as much as $35,000 in Korea)."[30]

Popular disgust with the growing concentration of wealth and power was expressed by the famous poet Kim Chi-ha in one of his best-known poems, "The Five Thieves." The five thieves referred to by Kim were the generals, high bureaucrats, millionaire industrialists, cabinet members, and national assemblymen. Kim had the following to say about the cabinet ministers:

> They waddle from obesity.
> And sediment seeps from every pore.
> With peerless, shifty mucous-lined eyes,
> They command the national defense,
> With their golf clubs in their left hands,

> While fondling the breasts of their mistresses
> With their right.
> And they softly write on their mistresses' breasts,
> "Increased production,
> Increased export and construction."
> The women giggle,
> "Hee, hee, hee; don't tickle me!"
> Then, jokingly, the ministers reproach:
> "Hey, you ignorant woman,
> Do affairs of state make you laugh?
> Let's export even if we starve;
> Let's increase production even if products are not sold;
> Let's construct a bridge across the Strait of Korea,
> With bones of those who have starved to death—
> So we can worship the god of Japan!"[31]

The poem was published in May 1970, and less than one month later, the government put both Kim and the editor of the journal which published the poem in jail. The journal itself was never allowed to publish again. The charge: the poem was intended to stir up class struggle in violation of the law.

Dictatorship

The social and political conditions described above provide the context for the April 1971 presidential election in which Park successfully used fraud and voter intimidation to defeat his opponent, Kim Dae Jung. The victory, however, settled nothing: the economy remained stalled. Rural and urban unrest continued.

Park's response to this increasingly threatening situation was a declaration of national emergency on December 6, 1971. On December 27, 1971, in an illegal secret session, he had the National Assembly pass the Law Concerning Special Measures for Safeguarding National Security which gave him the authority to ban public demonstrations; freeze wages, rents, and prices; and "mobilize any material or human resources for national purposes."[32]

As part of this special law, the legislation limiting labor activities at foreign firms was both tightened and expanded to include all workers at all enterprises. While it remained legal for workers to form unions, the Office of Labor Affairs itself would now dictate the terms of collective bargaining for all workers. The Office of Labor Affairs would also act as the sole mediator of all labor disputes, its rulings to be final and binding on all parties.

All of these actions were justified as necessary to guard the nation's national security. But, as Choi Jang Jip, an expert on South Korea's labor movement, explains, Park's fundamental motivation for seeking these new powers "derived from an urgent need to control the nation's economy. Its immediate target was the working class."[33] Not surprisingly, the chaebol also found the national security cover useful. To build their case against worker activism of any kind, they would commonly charge that "labor unions are communist organizations" or that "organizing labor unions contravenes the state's export policy."

These new restrictions on working-class activism were soon followed in August 3, 1972, by Park's decree which, as discussed earlier, enabled the chaebol to escape their financial liabilities. Finally, on October 17, Park declared martial law with the announced purpose of rewriting the constitution so as to institutionalize his newly acquired powers.

He called his new constitution the Yushin Constitution. Yushin, meaning "revitalizing reforms," was a term borrowed from the Japanese which referred to the period of the Meiji Restoration and Japan's aggressive industrial and military growth. Park claimed that his new constitution was necessary because Western-style democracy had proven unsuitable for South Korea. What was needed, he argued, was "Korean-style democracy." Yushin was designed to make Park a dictator for life.

The Yushin Constitution gave Park tremendous power, including the right to appoint one-third of the National Assembly; to dissolve the National Assembly at will; to appoint all judges; and to appoint all members of the constitutional committee, which determined whether laws passed by the National Assembly were constitutional. More generally, the new constitution gave Park the authority to take whatever emergency measures might be needed, whenever "the national security or the public safety and order is seriously threatened or anticipated to be threatened."[34]

Ironically, while Park used national security, or more specifically the threat from North Korea, as justification for his 1971 crackdown, he now used ongoing negotiations with North Korea as justification for Yushin. On July 4, 1972, the governments of North and South Korea issued a surprise statement pledging to work together to achieve an independent and peaceful reunification of Korea. To win support for his new constitution, Park told the South Korean people that Yushin was necessary to ensure the success of his negotiations with the North. A vote against Yushin, he announced, was a vote against continuing the North-South dialogue.

No public discussion of the Yushin Constitution was allowed, and a referendum to approve the new constitution took place while the country was still under martial law. According to the government, 91.9 percent of all eligible voters cast votes with 91.5 percent voting for Yushin. With the new constitution in place, martial law was lifted on December 13. Ten days later, Park had himself re-elected President by the newly created National Congress for Unification under terms specified by the new constitution. The South Korean people would have to wait until 1987 for the chance to once again directly elect their president.

Using intimidation, torture, and bribery, Park had succeeded in restoring order. But, while his hold on power was now unquestioned, people never stopped fighting to defend their rights as best they could. Fishermen destroyed government property to protest expropriation of their anchovy beds. Farmers demonstrated against government confiscation of their land for the purpose of building new factories. Workers fought for trade union rights with illegal sit-down strikes and walk-outs. The *Far Eastern Economic Review* described the overall political situation during this period as follows:

> South Korea's jails are rapidly filling up with political prisoners. Although martial law ended last December, the rate of arrests is increasing: in March [1973] alone, no fewer than 48 persons were arrested for speaking out against the Government. Most of the arrests . . . have been among the peasants, workers and students.[35]

Conclusion

South Korea's first decade under Park's rule was far from crisis free. After a few strong years of growth, weaknesses in the country's export strategy became apparent. Growth, rather than solving the balance of payments problem, had only intensified it. Moreover, increasingly militant opposition to the government and its economic strategy was generated by the very logic of the growth process.

As seen above, Park took a series of decisive actions to sustain his regime and ensure that the chaebol and foreign multinational corporations could continue business as usual. In other words, that they could continue to make profits and pay kickbacks to the government. But, while the benefits of such actions were enjoyed by those in positions of authority and power, the population was forced to sacrifice its political and economic rights. Because farmer and worker demands for reform were seen as a threat to the system's profitable operation, the state and chaebol were drawn to support each other and a political program of repression. Thus, rather than advance the country's democratic political development, the economic success celebrated by most economists had led to dictatorship.

CHAPTER 9

THE POLITICAL ECONOMY OF GROWTH AND CRISIS: 1973 TO 1981

As I outlined in the previous chapter, South Korea's economic strategy produced considerable industrial growth, an increasing concentration of wealth and power in the hands of a few chaebol owners and government leaders, economic and political instability, and finally, in 1972, dictatorship. But dictatorship alone was not sufficient to stabilize the South Korean political economy. Global developments, including a reduction in direct U.S. political and economic support and a rise in international protectionism, continued to threaten South Korean growth and Park's hold on power.

Survival required a bold new economic initiative and, following the thrust of an earlier Japanese proposal, Park responded with his 1973 Heavy and Chemical Industrial Development Plan. In this chapter, I continue my analysis of the South Korean experience by examining the workings as well as economic and political consequences of this plan.

The Dynamics of Export-Led Growth

According to the Heavy and Chemical Industrial Development Plan, iron and steel, nonferrous metals, shipbuilding, machinery, electronics, and petrochemicals were to become the heart of a restructured and revitalized South Korean economy. It was Park's hope that development of these industries would, by reducing imports and establishing new higher value-added exports, enable

South Korea to solve its balance of payments problems. These industries also offered South Korea an expanded military production capability, and thus greater foreign policy independence from the United States.

Because this program of industrial restructuring did not have the support of either the World Bank, the IMF, or United States officials, Park did not rely on normal policy channels for its development. Fearing that Western influence in the Economic Planning Board had grown too strong and was likely to cause unwanted policy debates and delays, Park decided to give responsibility for the heavy and chemical industry plan to his presidential secretary rather than the Economic Planning Board.

Development of these new industries was also combined with a new land-use plan. The goal was to create a large industrial complex for each of the targeted heavy and chemical industries as well as reduce the concentration of economic activity in Seoul. Approximately 45 percent of industrial output was produced in the Seoul area in 1970; the plan called for reducing that figure to under 30 percent by 1981. Although there are no exact figures, it appears that this target was, in fact, reached.[1] Toward that end, the Yosu-Yochon complex was created for petrochemicals, the Changwon complex was built for machine building, Pohang was targeted for steel, Okpo was designated to become a shipbuilding center, the Kumi complex was built for electronics, and Onsan was developed to support the nonferrous metal industry.

The establishment of these new heavy and chemical industry centers was a major undertaking and required enormous government intervention. To develop them, the Ministry of Construction was given responsibility for obtaining ownership of the desired land, often forcibly removing farmers, and building the required industrial infrastructure of roads, ports, and buildings. In the case of industries such as electronics and machinery production, the Ministry of Trade and Industry then used various financial incentives to attract private producers. For bigger projects, such as the establishment of steel mills or petrochemical facilities, the state created its own companies to undertake production or, as was more often the case, promoted joint ventures with foreign capital.

Nothing was left to chance, and decisions were always highly political. Masan and Changwon were selected to become production centers, for example, because of the wishes of officials close to Park. More significant in terms of the development of the South Korean political economy was the process for selecting firms to dominate these new industries. Not surprisingly, the Ministry of Trade and Industry used its licensing authority to reward the chaebol for their loyalty to Park. And, as a result, it was during this period that the chaebol established their dominance over the South Korean economy: the combined net sales of the top ten chaebol rose from 15.1 percent of GNP in 1974, to 30.1 percent in 1978, and to 55.7 percent in 1981.[2]

With the South Korean government in control of all stages of this industrial transformation and increasingly fearful that U.S. foreign policy under President Carter would leave South Korea militarily and economically isolated, the chaebol were pushed to develop these new industries as fast as possible. Thus, approximately 97 percent of all heavy and chemical industry investments scheduled from 1977 to 1981 were completed by 1979. By contrast, only 46 percent of scheduled investments in light manufacturing were completed.[3]

The results of this big push were impressive. The share of heavy and chemical industries in manufacturing output went from 39.7 percent in 1972 to 54.9 percent in 1979. Moreover, the percentage of heavy and chemical exports in total exports rose from 13.7 percent in 1971 to 37.7 percent in 1979.[4] Overall economic growth also picked up: from 1973 to 1978, the rate of growth of GNP averaged 11 percent a year. And, between 1974 and 1977, exports increased faster than imports (Table 9.1), producing a significantly smaller balance of trade deficit (Table 9.2).

By 1978, it appeared that South Korea had solved its major economic problems. It became the number one third world exporter of manufactures to the developed capitalist countries. Its efficient steel industry, its modern shipyards, its production of advanced electronics all bespoke a successful economic transformation. To most observers, it was obvious that South Korea had become a major industrial power and model of third world development.

But, as we will see further on, the South Korean experience during the 1970s was far more complex and contradictory than the standard economic pronouncements of the time would have us believe. For reasons similar to those discussed in the previous chapter, South

TABLE 9.1
Ratio of Exports to Imports

Year	Ratio
1973	.76
1974	.65
1975	.70
1976	.88
1977	.93
1978	.85
1979	.74
1980	.79

Source: International Monetary Fund.

Korea's economic success proved to be short-lived. By 1979, the country was again facing serious balance of payments problems and, this time, headed into serious recession. With people rioting in the streets in protest against the Park regime, the South Korean political situation was even more troubled than the economy. The resulting tensions finally triggered the assassination of Park.

Park's death created an opportunity for the South Korean people to express their own preferences concerning the future of South Korea's political economy. But, fearful that existing economic and political arrangements did not have the support of the people, the military once again intervened. In 1980, a bloody military coup enabled the South Korean political economy to survive Park's death. In short, the South Korean experience during the Park era shows that while the country's specific growth strategy is worthy of careful study, it is far from deserving of its status as a model for other countries to follow.

Economic Instabilities

My initial presentation of Park's heavy and chemical industrialization drive highlighted its successes. However, a more careful examination of Tables 9.1 and 9.2 also shows that many of the gains, especially in the trade area, were only short term. Beginning in 1978, for example, imports once again rose faster than ex-

TABLE 9.2
Balance of Trade
(billion U.S. dollars)

Year	Balance of trade
1973	- .57
1974	-1.94
1975	-1.67
1976	- .59
1977	- .48
1978	-1.78
1979	-4.40
1980	-4.38

Source: International Monetary Fund.

ports, driving the balance of trade deeper into deficit and necessitating ever greater foreign borrowing. There were a number of reasons for this economic reversal.

First, to attract the chaebol and fund the large investments necessary to launch industries such as steel, chemicals, and shipbuilding, the state aggressively mobilized domestic savings, increased its foreign borrowing, and extended policy loans. This expansionary credit policy produced a significant increase in the inflation rate. Inflation averaged less than 13 percent from 1965 to 1973. In 1974, prices rose by more than 29 percent. The rate of inflation remained above 20 percent in five of the next six years.[5] Such high rates of inflation tended to undermine the export competitiveness of South Korea's manufacturers, especially those in light manufacturing.

Second, state support of chaebol activities through highly subsidized credit led to greatly increased corporate debt-equity ratios, leaving the chaebol increasingly vulnerable to future economic instability. It also led to over-investment and excess capacity in a number of industries. From 1978 to 1980, for example, the overall capacity utilization rate in manufacturing fell from 83.4 percent to 69.5 percent. The problem was much worse in specific heavy and chemical industries. In the machinery sector, for example, the ratio fell from 74 percent in late 1977 to 35 percent by late 1980.[6] In transport equipment, rates from 1978 to 1980 were 40.4 percent,

38.8 percent, and 41.9 percent, respectively.[7] When the economy finally began to slow in 1979, this over-investment greatly added to the chaebol's financial burden and the economy's instability.

Third, many of the newly established industries were technologically and structurally dependent upon foreign capital. This dependence was partly the result of South Korea's insistence on rapid development of a broad range of heavy and chemical industries. It was also the result of the fact that Japanese corporations, eager to relocate many of the labor and processing-intensive sectors of these industries to South Korea, were not interested in yielding control of the underlying technology.

Most of the technology used by these new heavy and chemical industries had to be imported, giving rise to substantial royalty payments.[8] Such dependence also made production itself heavily dependent upon imports: while South Korea built one of the largest corporate shipyards in the world, only the hulls were produced in South Korea. All the machinery, engines, and instruments had to be imported from Japan.[9] This dependence clearly created balance of payments difficulties for South Korea.

The South Korean state did make efforts to increase technology transfer by forcing foreign firms to accept, whenever possible, joint venture agreements with a maximum 50 percent foreign ownership and management control. However, as one South Korean government report noted, "excessive emphasis on retaining control in the hands of Korean enterprises has served as a disincentive for foreign investors to utilize their most up-to-date manufacturing processes . . . "[10]

When modern technology was used, foreign capital often took steps to ensure its control. For example, when textile machine production was undertaken through joint venture with Stone-Platt (Great Britain), the United Nations Conference on Trade and Development reported that "Stone-Platt retain[ed] proprietary control over the technology as well as final say over choice of markets."[11]

The struggle between the South Korean state and Dow Chemicals illustrates some of the tensions of the period. The South Korean chemical industry was perhaps the most dependent of all heavy and chemical industries on foreign direct investment and technical assistance. Dow Chemicals, one of South Korea's largest foreign investors, was charged with inflating prices of key inputs to its South Korean partner in order to transfer profits from its joint venture to its own wholly owned plant outside of South Korea. When the South Korean partner objected, and the South Korean government intervened in support of the local firm, Dow Chemicals simply pulled out of its joint venture.

Fourth, South Korea's growth strategy led to a rapid increase in wages. In response to the Middle East oil boom, the South Korean state negotiated and directed a massive construction program in the region. According to Ministry of Labor data, approximately 293,000 male workers were sent overseas between 1977 and 1979 for construction work, a number equal to more than one-fourth of the entire South Korean male manufacturing work force.[12] This helped drive real wages up at a faster rate than productivity, squeezing profits in light manufacturing and intensifying inflationary pressures.

Thus, while massive state spending and subsidized credit spurred economic growth and profits for the large chaebol, foreign corporations, and state officials, the economy became increasingly unstable and unbalanced. The overbuilt new industries proved unable to meet the government's ambitious export targets, while the traditional export earning sector, light manufacturing, lost its international competitiveness. The growth in export volume slowed drastically from its post-1965 historical trend of approximately 30 percent a year to only 14 percent in 1978, and to -1 percent in 1979.[13] Simultaneously, the country's rapid industrialization pulled in ever greater imports of technology and capital goods. The result was a rapidly widening trade deficit and forced foreign borrowing to sustain growth.

By mid-1979, it had become clear to the government that the expansion could no longer be sustained. To avert a debt crisis, Park had to take steps to reduce imports and restore export competitiveness in light manufacturing. His response, a reduction in government spending and money creation, triggered a recession. GNP growth slowed to 6.5 percent in 1979 and then fell by more than 5 percent in 1980, the first year of negative growth since the Korean War.

South Korea's industrialization policy also left it, by the end of 1980, the world's third-largest debtor, trailing only Brazil and Mexico. South Korea's foreign debt skyrocketed from approximately $20 billion in 1979 to $40 billion in 1983; one can only speculate on the negative effect such a debt load would have had on the South Korean economy if the Japanese did not offer the highly subsidized $4 billion loan discussed earlier.

Thus, in spite of its accomplishments, Park's heavy and chemical industry drive left South Korea facing a number of serious economic problems. This is not to say, however, that the plan was responsible for all of the country's difficulties. Many of South Korea's new industries, such as shipbuilding, came on line just as a global economic slowdown was gathering momentum. Moreover, as discussed earlier, without the establishment of these new industries, South Korea's mid-1980s export revival would not have been possible.

My point, then, is not that South Korea ended the 1970s as a hopeless economic case, but rather, after almost twenty years of rapid growth, Park's state-driven economic strategy produced neither a balanced nor stable economy. As the discussion in this chapter highlights, the end result was an economy increasingly export oriented, dominated by a handful of chaebol, dependent on foreign capital and crisis oriented. An even more significant weakness in Park's industrialization strategy, however, was its underlying class bias, which, as we will soon see, meant that growth itself continued to intensify already serious social contradictions.

Political Conditions

As discussed in the previous chapter, Yushin gave Park the powers of a dictator. The following commentary from a foreign journalist in South Korea, entitled "A New Hero Worship in Asia," offers insight into how Park viewed his own importance:

> His every thought and his tireless energy are wholly dedicated to the future of our people. By his unbounded kindness and complete sincerity we are led forward continuously in progress toward a better future . . .
>
> He sets new faith aflame in our hearts, and from our labors brings forth a national harvest without equal.
>
> Is the great hero lauded here Chairman Mao? Chairman Kim Il Sung? Superman? Not any of these. The object of all this praise is Korea's own daring, dauntless Park Chung Hee.
>
> After sweeping away all political opposition in last October's complete takeover of power, Park has been surrounded by efforts to elevate him to hero status. These efforts would attribute to him all national strength, all state decisions, all creative ideas.

This is, of course, no easy task. A man of few words, Park has no charisma whatsoever. Still, no newspaper in the country could last more than a day without printing pictures of the stern-faced Park grouped with his officials or meeting foreign dignitaries. . . .

The credit for all industrial progress is his: "The remarkable growth in industry is due to cooperation of the people with the leadership of our wise and brave president." . . .

President Park holds only one press conference each year. The general public rarely have a chance to see him. A recently published book nonetheless has this to say: "The pulse of the president's will beats throughout this land to every shore, awakening us from a 5,000-year slumber to go forward to ever greater achievements in the future." . . .

Now that Park's control of the presidency has become permanent, the people who must obey him are told that they also ought to love him.[14]

Park, of course, never succeeded in winning the support of the great majority of South Korean people, and opposition to the Yushin Constitution and Park's rule, led by students and church leaders, was quick to develop. In response, Park issued a series of emergency decrees. For example, Emergency Decree No. 1, which was issued January 1974, made it illegal to "deny, oppose, misrepresent or defame the constitution of the Republic of Korea" or "seek revision or repeal of the constitution." Hundreds of students, intellectuals, and religious leaders were arrested, tortured, and sent to prison for violating this decree.

When students refused to be intimidated, continuing their efforts to overturn Yushin, Park issued Emergency Decree No. 4 in April 1974, which made it illegal for any person "to organize or join the National Democratic Youth and Student Federation or any organization affiliated with it; to praise, encourage, or sympathize with the activities of the said organization or its members; to assemble with its members or contact them by formal means of communication or by any other means; to provide a place, articles, money or any other accommodation for its members to help them hide, establish contact, or engage in other activities; or to participate directly or indirectly in the activities of the said organization or its members." Fourteen people were sentenced to death for violating this decree, eight of whom were actually executed.

In May 1975, Park issued Emergency Decree No. 9, the most

sweeping of all his decrees. It prohibited making any "false" statements about Park or the government. It prohibited any criticism of the constitution, any political activity by students, or any public presentation or statement describing or discussing any act which might violate the decree. As a result of this decree, it became illegal for any South Korean to call for democracy, object to any government act, or say or do anything that might defame or harm the "welfare" of South Korea while abroad or with a foreigner while in South Korea. Given the scope of Emergency Decree No. 9, Park had no need for further decrees.

Economic Conditions

While students and religious leaders were among the most outspoken opponents and earliest victims of Park's dictatorship, workers also paid a price for Yushin and industrialization. As noted in the previous chapter, the expansion of Park's dictatorial powers was largely driven by the need to defend the interests of those who dominated the South Korean economy. Greater restrictions on labor were, therefore, always central to each new step on the road to what Park called "Korean-style democracy."

Yushin was no different. It codified the labor restrictions which were introduced on December 27, 1971, as part of the Law Concerning Special Measures for Safeguarding National Security. Additional labor law revisions were also made in 1973 and 1974, further weakening union autonomy and responsibility. But South Korea's workers sacrificed more than just their civil liberties and democratic rights during the 1970s. As we will see next, the country's industrial restructuring and renewed growth was also accompanied by growing income inequality and increasingly oppressive working conditions for most South Koreans.

Income

Economists have long praised South Korea for having one of the world's most equitable distributions of income. The South Korean income experience has, in fact, often been cited by economists to demonstrate the possibility of growth *with* equity. Income distribution is commonly measured by the Gini index, a summary statistic

TABLE 9.3
Distribution of Household Income, 1965-1980

Income group	1965	1970	1976	1980
Top 20%	41.81	41.62	45.34	45.39
Bottom 40%	19.34	19.63	16.85	16.06
Top/bottom	2.16	2.12	2.69	2.83
GINI Index	.344	.332	.391	.389

Source: Economic Planning Board, *Social Indicators in Korea, 1987* (Seoul, South Korea: Economic Planning Board, 1987), p. 80.

which ranges in value from 0, representing perfect equality in the distribution of income, to 1, representing maximum inequality. The Gini index for South Korea in 1970 was .332 which compares favorably with the 1970 Swedish index value of .387 and the 1972 U.S. index value of .417.[15]

However, South Korea's relatively equal distribution of income has little to do with the country's export-led development strategy. Far more important was the legacy of Japanese colonialism and the Korean War: Japanese colonialism hindered the development of a South Korean capitalist class, and the Korean War forced the South Korean government to complete its proposed land reform. Park, therefore, inherited a society with an unusually equal distribution of income. The initial stages of his export-led development strategy, based on the rapid expansion of light manufacturing, had a positive impact on income equality. But, with the initiation of the heavy and chemical industrialization drive, conditions began to worsen.

Table 9.3 shows changes in income distribution using two different measures of inequality, the Gini index and relative income shares. Both measures reveal an improvement in income distribution from 1965 to 1970 and then a sharp increase in inequality over the first half of the 1970s. While the Gini index remained stable over the second half of the decade, the movement in relative income shares indicates a further growth in inequality. Regardless of which measure is used, inequality was far greater in 1980 than it had been in 1970. The growth in relative poverty during the 1970s lends support to this conclusion. The percentage of the population earning

TABLE 9.4
Increases in Labor Productivity
and Real Wages in Manufacturing, 1971-1981

Year	Labor productivity	Real wages
1971	9.7	2.4
1972	8.7	2.0
1973	8.8	14.3
1974	11.4	8.8
1975	11.6	1.4
1976	7.5	16.8
1977	10.4	21.5
1978	12.0	17.4
1979	15.8	8.4
1980	10.7	-4.7
1981	15.8	-2.6

Source: Economic Planning Board, *Major Statistics of Korean Economy, 1982* (Seoul: Economic Planning Board, 1982), p. 175.

less than one-third of the national income, the definition of relative poverty, rose from 5 percent in 1970 to 14 percent in 1978.[16]

There is also good reason to believe that these figures seriously underestimate the problem of income inequality in South Korea. Government statistics are based on selected data "derived from surveys that exclude wealthy households, single-person households, nonfarm households in rural areas, and small farmers."[17] Urban statistics exclude families earning more than $5,000 a year.[18] Moreover, neither corporate income, profits from real estate activity, or interest earnings from curb market lending are included in the statistics. All of these omissions bias the data to suggest a far greater degree of income equality than actually exists.

Economists have also praised South Korea's wage performance. International comparisons of wage gains over the 1970s are certainly favorable to South Korea. For example, South Korea's index of real wages rose from 100 in 1970 to 238 in 1979, an increase of 138 percent. Over the same period, Brazil's index grew by only 34 percent, Mexico's by 21 percent, Turkey's by 55 percent, and Taiwan's by 63 percent. Argentina's wage index actually fell by 13 percent.[19] However, while most South Koreans are financially better off as a result of their country's industrialization, South Korean government statistics significantly overstate worker gains.

Table 9.4 presents government data on real wages and productivity in the manufacturing sector through the 1970s. Two trends are worthy of discussion: first, productivity increases were greater than real wage increases for seven of the eleven years shown. Over the entire period, productivity rose at an average annual rate of 11.13 percent compared with real wages which rose at an annual average rate of 7.79 percent. This productivity advantage enabled the chaebol to lower their production costs and boost profits. It also contributed to a redistribution of income from workers to owners.

The data also show that workers in manufacturing earned real wage increases every year during the 1970s. These figures are suspect for several reasons. First, the government's determination of real wages is based on a comparison of nominal wage increases with movements in the consumer price index. This price index has been commonly manipulated downward, however, leading to a serious underestimation of actual increases in the cost of living and, as a result, overestimation of worker real wage earnings.[20] In 1978, for example, government data showed a 17.4 percent gain in real wages as a result of a 34.4 percent increase in nominal wages and a 17 percent increase in the consumer price index. In fact, it was commonly understood by most South Koreans that the actual increase in the consumer price index that year was 30 percent to 40 percent.[21] Substituting an inflation rate of 35 percent for the government's figure of 17 percent, yields a real wage *decline* of 0.6 percent.

Second, the wage figures shown in Table 9.4 are based on total *monthly* wages paid. They are not adjusted to take account of changes in the number of hours worked during the month and include earnings for all workers, production *as well as* white collar. Finally, small firms, among the lowest paying in the manufacturing sector, are not included in the wage survey that provides the data for government income calculations.[22]

In spite of government data showing consistent and often large annual real wage increases, most workers, even as late as 1978, continued to earn extremely low wages. According to government statistics, approximately 65 percent of all manufacturing workers earned less than that year's average monthly wage of 100,000 won ($207). Approximately 38 percent of all manufacturing workers earned below the government-defined subsistence wage level.[23]

A similar picture of worker poverty emerges from Ministry of Finance data on tax revenue. In 1978, 76.7 percent of all employed workers were paid wages below the point of income tax exemption. This was primarily due to poorly paid workers rather than an unusually high tax exemption point. In comparison, only .3 percent of all employees paid 43.1 percent of the nation's total income taxes.[24] In short, while the South Korean economy grew more industrialized and South Korean capitalists richer during the 1970s, most workers continued to live under difficult economic conditions.

Perhaps more relevant for our analysis of South Korea's economic strategy is the fact that worker income varied considerably according to whether employment was in the export or domestically oriented sector: in 1976, for example, wages in export firms were, on average, only 70.5 percent of those earned in firms producing primarily for the domestic market.[25] More specifically, while the average monthly wage in 1976 was $130 for all nonfarm wage earners and $108 for all manufacturing workers, average earnings were only $90 a month in textiles, clothing, and leather ($60 in clothing alone); $90 in rubber; and $104 in electronics.[26]

This earnings disadvantage for workers in the export sector can be explained primarily by the extremely low wages paid to women workers employed in the country's key export industries. Women earned far less than men, even when employed in the same industry. Mid-1980s survey data show that the average monthly wage of women was only about 59 percent than that of men in textiles; 63 percent in basic metal manufacturing; and 52 percent in metal assembling and machine manufacturing.[27] South Korea's rapid export-driven growth was thus largely supported by the exploitation of those workers, especially women, who produced the products sold abroad. Thus, in spite of the real gains that came with industrialization, most workers, especially those employed in the export sector, had reason to feel that they were being denied a fair share of the wealth they were creating.

Working Conditions

In addition to low wages, South Korean workers also faced extremely oppressive working conditions which tended to worsen during the period of heavy and chemical industrialization. According to the International Labor Organization, for example, South Korean workers had the world's longest work week throughout the 1970s. And, in contrast to trends in most other countries, their average work week actually lengthened from 50.5 hours a week in 1975 to 54.3 hours in 1983.[28]

The following statement by the workers at Pangrim Textile Company translates these numbers into human terms:

> At our factory, we work three 8-hour shifts, but from when to when we do not know. We are forced to come 30-60 minutes early and work until the job is finished—however long it may take! If we are supposed to finish by 10 p.m. we often don't get home until just before curfew at 12 a.m. If we live in the dormitory we sometimes work until 1 a.m. or 2 a.m. If for some reason a worker comes at the scheduled starting time then the foreman and lead girl worker give her a hard time. . . . Each worker wants to avoid being last to arrive and so tries to arrive before her co-workers. After work, no one wants to be the first to leave, so all stay longer. Even animals have a rest time, why must we work harder than animals? Because the machines run continuously we are so busy that we often cannot have a meal break. If the machine needs fixing we must do it immediately or be reprimanded. We are ashamed to say that sometimes we cannot go to the toilet and so must use the factory floor. The machine never stops![29]

Not only did the machine not stop, in the interest of maximizing profits, companies paid no attention to health and safety conditions. The result, as Table 9.5 illustrates, was that workers suffered from high and growing numbers of industrial accidents. In fact, these figures understate the seriousness of South Korea's occupational health and safety problems. For example, these accident records are based only on filed reports, and many accidents are never reported by companies in order to minimize insurance costs. Equally important, workplaces with fewer than 10 workers, among the most dangerous, were not included in the statistics. According to the Ministry of Labor, adjusting the 1983 data to include these small firms would raise the total number of accident victims from approximately 157,000 to 317,000. This corrected number translates to two workers injured on the job for every minute of work time in 1983.[30]

TABLE 9.5
Victims of Industrial Accidents

Year	Number
1969	31,705
1970	37,752
1971	44,545
1972	46,603
1973	59,367
1974	70,142
1975	81,641
1976	97,716
1977	118,011
1978	139,242
1979	130,307

Source: *Social Justice Indicators in Korea,* 2nd ed., Christian Institute for the Study of Justice and Development (Seoul: Minjungsa, 1987), p. 121.

Perhaps the worst overall employment conditions during the 1970s were found in the female-dominated export industries such as garment, textile, and electronics. One former sewing-machine operator described conditions in her garment factory as follows:

> When [the apprentices] shake the waste threads from the clothes, the whole room fills with dust and it is hard to breathe. Since we've been working in such dusty air, there have been increasing numbers of people getting tuberculosis, bronchitis, and eye disease. . . . It makes us so sad when we have to have pale, unhealthy, wrinkled faces like dried-up spinach. . . . It seems to me that no one knows our blood dissolves into the threads and seams, with sighs and sorrows.[31]

While women workers faced the most oppressive work conditions, male workers in the newer heavy and chemical industries also were exploited. Little concern was given to health and safety conditions in either the construction or operation of these new industries. Moreover, the chaebol were given the green light to violate the already weak labor laws in order to cut production costs. At shipyards and steel mills, for example, the law allowed companies to hire workers on an initial probationary basis not to exceed six months. At places like Hyundai Shipyards, however, workers were regularly fired at the end of their probation period only to be immediately rehired back on a probationary basis. The advantage to the company: workers on probation were not entitled to regular wages or bonuses and could legally be forced to work extra-long days.

The conditions described above reveal that there was very little miraculous about the so-called South Korean "economic miracle." South Korea's economic success during Park's reign can more accurately be described as the result of a forced march, and one in which workers enjoyed few of the benefits.

The Changing Strategy of Resistance

During the 1960s, resistance to Park's political and economic agenda was led by students and church officials whose primary demand was for "democracy," by which most meant respect for established electoral procedures and basic civil rights. Little attention or support was given to the isolated and spontaneous struggles of workers, farmers, and the urban poor. While this remained true throughout the early part of the 1970s, political and economic developments soon began to produce a more united and increasingly effective working-class-centered opposition movement.

Student and church leaders initially hoped that symbolic acts of resistance and civil disobedience would highlight the undemocratic nature of Yushin, leading to the international condemnation and isolation of the Park regime. The result, they hoped, would be, as in 1960, the forced resignation of the president. Times had changed, however, and the strategy proved unsuccessful.

Park's imposition of Yushin, for example, was met with silence, and not disapproval by the United States. A U.S. House of Representatives report on South Korean-American relations illustrates this point with the following statement:

> When the Yushin declaration was made, the United States had to put its policy together quickly. At that time Seoul was in considerable favor in Washington because of the economic achievements and the negotiations with the North. Therefore, the policy adopted was one of noninterference. President Nixon reiterated the policy when he told Prime Minister Kim Jong Pil in January 1973 that "unlike other Presidents, I do not intend to interfere in the internal affairs of your country."[32]

Thus, even though a number of South Korean students, intellectuals, and church officials suffered arrest, torture, imprisonment, and in some cases death, from acts as simple as signing petitions calling for revision of the Yushin Constitution, the U.S. government was neither interested in nor moved by their plight. The same was generally true for the Japanese government. The result: growing numbers of activists soon reached the conclusion that continued civil disobedience by a few would not succeed in bringing down a police state that was internationally celebrated for its economic achievements.

Many church and student activists were also forced to re-evaluate their strategy and goals by the November 1970 self-immolation of Chun Tae-il, a young garment worker at the Peace Market. His death shocked the nation and focused attention on the horrors of industrialization for millions of workers as well as their struggles for change. In response, a small but significant core of church and student activists began to broaden their understanding of democracy to include meaningful and direct popular participation in workplace and community decision-making. This led to a new commitment to labor and farmer organizing and support work.

In the view of these activists, South Korean growth was dependent upon the exploitation of those who produced the growth. If workers could be helped to end their exploitation, not only would the regime collapse, but the resulting worker activism would make it possible to build a truly democratic society.

The process of industrialization itself further drew student and church activists together with workers. The rapid growth and oppressive workplace conditions gradually increased both worker solidarity and militancy. When repeated attempts to improve working conditions were frustrated by the combined actions of the police, bosses, and state-controlled union federation, many workers became convinced that even basic economic gains would be impossible without allies and active involvement in political struggle. We will see later that the developments described above helped to lay the groundwork for an increasingly powerful movement for social change, one that began the decade by seeking political and economic "reform" and ended it by pursuing a more fundamental social transformation of the South Korean political economy.

The Church and Labor Resistance

Church-related institutions played an especially key role in breathing new life into the South Korean labor movement, the two most important being the Urban Industrial Missions (UIM), affiliated with the United Methodist Church, and the Young Christian Worker (JOC), affiliated with the Catholic Church. Both JOC and the UIM have relatively long histories, dating back to 1958 in the case of the former and 1960 in the case of the latter. But, it was not until the early 1970s, that a number of the priests and pastors involved with these organizations came to view helping workers end injustice at the workplace as a central part of their religious mission.

By offering workers not only basic religious training but also a safe place to talk about workplace concerns and learn about labor law and organizing, these organizations had an enormous impact on labor activity. The Korean National Council of Churches and their Urban Industrial Missions, for example, worked with some 40,000 workers during the years 1970 to 1974. During the years 1975 to 1976, the various UIM gave support and training to approximately 12,000 factory workers each year. This was far more than reached by labor unions.[33]

The UIM and JOC were so successful in supporting labor activism that, by the mid-1970s, the government, companies, and the Federation of Korean Trade Unions (FKTU) were expending considerable effort to destroy them. The KCIA and police regularly spied on their activities and often arrested and tortured their staff. Workers would commonly be fired and blacklisted if they were found to be members of, or attended meetings organized by, either organization.

This attack on the UIM and JOC was just one part of a more general anti-union strategy. In some cases, owners would undermine worker efforts by organizing their own company-controlled union. Since the law allowed only one union to exist per workplace, this maneuver effectively denied workers any meaningful representation. More often, companies relied on beatings and firings to force workers to abandon unionization efforts. Companies would normally hire their own thugs to carry out the attacks but, if the workers proved too well organized, management could always count on FKTU and police support. The government, through the KCIA and special labor police, always kept a careful eye on labor activities. If the government felt that a company was creating a dangerous precedent by yielding to worker demands, it would occasionally force a renegotiation of the labor contract or, in extreme cases, use its control over the banking system to drive the firm into bankruptcy and then reassign ownership.

Yet, in spite of these difficulties, women workers, with the support of the UIM and the JOC, waged struggle after struggle for democratic unionism. One such struggle took place at Dong-il Textile Company. In 1972, union members, with the active support of the UIM, succeeded in expelling their corrupt union leadership and electing a new president, the first woman union president in the Park era, as well as an all-female executive board. The company grudgingly accepted the union for several years but, prodded by the National Textile Workers Union and the government, decided to try and regain control through manipulation of the union's 1975 presidential election. The women were too well organized, however, and succeeded in electing the president of their choice.

Angered by defeat, the company turned to violence: union activists were threatened, beaten, and fired. The women responded with strikes and sit-ins. Finally, in 1976, the company was able to arrange the arrest of the union president and, through bribery and force, outmaneuver the women to elect a company man to the union presidency. When the women demonstrated, the company called in the police who beat and arrested over seventy workers; fourteen were hospitalized.

Still the struggle continued. In 1978, when union activists went to the union hall, which was on company grounds, to prepare for new elections, they found a gang of men waiting for them. The men, after covering the office with human excrement, attacked the women and destroyed the ballot boxes and office furniture. The company, obviously prepared, immediately charged the women with provoking a riot and fired over one hundred union activists. The National Textile Workers Union then delivered the death blow to the efforts of the Dong-il workers by revoking the union's charter.

The basic pattern described above—with company, police, and national union federation joining forces to defeat democratic unionization—was repeated over and over in workplace struggles throughout the 1970s. The Bando Fashions struggle in early 1974 is another example. Led by a strong core of approximately thirty women who had gone through a UIM organizing and educational program, more than 1,000 women took part in a militant sit-in strike to protest company control over their union, and to win better wages and end the violent treatment of workers by management. The company stood firm, however, and when the women refused to accept the company's hand-picked union leader, the National Textile Workers Union ordered the local union to disband. The end came when the police forcibly evicted the women from the factory and the company fired the entire union leadership.

Not all efforts ended in defeat however. One important effort was the Chunggye Garment Workers Union, formed at the Peace Market shortly after Chun Tae-il's death. This union remained under strong rank-and-file control from its founding in November 1970 to its forced dissolution in January 1981. A worker-controlled intraunion education program "made the workers, most of whom are only elementary school graduates, with the lowest education level in the manufacturing sector, more conscious, forming them into a stable block of alert rank and file members."[34] Through constant effort, the union succeeded in winning a number of improvements for workers, including increased wages, shorter hours, weekly holidays, and improved working conditions.

Struggles such as these, although mostly unsuccessful, were important for keeping the spirit of democratic unionism alive in South Korea. The fired Dong-il workers, for example, formed a dismissed workers association and, operating out of a UIM office, continued to advise and support the unionization efforts of other workers. As a result, as George E. Ogle explains, "When in the mid-1980s male workers began to take action of their own, they found that they were standing on the shoulders of women who had been struggling for justice for more than ten years."[35]

While most of the union activity that took place during this period was led by women who worked for non-chaebol companies in light manufacturing, worker protests did take place in the chaebol-owned heavy and chemical industries as well. More than 2,000 workers rioted at the huge Hyundai shipyard in Ulsan to protest working conditions. They paralyzed the entire town. Many labor disputes also arose among the thousands of South Korean workers sent to earn foreign exchange in Middle East construction work. In early 1977, approximately 2,000 South Korean workers employed in Saudi Arabia rioted for three days to protest oppressive working conditions. Company officials were attacked and five dormitories and thirty vehicles set on fire.[36]

Because the labor unrest described above concerned chaebol, the state was quick to intervene: in both cases violence was used to suppress the protests and many workers were seriously injured. For the state and chaebol, unions (even company-controlled unions) were unacceptable. This philosophy was most clearly expressed by Lee Byung-Chull, the founder of Samsung: "I will have earth cover my eyes before a union is permitted at Samsung."[37]

But while unionization at the chaebol was, for the moment, impossible, the dynamics of the heavy and chemical industrialization drive were working to increase both the anger and organizational capacities of workers. The new industries were almost always large scale and located in newly established working-class cities. This large working-class concentration, at both the plant and in the community, helped to create a new and stronger base for working-class solidarity. Moreover, by hiring mostly young male workers, these new industries were also helping to build a new vision of trade unionism among men. Thus, while the chaebol were successful in keeping themselves union-free over the decade, underneath the surface a labor explosion was building, one so powerful that when it finally broke out in 1987 even the chaebol were affected.

Farmer Organizing and Resistance

Farmers also became increasingly active throughout the 1970s. Early in the decade, Park reversed his past anti-farmer agricultural policies, boosting grain prices and increasing rural credit allocations. These changes were largely the result of the government's desperate need to stimulate food production to compensate for declining U.S. food aid. As Table 9.6 shows, farmers benefited from these new policies, enjoying a rapid rise in both absolute and relative income.

As the heavy and chemical industrialization drive picked up, however, government policies once again shifted against the rural economy. As a result, farmers suffered declines in their household income compared with urban worker households. Even the absolute rural income gain shown in Table 9.6 is not as significant as it might appear. Between 1975 and 1980, average farm debt grew more than three times as fast as did average farm income.[38]

TABLE 9.6
Comparison of Real Farm Income and
Real Urban Worker Household Income
(1975 prices)

Year	Farm household income (thousand won)	Urban worker household income (thousand won)	Income farm/urban
1970	580	776	74.7
1971	715	811	88.2
1972	761	831	91.6
1973	783	857	91.4
1974	833	808	103.1
1975	873	859	101.6
1976	926	999	92.7
1977	980	1,106	88.6
1978	991	1,319	75.1
1979	1,030	1,530	67.3
1980	999	1,448	69.0

Source: *Social Justice Indicators in Korea*, 2nd ed., Christian Institute for the Study of Justice and Development (Soeul: Minjungsa, 1987), p. 91.

Farmers were not passive in the face of Park's antirural policies. In early 1974, for example, they battled construction crews who were trying to clear land for the development of factories in the Changwon district. Riots in the industrial zone at Kumi, President Park's home district, forced the KCIA to call in helicopters to evacuate technicians and construction crews.[39] As rural conditions worsened throughout the late 1970s, farmers continued to increased their level of organization and militancy. As with labor organizing, the church played an important role. The Korea Catholic Farmers Movement and the Korea Christian Farmers Federation were among the most important rural groups lending momentum to the farmers struggle.

A Growing People's Movement

By early 1977, opposition to Park's dictatorship had become qualitatively different from what it had been at the start of the decade. First, organized and active labor and farm movements were now involved. Second, these movements enjoyed considerable contacts with church and student-based human rights and democratization movements. Finally, and most important:

> The minjung [people's] movement began to undergo a slow transformation from concentrating on simple economic struggles to undertaking political struggles. This indicated the awakening of the political consciousness in the minjung movement. That is, they began to identify the state power and the state social structure as the fundamental cause of the suffering and oppression they faced in their daily lives.[40]

Strikes picked up in number and intensity during both 1978 and 1979. By the summer of 1979, in the midst of the country's economic slowdown, student and worker demonstrations were ongoing in most of the country's major cities. Unlike past demonstrations, workers and students were now directly supporting each others' demands; calls for democracy were now combined with demands for better working and living conditions.

Increasingly worried about the deteriorating political and economic situation, Park went on the offensive. New political trials were organized to separate labor and farmer activists from their movements. For example, a branch chief of the Catholic Farmers Association was kidnapped twice by the KCIA in an attempt to intimidate him. When that proved unsuccessful, he was taken to court, convicted, and sent to jail for falsely claiming to have been kidnapped, a violation of Emergency Decree No. 9.

Perhaps the most important event of this period was the "Y.H. incident." The Y.H. Trading Company was a typical labor-intensive, export-oriented firm employing mostly young women and forcing them to work extremely long hours for low wages. During the late 1960s, it had been South Korea's largest wig exporter and, in 1970, the country's fifteenth largest foreign exchange earner. Its importance declined over the decade, however, as wigs gave way to electronics and other exports. Reflecting this trend, the company's total employment fell from 4,000 workers in 1970 to only 500 in 1978.

Fearful of further job losses, the women at the plant formed a union to defend their positions and boost wages. While it initially appeared that an agreement acceptable to the workers would be signed with the company, the president, a Korean living in America, suddenly announced a change of mind. Rather than agreement, the plant would be completely closed. Outraged, the union engaged in sit-ins, petition drives, and demonstrations in an attempt to get the company to reverse its decision. The workers also appealed to students, the UIM, and opposition political groups for assistance.

The Y.H. Trading Company closed on August 7, 1979. Five hundred women were now out of work. When they occupied the plant, they were brutally forced out by police. A number of workers then went to the headquarters of the opposition New Democratic Party to publicize their plight. Although the New Democratic Party had not objected to the presence of the workers, Park ordered the police to clear the party headquarters. In the police assault that followed, many workers and supporters were beaten and arrested. One worker died.

Shortly afterwards, the KCIA engineered the suspension and then removal of Kim Young Sam, the head of the New Democratic Party, from the National Assembly. The official charge was that by supporting the Y.H. workers and making critical remarks to the *New York Times* about the Park regime, Kim had engaged in anti-state behavior.

The tension of the period finally exploded when, in mid-October 1979, thousands of students and workers, demanding Park's resignation, clashed with police in the industrial cities of Pusan and Masan. Park declared martial law in Pusan and sent troops to both cities to restore order. The demonstrators in Pusan had attacked police cars and stations, government buildings, and the headquarters of the ruling party. Street battles continued in both cities in spite of the presence of troops.

Fearful of a replay of the events of 1960, when student-led demonstrations drove President Rhee from office, Park reportedly planned a major military offensive against those demonstrating in Pusan and Masan. But before he could issue the order to the troops, Park was himself shot and killed by the head of the KCIA on October 26, 1979. At his trial, the KCIA chief claimed that he acted to avoid a major bloodbath.[41]

The Park regime came to a swift and sudden end. And, in spite of having engineered almost two decades of rapid economic growth and social change, the overwhelming majority of South Koreans were thankful for the opportunity his death opened. Students marched for a democratic constitution, reunification, and dismissal of hard-liners in the government; workers joined them and also struck for higher wages, better working conditions, and labor reform.

No clear vision of a future South Korea emerged from these initial demands for change. Yet while these mass movements were far less organized and far more oriented toward a vision of "democratic capitalism" than those in 1960, it is difficult to say what choices the South Korean people would have made if given the freedom to debate and consider alternative political and social arrangements. Nevertheless, one thing was clear: there was little, if any, popular support for the national security state, the chaebol, or the country's export-first economic strategy.

Tragically, those who benefited most from the operation of the South Korean political economy—the military, the chaebol, foreign corporations, and the United States and Japanese governments—were unwilling to allow the South Korean people an opportunity to explore alternative arrangements. Once again, the South Korean political economy was to be secured by military dictatorship. The next section describes how this forced march continued.

Military Dictatorship Once Again

With Park's death, the powers of state officially transferred to Prime Minister Choi Kyu Hah. While the great majority of South Koreans wanted an immediate repudiation of the Yushin Constitution and direct election of the country's next president, Choi insisted that he finish out Park's uncompleted term of office according to the indirect procedures of Yushin. His wish was granted and the National Conference for Unification elected him to the Presidency on December 6, 1979.

While public attention was focused on constitutional questions, forces within the military moved quickly to foreclose any democratic option. On December 12, 1979, Major General Chun Doo Hwan, head of the Army Security Command and the investigation into Park's assassination, sent troops to arrest the army chief of staff and martial law commander. A brief shoot-out occurred. Backed by thousands of troops secretly recalled from the border area with North Korea, Chun Doo Hwan emerged victorious. Chun, in total charge of the military, was now the most powerful person in the country. Unable or unwilling to stand up to Chun, President Choi bowed to his wishes and allowed the Yushin system to remain in place with politically motivated trials and torture of prisoners continuing into 1980.

As noted, workers and students had taken advantage of Park's death to press their own demands. Labor, in particular, faced difficult times as the economy continued to contract. With inflation up sharply, real wages fell by 4.7 percent in 1980. Many firms actually withheld wages that workers had already earned. But with the government and its hand-picked union leadership in disarray, workers turned to direct action to improve their situation.

Official government statistics show a decline in the number of labor disputes from 1970 to 1982: 427, 407, 186, and finally, 57 respectively. These statistics, however, especially the 1980 figure, were designed to manage impressions, not convey actual trends. The *Korea Times*, for example, reported that there were 897 labor disputes in the first five months of 1980 alone.[42] During that year, garment workers, pharmaceutical workers, machine tool workers, nylon factory workers, and miners, among others, all struck for higher pay, improved work conditions, and democratic unions.

The most highly publicized labor action was the four-day miners' strike at Tongwon Mine in Sabuk in April. The miners had many grievances, including low pay, an overpriced company store, and a corrupt union. The strike was triggered when workers learned that they had been sold out, once again, by their union leadership in contract negotiations. When three miners walking picket lines were hit by a car driven by the local chief of police, the miners' anger erupted. More than 3,500 stormed into town and seized control. Armed with rifles and dynamite, they fought off attacks by combat police. The strike finally ended with the mine owners agreeing to substantial wage increases. Afraid to enter the town, they communicated the terms of the new contract by hiring a helicopter to drop leaflets into the city.

The Sabuk action was not unique. Workers at the Tongguk Steel Company in Pusan, for example, tried unsuccessfully to form a union to improve their pay and working conditions in 1979. Finally, in April 1980, more than 500 workers went on strike. When confronted by the police, the workers responded with force: they fought street battles and set fire to company buildings. They succeeded in gaining recognition for their union.

Unionization also spread to foreign-invested firms. Three unions were formally recognized in the Masan Free Trade Zone and organizing campaigns launched at seventeen other plants. The Chemical Workers Union sent organizers to the Ulsan petrochemical area and succeeded in organizing seven companies. Low-level white collar workers, in particular nurses and orderlies, also formed unions. Within the first few months of 1980, more than 80,000 workers became unionized. Almost all of this union activity was technically illegal according to the country's existing labor laws.

With workers demonstrating their disregard of Yushin, and capitalists, both foreign and domestic, demanding government action to restore order, Major General Chun slowly emerged from behind President Choi's shadow. By mid-March 1980, Chun began giving and not taking orders from Choi. Students responded by organizing large demonstrations throughout the country demanding the resignation of Chun, an end to martial law, and revision of the constitution. Chun, in turn, had himself named acting director of the KCIA while keeping his position as head of the Defense Security Command. This joint appointment was in violation of the South Korean constitution, but no one in the government opposed him.

On May 15, one of the largest demonstrations took place, as some 100,000 students gathered in Seoul to demand democracy. The National Assembly, yielding to student and citizen pressure, finally announced that it would meet on May 22 to vote for an end to martial law. Chun, however, acted first. On the evening of May 17, the government, in response to Chun's orders, declared an expansion of martial law and sent troops to all major cities.

Under the new conditions of martial law, the National Assembly was dissolved, all political activity was banned, the media was placed under prior censorship, all colleges and universities were closed, and all labor strikes and unexcused absences were prohibited. A number of important political leaders were also arrested to ensure that they would be unable to organize opposition. The rationale for Chun's act: the need to fight corruption and restore order.

Workers and students throughout South Korea demonstrated against this new military coup, but the most organized and significant resistance took place in the southwestern city of Kwangju. There, on May 18, police fought with thousands of students who were demonstrating against martial law. Determined to crush all opposition, the military sent special combat paratroopers to the city. These troops went on a rampage, indiscriminately killing people.

Outraged by the brutality of the troops, more demonstrators took to the streets the following day. The response of the special troops is described as follows by an Asia Watch report:

> They repeated the same actions of the day before, beating, stabbing, and mutilating unarmed civilians, including children, young girls, and aged grandmothers. They forced both men and women to strip naked, made others lie flat on the ground and kicked them. Several sources tell of soldiers stabbing or cutting off the breasts of naked girls; one murdered student was found disemboweled, another with an X carved in his back. About twenty high school girls were reported killed at Central High School. The paratroopers carried out searches in side streets, fired randomly into crowds, carted off the bodies in trucks, and piled them in the bus terminal. They even took the wounded out of hospitals.[43]

The people of Kwangju responded with anger to what they had witnessed. The entire city mobilized: people set fire to TV and radio stations that refused to report what was happening; businessmen set fire to government buildings; students erected barricades. And on May 20 townspeople seized weapons from abandoned police stations. Students set up machine guns on campuses and armed citizens occupied key buildings in the city. Intense fighting followed and on May 22 the soldiers were forced to withdraw from the city. During this entire period, the government did its best to stop all communication between Kwangju and the rest of South Korea. The rest of the country was told only that there was unrest in Kwangju because of "impure elements," and that order would soon be restored.

"Order" was, in fact, soon restored. After the troops withdrew, a citizens' committee was formed in an attempt to find a peaceful solution to the conflict. However, on May 27, 1980, while negotiations were still being attempted, tens of thousands of troops attacked the city, killing hundreds more people, and finally ending all resistance. The government claimed that only 191 people died during the period of the Kwangju uprising. According to almost all other sources, at least 2,000 civilians died and about 15,000 were injured. By carrying out a slaughter of South Koreans, Chun succeeded, at least temporarily, in halting the democratic reform process.

The "Economic Miracle" Reborn

Having militarily overwhelmed his opposition, Chun "retired" from the military, announced his candidacy for the presidency, and was elected on August 27, 1980, by the Yushin-created National Conference for Unification. Choi helped simplify the process by resigning and offering Chun his support. Shortly after Chun's election, a specially appointed military-controlled committee drafted a new constitution which was approved by national referendum under conditions of martial law.

In an attempt to give legitimacy to his rule, Chun formed a new political party, the Democratic Justice Party (DJP). Following the procedures specified under the new constitution, he was re-elected president in February 1981, this time as the candidate of the DJP. A new National Assembly was then elected in March.

The nature of the Chun regime was, however, revealed long before the staging of these presidential and National Assembly elections. Determined to stamp out any possibility of political challenge, Chun quickly followed his seizure of power by initiating a reign of terror on the nation. Many professors, for example, were forced to resign, and more than 1,000 students were expelled from school. Those students caught demonstrating on campus were arrested, beaten, and sent to prison. In special cases, arrested students were sent directly into the military. Six or possibly eight students died while in military custody. Although Park used a similar conscription policy, not a single student died while in military custody during his regime. Leaving nothing to chance, spies were also stationed on most campuses, and teachers were forced to monitor and write regular reports on student behavior for the Agency for National Security Planning (ANSP), formerly the KCIA.

The church also suffered greatly from government repression. Fearing church involvement in the defense of human rights, the ANSP often broke up Sunday worship services, beat worshipers, and spied on clergy. Those clergy found active in defending human or labor rights were pressured to resign and often arrested.

Chun's offensive against the South Korean people was coupled with a complete government takeover of the county's media. Over 800 journalists were fired and more than 170 publications banned. All papers and publishers had to be licensed and operated under terms of prior censorship,and all existing news agencies were merged into one government-controlled agency. With the exception of Seoul, each province was allowed only one newspaper. The government also took control of all existing TV and radio stations, creating a new state-run system out of forced mergers. The only exception to this nationalization policy was the Christian Broadcasting Service, but it was forbidden to broadcast any news.

While such actions provided Chun with political breathing space, they did little to help him with his main task, the revitalization of the South Korean economy. Not surprisingly then, one of his earliest targets was the South Korean labor movement. Almost immediately after the coup, thousands of union leaders, including the senior officers of most of the sixteen existing national union federations were ordered fired. Hundreds of union leaders and activists were also arrested and sent to military-run re-education camps. Simultaneously, new labor guidelines, the most restrictive and oppressive in South Korean history, were issued in July 1980 and codified by the end of the year in new labor laws.

Under the new laws, all union activity was to be restricted to a single workplace. As a result, industrywide or regionally coordinated union negotiations with one or more employers became illegal. Unionization itself was also made illegal at workplaces with fewer than thirty employees, thereby allowing many light manufacturing firms such as those in the garment industry to operate union free.

The government also retained the right to intervene and change any union agreement if it believed it to be contrary to the "public interest." The law also gave the government the authority to order the election of new officers or dissolution of an entire union "when a union violates the law or an order concerning labor or is considered likely to harm public benefits."

Perhaps the most important change in the country's labor laws was the introduction of a measure restricting so-called "third party" involvement in labor activity. According to this measure, "persons other than an employee who has actual employment relations with the employer, or persons other than having legitimate authority under law, shall not engage in an act of interference, in a dispute, for the purpose of manipulating, instigating, or an other act to influence the parties concerned."

This law was designed to destroy both the effectiveness of unions as well as their ties to the broader progressive community, especially student and church groups. As interpreted, this law made it illegal for anyone, even officials from the FKTU, to advise a workplace union on labor law or organizing, or to offer it direct support in a labor dispute. This, of course, put workers at a tremendous disadvantage in bargaining with employers, especially the large chaebol. More important, this law allowed the government to completely and legally isolate workers from each other, UIM or JOC organizers, and students. Even fired workers were forbidden, under terms of this measure, from maintaining any contact or involvement with ongoing union activity at their former workplace.

To jump-start the economy, the government made swift and effective use of its new powers to discipline labor. One of its earliest actions was aimed at the Chunggye Garment Workers Union. The government ordered the union dissolved on the grounds that it illegally represented workers at more than one enterprise. When the union refused to stop collecting dues, 600 police were sent to close the union office. When the workers organized a protest at the office of the Asian American Free Labor Institute, an arm of the U.S. AFL-CIO, fearful U.S. labor officials called for police support. The police stormed the office and arrested the entire union leadership.

Similar attacks were directed at all progressive unions, including the union at Wonpoong Textile Company. To destroy this union, among the strongest and most democratic in South Korea, Chun had its president arrested on charges of having engaged in illegal activities associated with the Kwangju Uprising. The company then began firing union activists, many of whom were also arrested by the government for alleged labor law violations.

Female paratroopers were sent to the women's dormitories to intimidate the workers but, despite their presence, the women elected a new slate of progressive union leaders. In September 1982, the new union president was severely beaten by company-hired thugs and then fired. When a new president was elected two weeks later, she too was beaten. The workers declared a sit-in strike to protest company violence, but police and company-hired thugs attacked the workers, dragging them out of the factory. Sixty-six workers were hospitalized. A number of students who had come to the factory to lend support to the workers were either beaten, arrested, or immediately drafted into the army. When the company finally reopened, it rehired only those workers who agreed not to engage in union activity.

Such attacks on labor had their desired effect. According to the *Far Eastern Economic Review*: "Alarming was the 1981 figure from the Ministry of Finance that half the nation's workforce was earning less than 100,000 won a month [$140], which in 1982 was equivalent to a single person's minimum cost of living minus housing expenses."[44] A study by the Federation of Korean Trade Unions paints a similar picture. According to the Federation, the minimum monthly income necessary for a family of 4.4 members in 1982 was 431,130 won. The average union member's monthly wage, however, was only 247,759 won.[45]

Creating forced labor conditions, under which wages fell and productivity soared, was a central part of Chun's strategy for restoring South Korea's economic competitiveness as well as its attractiveness to multinational capital. And, in the short run, it proved to be a successful strategy. Relying heavily on its anti-labor policies, the government succeeded in driving down the rate of inflation from over 20 percent in 1980 and 1981 to only 3.4 percent by 1983.

By 1983, after two years of relatively slow growth had stabilized economic conditions, the economy was once again ready for expansion. Led by exports, GNP rose by approximately 11.9 percent that year. According to many analysts, this GNP performance demonstrated that the South Korean economy had weathered the storm, and was back on its high-growth track. These same analysts tended to overlook the forced sacrifices of workers which played a major role in making this recovery possible. The relationships among the country's return to rule by military dictatorship, the working conditions described above, and the apparent revitalization of the South Korean growth strategy were clear and probably best illustrated by the following quote from a U.S. corporate executive in 1982: "It is in our own selfish interest to have a strong government [in South Korea] that controls the students and labor so that everything will blossom and grow and we can continue to make profits."[46]

Foreign Support for Dictatorship

Chun's reign of terror was, if not welcomed by U.S. and Japanese government leaders, at least given substantial support. Both the United States and Japan had become very nervous about the mass political movement in South Korea during the last few years of Park's rule. Radical students were playing an increasingly important role in the country's democratization and labor movements. As a result, their critique of South Korea's dependence on the United States and Japan and advocacy of an independent and unified Korea were being taken more seriously in both intellectual and activist circles. Such thinking, if allowed time to spread throughout the society, had the potential to weaken the entire structure of U.S.-organized regional military and political alliances. U.S. and Japanese government and corporate fears for the future grew still greater as a result of the increase in labor activity and support for reunification in the period immediately following Park's death.

The South Korean political economy of Park Chung Hee had served foreign interests well, and these interests, both governmental and corporate, were strongly committed to its survival regardless of the cost to the South Korean people. This commitment was expressed in both word and deed. In February 1980, for example, when the South Korean military was clearly preparing to impose its own rule in South Korea, the joint South Korea-U.S. military command announced that massive military maneuvers would soon be held in South Korea and that the exercise, named Team Spirit, would include drills to combat domestic riots and unconventional warfare.

During the actual Kwangju uprising, when the Kwangju citizen's committee sought to negotiate a truce with government forces, committee members had also contacted the U.S. embassy to ask for its help. The U.S. embassy refused, claiming that it was not empowered to involve itself in the internal affairs of South Korea. The U.S. commander of the joint South Korea-U.S. military command, U.S.

Army General John Wickham, obviously felt no such limitation. He approved General Chun's request to use South Korean military personnel and equipment to restore order in Kwangju. Those forces were used in the final assault on Kwangju.

While the U.S. government has claimed that under the terms of the joint military command structure it could not deny Chun the right to use South Korean troops for purely internal purposes, there is substantial evidence that, legalities aside, the United States fully supported Chun's actions. The *Los Angeles Times*, for example, quoted General Wickham as saying, not long after Kwangju, that " . . . lemming-like, the people are kind of lining up behind [Chun] in all walks of life." The *Los Angeles Times* also reported Wickham voicing the opinion that Chun had come to power "legitimately."[47]

Chun, at least, had no doubts about U.S. intentions. He publicly announced on May 30 that he received support for his handling of the Kwangju Uprising from U.S. Ambassador Gleysteen. The U.S. State Department issued the following statement to clarify the United States position on Kwangju:

> We believe this rebellion was a major breakdown of law and order. Our situation, for better or worse, is that Korea is a treaty ally, and the United States has a very strong security interest in that part of the world.[48]

Chun's next challenge was to solve South Korea's serious international trade and debt problems. Once again, the United States was helpful, providing Chun with essential economic and political support. Less than two weeks after Kwangju, U.S. President Jimmy Carter gave approval for John Moore, head of the U.S. Export-Import Bank, to go to South Korea and finalize terms for more than $600 million worth of import credits. Moore's visit was soon followed by visits from David Rockefeller, head of Chase Manhatten Bank, and William Spenser, head of First National Bank, both of whom reassured the new South Korean government of continued financial support. Finally, Chun himself was invited to Washington in February 1981, becoming the first head of state to visit newly elected President Ronald Reagan. Expressing his support for Chun, Reagan announced that the United States would sell South Korea almost $1 billion worth of advanced military equipment.

Japan also played its part in offering support to the new dictatorship. As previously discussed, Japan, in response to an appeal for aid, extended approximately $4 billion in loans and credits to South Korea. The $1.85 billion in official governmental credits and $2.15 billion in EXIM bank financing came to almost 13 percent of South Korea's net external debt; more than 5 percent of its GNP, and almost 20 percent of its total investment in 1983.[49]

U.S. and Japanese political and financial support was crucial for Chun. Without it, South Korea might well have been forced into a foreign debt-driven austerity crisis, similar to one Brazil experienced in 1981. It is doubtful that Chun could have survived the political repercussions of such a prolonged economic crisis. As it was, South Korea proved able to struggle through the global recession, eventually exporting its way out of economic difficulties thanks to the U.S. economic recovery which began in 1983.

Conclusion

Most economists have praised South Korea for its economic achievements during the Park Chung Hee years, and these achievements are indeed noteworthy: in less than twenty years, South Korea was transformed from one of the world's poorest and least industrialized nations to one of the richest and most successful of all the newly industrialized countries. And, on the basis of this record, these economists have argued that the South Korean development strategy represents an attractive model for other countries to follow.

As we have seen in Part II, this "argument" is itself refuted by a careful examination of the South Korean experience. First, South Korea's state-directed development strategy is not one that other countries would find easy to follow. South Korea's strong state was not simply willed into existence by economists in order to promote the country's development. Instead, it was the result of a rather unique history shaped largely by foreign forces. In fact, since dominating states are more likely to arise from social revolution rather than a policy consensus on the part of an existing capitalist elite, South Korea's experience is far from an endorsement of capitalism.

Moreover, South Korea's rapid growth and industrialization was not simply a product of its own planning and production efforts.

Without substantial and timely foreign support, South Korea's economic success would have been impossible. Such support is unlikely to be available to other third world nations.

Last, and even more important, by broadening our analysis of state economic planning and policy to include the class origins and consequences of that policy, we see that the country's growth strategy falls far short of model status. As our examination of the South Korean experience makes clear, the South Korean people have paid an unacceptably high price for their country's economic progress.

Because of the class nature of South Korea's economic and political institutions, economic growth led to new and intensified forms of oppression and exploitation, forcing farmers and workers into growth-threatening resistance. This resistance was contained, and the conditions necessary for further growth maintained, only by political repression. The result: a vicious spiral of resistance and repression. Seriously flawed by its undemocratic nature, South Korea's growth strategy proved incapable of winning the support of the great majority of South Korean people. In fact, quite the opposite was true.

My critique of the South Korean approach to development goes beyond even its undemocratic nature. As I will argue in Part III, economic and political trends now call into question the benefits of this approach on even the narrowest of economic grounds. Thus, although still praised by many analysts, I believe that the existing South Korean growth strategy has exhausted its economic potential while remaining incapable of accommodating democratic reforms. As a result, South Korea's future prospects now appear to depend largely on the ability of the country's increasingly organized and politicized working class to help articulate a vision of, as well as lead the fight for, a radically transformed South Korean political economy.

PART III

THE GATHERING STORM: CONTRADICTIONS, CONFLICT, AND CRISIS

CHAPTER 10

THE GATHERING STORM:
ECONOMIC TRENDS

As we have seen, South Korea's rapid industrialization was largely
due to effective state direction of chaebol activity, management of
international trade and investment, and domination of the population. However, in this section we will see the contradictions inherent
in South Korea's growth process begin to erode the power of the
state and thus its ability to further the country's economic growth;
in other words, South Korea's growth strategy is seriously flawed
even if one accepts political repression as an unpleasant but necessary cost of economic growth.

In this chapter I will examine how trends set in motion by South
Korea's economic strategy have weakened state control over both
the chaebol and foreign trade. Effects of this process can already
be seen: growing financial speculation, corruption, and income inequality; the premature hollowing out of the South Korean industrial base; and growing foreign trade and debt problems. In the
next chapter, I will look at another unintended consequence of South
Korea's economic strategy: the development of social movements
increasingly capable of blocking state initiatives designed to solve
South Korea's economic problems at popular expense.

Discussion of what lies ahead for South Korea is the topic of the
final chapter of this book. As we will see, many South Koreans are
themselves coming to realize that without a fundamental change
in their country's economic strategy, South Korea is more likely to
head backward into the third world instead of forward to higher
levels of economic development. Moreover, while mainstream
analysts continue to point to the South Korean experience as proof

of the superiority of capitalism over socialism, a small but growing number of South Koreans are looking to a socialist-oriented political economy rather than a reformed state-capitalism as the basis for establishing a more secure, democratic, and prosperous future. In short, political and economic trends strongly suggest growing class conflict over the future shape of the South Korean political economy.

The Erosion of State Power: The Rise of the Chaebol

The events of 1980-1983, in particular the renewal of military dictatorship and export-led growth, appeared to signal the start of another long period of growth based on the policies of the past. Chun's approach to politics was similar to that of Park: force and terror were used to silence all opposition to his rule. Military men were placed in charge of the police, the ruling party, the intelligence network, and planning the Olympics. Hundreds of retired officers were given political positions as ambassadors or mayors. As one observer commented, "Chun's got his guys all out there. You've got a formal government, and then you have this sort of informal government that really controls things."[1]

Chun's initial approach to solving South Korea's economic problems was also similar to that followed by Park: labor repression was used to fight inflation, restore competitiveness to light manufacturing industries, and boost chaebol profits. Direct state intervention was also used to support financially troubled chaebol as well as shrink excess capacity and reorganize production.

These "traditional" state policies produced impressive results. As Table 10.1 and Table 10.2 show, inflation fell, growth picked up, and the balance of trade improved. Any remaining doubts about whether the new dictatorship was capable of restoring the South Korean "economic miracle" were seemingly put to rest from 1986 to 1988, a period of extremely rapid growth and record trade surpluses. However, while outward appearances seemed to confirm the stability and durability of South Korea's economic strategy, growth itself was leading to a fundamental realignment in one of the key relationships supporting that strategy: that between the state and chaebol.

TABLE 10.1
Growth and Inflation

Year	Real GNP growth (in percent)	Rate of inflation (Consumer price index)
1981	6.62	1.3
1982	25.4	7.3
1983	11.9	3.4
1984	8.4	2.3
1985	7.0	2.5
1986	12.9	2.8
1987	12.8	3.0
1988	12.4	7.1
1989	6.8	5.7
1990	9.0	9.5
1991	8.4	9.7

Source: Economic Planning Board.

The Growing Independence of the Chaebol

Although the chaebol were initially a creation of the South Korean state, they had become, by the end of Park's heavy and chemical industrialization drive, a significant political force in their own right. As we have seen, Park used subsidized credit along with protected markets to attract the chaebol into the newly targeted industries. This process left the chaebol in a financially vulnerable and thus subordinate position relative to the state. But, by also encouraging chaebol monopolization of economic activity, the state eventually enabled the chaebol to turn their weakness into a strength.

The shift in power relations between the chaebol and the state became apparent during the early Chun years. Hoping to restructure the economy, Chun introduced a number of initiatives designed to force chaebol mergers as well as limit chaebol access to credit. While some reorganization did take place, the chaebol also succeeded for the first time in resisting a number of state directives, including state proposed mergers and liquidation of nonbusiness properties.[2] Most important, the state found it impossible to break the chaebol's hold on credit markets.

Chun's difficulties had a lot to do with the fact that the major

TABLE 10.2

Trade

(in billion U.S. dollars)

Year	Merchandise exports	Merchandise imports	Merchandise trade balance	Current account	Export growth	Import growth
	(in billions of U.S. dollars)				*(in percent)*	
1981	21.25	26.13	-4.88	-4.65	21.41	7.2
1982	21.85	24.25	-2.40	-2.65	2.8	-7.2
1983	24.45	26.19	-1.74	-1.61	11.9	8.0
1984	29.25	30.63	-1.38	-1.37	19.6	117.0
1985	30.28	31.14	-.86	-.89	3.5	1.7
1986	34.71	31.58	3.13	4.62	14.6	1.4
1987	47.28	41.02	6.26	9.85	36.2	29.9
1988	60.70	51.81	8.89	14.16	28.4	26.3
1989	62.38	61.46	.92	5.06	2.8	18.6
1990	65.02	69.84	-4.83	-2.18	4.2	13.6
1991	71.87	81.52	-9.65	-8.83	10.5	16.7

Source: Economic Planning Board.

chaebol now dominated both production as well as credit markets. In terms of production, the combined sales of the top ten chaebol had risen from 15.1 percent of GNP in 1974 to 48.1 percent in 1980.[3] As for credit, in 1980, the top twenty-six chaebol held a third of total commercial bank loans, as well as the overwhelming majority of loans extended by state investment banks.[4] In short, the health of the South Korean economy and thus the well-being of the state was now dependent upon the health of the chaebol.

If restructuring forced too many chaebol into bankruptcy, the entire financial system would be endangered. Moreover, the government could not hope to simultaneously restart the economy's export drive and at the same time deny the chaebol access to the credit they needed to boost production. Further complicating the situation was the fact that even if new credits were made available to the chaebol, the state could no longer be confident that they would be used for productive purposes. In fact, the chaebol were increasingly using their funds to speculate in real estate or to buy up smaller non-chaebol firms. So even though the state still remained more powerful than the chaebol, its ability to dictate economic activity was no longer as total.

Uncertain how best to discipline the chaebol, Chun decided on a new strategy—market liberalization. This decision, as we will see later, was also designed to help the new regime win favor with the United States. Although some import restrictions were relaxed, the heart of Chun's liberalization program was the privatization and deregulation of the financial system. Chun supported this marked departure from past policy, in the hopes that privatization of the banking system would enable the government to avoid total financial responsibility for losses resulting from chaebol bankruptcies, while deregulation would make it harder for the chaebol to dominate the allocation of credit.

Both the chaebol and the United States supported Chun's financial liberalization policy. The chaebol hoped that greater financial freedom would enable them to become more independent of government control. The U.S. government supported liberalization, believing that it would help U.S. financial and industrial corporations seeking to do business in South Korea. However, because the government's financial strategy was more a tactical move designed to weaken the chaebol and win U.S. support than an embrace of free market ideology, the liberalization was far from the complete market opening either the chaebol or the U.S. government had hoped for.

The government's program began in 1981 and included privatization and deregulation of the five existing national commercial banks, the ten local or provisional banks, and all nonbank financial institutions. All five national banks were privatized by 1983. Moreover, the government allowed the establishment of two new privately owned national banks, one each in 1982 and 1983.

At the same time, the South Korean state continued to restrict the activities of foreign financial institutions. The government also took a number of steps to try to limit the ability of the chaebol to gain control over these newly privatized national commercial banks: an 8 percent ceiling was placed on the percentage of shares that a single shareholder was allowed to own. Moreover, even after privatization, the government continued to reserve the right to select the management of the banks, set interest rate and loan allocation guidelines, and mandate policy loans.

Even so, the chaebol, individually and collectively, found legal and illegal ways to gain considerable control over these newly privatized banks. In three of the original five banks, for example, the top chaebol came to collectively own more than 30 percent of the total shares. The situation was somewhat different in the case of the country's provincial banks. Because the privatization directive placed no restrictions on share ownership of these banks, the chaebol quickly came to dominate them.[5]

Liberalization also produced significant changes in both the ownership and operation of the country's "nonbank financial institutions" (NBFI). The government had originally encouraged the growth of this sector after its August 3, 1972, decree as a way of drawing money away from the unregulated curb market and into regulated financial institutions. To accomplish that goal, the NBFI was allowed to pay considerably higher interest rates on deposits than were commercial banks. Now, under the terms of the liberalization program, the state was committed to privatize and deregulate this sector as well. Government shares were sold off, barriers to entry were reduced, and the various NBFI were allowed greater freedom to set interest rates and offer new services.

The chaebol, of course, were best placed to take advantage of this privatization. By the end of 1983, eleven of the twenty-six existing insurance companies were under the ownership of a single chaebol. Several chaebol in combination dominated the remaining companies. As for the six life insurance companies, all except one is owned by a single chaebol.[6] As a result of deregulation, the NBFI have grown in both number and significance. The share of NBFI deposits as a percentage of total deposits, for example, rose from less than 20 percent in 1975, to 30.1 percent in 1980, 45.5 percent in 1984, and 51.3 percent in 1987.[7]

This reorganization of the South Korean financial sector had a different impact on the state-chaebol relationship than that which Chun had intended. Chun had begun the decade hoping that his policies would both weaken chaebol power and force them to become more efficient producers. More specifically, Chun hoped that by weakening their hold over credit markets, the chaebol would have no alternative but to satisfy their credit needs by selling off nonproductive land and subsidiaries and concentrate their investments in state-approved activities. Neither happened. In fact, as a result of deregulation, the chaebol secured a stronger foothold in the country's financial system. One effect of this development:

chaebol economic growth over the 1980s was achieved largely through mergers and buy-outs of non-chaebol businesses. Considerable chaebol money was also spent on additional purchases of nonbusiness land for speculative purposes.

The Birth of the Racketeering State

As the chaebol began to profitably exploit their new financial freedom, the state-chaebol relationship changed in still another important way. Chun soon tired of battling the chaebol and sought instead to negotiate a new understanding, one that would preserve the essential harmony between the two sides by ensuring that a significant share of chaebol income would pass into his hands. Thus, unable to direct chaebol activities, Chun came to care less about how the chaebol generated their profits and more about how to secure the largest share possible for himself, his family, and his supporters. In short, the South Korean state began acting more as a traditional "racketeering" state than as a "developmental" state.

Most significant in this regard were the largely invisible "political contributions" the large chaebol were forced to make to Chun. To regularize the payoff process, Chun established his own foundation, the Ilhae Foundation, in 1984, and selected Chung Chu-yong, the founder of Hyundai, to become the collector of "donations" from the various chaebol. The major chaebol, including Hyundai, are said to have each contributed approximately $6 million to the foundation in exchange for good relations with Chun. One business leader has stated that during the seven years of Chun's presidency, the top twelve chaebol were forced to give approximately $14 million a year to the Ilhae Foundation and the New Village Movement (a government rural development agency) which was run by Chun's younger brother. Chung Chu-young has also admitted that he made additional "donations" to Chun's political party, "always in the amount asked."[8]

Those chaebol leaders who refused to pay were dealt with harshly. This was demonstrated most clearly by what happened to the Kukje-ICC group in 1985. As described in Chapter 3, the group's founder, Yang Chang Mo, refused to give any money to the Ilhae Foundation and made only a small contribution to the New Village Movement. Chun responded to this slight by ordering the banks to call in Kukje's outstanding loans and refuse to extend additional credit. Within two weeks, Kukje was forced into bankruptcy and its assets redistributed to other chaebol, all of whom had previously made sizable contributions to the Ilhae Foundation.[9]

Symbolic of the corrupt nature of the Chun regime was the widespread participation of relatives of both Chun and his wife in illegal dealings.[10] Chun's younger brother was, as previously mentioned, in charge of the New Village Movement. This organization had a yearly budget of approximately $120 million dollars, yet was never required to make detailed budget presentations to the National Assembly or face an audit. Although there has still been no formal accounting of expenditures, Chun's younger brother is commonly understood to have greatly enriched himself at the public expense. Chun's older brother was apparently no better. Often called the "mafia boss," he was accused of selling promotions in the National Police Agency and using his influence with the President to take over various companies and win public construction contracts.

Chun's wife, Lee Soon Ja, and her family were also involved in various schemes. Lee Soon Ja founded and chaired The New Generation Foundation which she apparently used as her own personal conduit for kickbacks and bribes. Her father was thought to be a key player in land scandals involving advanced notification of land zoning changes and land purchases. Other members of her family supposedly profited from illegal financial schemes involving corporate loans.[11]

By the mid-1980s, this heavy financial burden of corruption had led the chaebol into open conflict with Chun. Seeking to free themselves from future obligations, they began a campaign to reduce the state's economic power. The Federation of Korean Industry, for example, called for an end to state micro-management of the economy. The head of Hyundai made his own personal call for greater corporate market freedom and complete autonomy for the banking system.[12]

While indicating a significant change in the state-chaebol relationship, the developments described above did not seem initially threatening to the growth of the economy. On the surface, in fact, all seemed the same: the state still dominated the chaebol, the chaebol still dominated production, and growth remained based on exports to the U.S. market. As noted earlier, the South Korean economy achieved its best overall economic performance from 1986 to 1988. However, as we will see next, this economic success, based largely on favorable short-term conditions, could not be sustained. Even more important, this period of rapid growth greatly accelerated the developments described above, leaving the state and economy far weaker than before.

Power Shift in the State-Chaebol Relationship

South Korea's economic accomplishments from 1986 to 1988 have been commonly attributed to the so-called "three lows"—low oil prices, low interest rates, and a low value for the South Korean won. These three lows enabled the country to cut its oil import bill, reduce the cost of its international debt, and boost exports. Other factors also contributed to South Korea's rapid economic growth: South Korean workers were grossly underpaid, the U.S. market was generally open to South Korean products, and South Korean export producers enjoyed relatively easy access to Japanese parts and technology. Under these conditions, South Korean exporters had great success, flooding the U.S. market with cars, computers, microwaves, and other consumer electronics. The conditions that gave rise to this success were far from stable, however. In fact, South Korea's rapid export-led growth undermined the very conditions that nurtured it.

For example, South Korean exports to the United States had come largely at Japanese expense. While Japanese products generally remained superior to South Korean goods, the chaebol enjoyed an especially great cost advantage during this period. Not only were South Korean workers paid considerably less than their Japanese counterparts, the South Korean won was also greatly undervalued compared to the Japanese yen. From September 1985 to May 1987, the yen rose 70 percent against the U.S. dollar while the won rose by only 7 percent. Determined to hold market share against the South Koreans, the Japanese began to withhold the components and technology the chaebol needed to remain competitive.

The United States, target for approximately 40 percent of South Korea's exports, was also driven by its own trade problems to slow South Korea's export offensive. The U.S. government demanded and eventually won an upward revaluation of the South Korean won by almost 16 percent in 1988 and greater market openings for

U.S. products. And, beginning in 1987, after years of intense exploitation and repression, South Korean workers exploded in a massive strike wave. Wages that had risen by only 9.2 percent in 1986 shot up by 19.6 percent in 1988 and over 25 percent in 1989.

These developments, taken together, hit the South Korean economy hard. As Tables 10.1 and 10.2 showed, by 1990, the country's trade balance was back in deficit, inflation was on the rise, and in spite of official statistics, growth was continuing to slow. Most South Korean economists believe that the government understated the actual rate of inflation in 1990 by approximately 5.5 percent and as a result overstated growth by a similar amount. It is likely that the economy actually grew by less than 4 percent in 1990.[13] With economists also doubting the government's claim that inflation was held below 10 percent in 1991, the official GNP growth figure once again appears to be overstated.[14]

The state has justifiably reacted with alarm to these trends, trying to reverse them with policies designed to, among other things, stimulate chaebol research and development as well as production of more highly valued exports. Significantly, however, financial developments made possible by South Korea's 1986-1988 expansion have so altered the state-chaebol relationship of the past that the state no longer appears to have the will or ability to dictate policy to the chaebol. Most important, this period of growth provided the chaebol with two new independent sources of income. First, the country's economic expansion generated a rapid increase in stock market values. For example, total market value went from 6.9 percent of GNP in 1980, to 9 percent of GNP in 1985, and to 56.6 percent in 1988. By 1990, the South Korean stock market had become the ninth largest in the world.[15]

A second and even more important source of chaebol income came from rising land prices, the result of land speculation. Land speculation, in turn, became a favorite chaebol investment activity, creating a self-reinforcing speculative dynamic. This was especially true after the stock market began its decline in April 1989.

This speculative activity was largely fueled by profits earned during the export-led expansion from 1986 to 1988. A May 1989 government report, for example, noted that housing prices rose nearly five-fold since 1975. The largest increase, however, dated from 1987. According to the report, real estate prices climbed more than 50 percent between 1987 and 1989. Thus, even as the economy began to slow, land and housing prices continued to rise.[16]

The winners in this speculative dynamic were, as in so many other aspects of South Korean life, primarily the chaebol and their executives. South Korean economists estimate that in 1988, 76.9 percent of all privately held land was owned by just 6.2 percent of the population.[17] That same year, the top chaebol were officially reported to own approximately 429 million square meters of land valued at some $15 billion as well as an additional 45,000 square meters of buildings. Moreover, less than 10 percent of total land holdings was designated for plant construction. The rest was apparently purchased for speculative purposes.[18]

These speculative activities created both political and economic problems for the state. With real estate prices rising 14.7 percent in 1987, 27.5 percent in 1988, 32 percent in 1989, and even higher in 1990, many people found it all but impossible to obtain housing. One South Korean analyst explains popular outrage over the housing situation as follows:

> People are furious. They see big businessmen getting richer and richer, and gobbling up all the real estate in the country, while the middle class can't afford to buy houses and the poor can't even pay their rent.[19]

Chaebol speculation has also meant that the economic gains of the 1986-1988 period were wasted rather than used to improve the country's international competitiveness. In the first half of 1989, for example, Samsung spent $230 million on land purchases, more than three times the amount it spent on investment in plant and equipment.[20] Samsung's behavior is the norm, not the exception.

This run-up in equity value and land prices, coupled with chaebol ownership of both banks and nonbank financial institutions, has given the chaebol more financial independence, enabling them to successfully resist a series of highly publicized state attacks on their speculative behavior. In mid-1990, President Roh Tae Woo announced that: "The tendencies of business to attempt to make profits through real-estate speculation, rather than genuinely productive activities, will be rectified."[21] To back up his pronouncements, Roh ordered the top forty-nine business groups to sell off a large percentage of their nonbusiness real estate. He also threatened the largest chaebol, including Hyundai, Daewoo,

Samsung, Hanjin, and Lucky-Goldstar, with tax investigations and new credit restrictions if they tried to purchase any more nonbusiness real estate or buildings.

While the chaebol announced some land sales and the government claims victory in its campaign, little has been accomplished. This fact is perhaps best highlighted by three recent events. The first concerns Lee Moon-ok, a government housing inspector. After hearing that the Bank Inspection Office had announced that the chaebol nonbusiness real estate ratio was only 1.2 percent, Mr. Lee leaked government reports to the press in May 1990 that showed the actual ratio to be 43.3 percent. Mr. Lee was jailed for two months before a public outcry finally forced his release. The official ratio still stands as the benchmark for evaluating chaebol compliance with the government's antiland speculation program.

The second event was a new land scandal in February 1991. In this incident, the chairman of the Hanbo group was found to have paid more than $1 million in bribes to get zoning changes enabling him to build a massive apartment complex on land not zoned for residential construction. As a result of this scandal, five National Assembly members and a former presidential aide were forced to resign. Roh was also forced to dismiss officials from the Ministry of Construction and the Economic Planning Board. Although the state prosecutor's office denied reports that payoffs went higher in the governmental chain of command than the presidential aid, there is, in fact, evidence that the top leaders of the ruling party were involved. Some sources say that President Roh himself was involved.

The government tried once again, in April 1991, to regain control over chaebol activity. President Roh ordered each of the top thirty business groups to choose three business subsidiaries for purposes of specialization. His hope was that by forcing the chaebol to concentrate their efforts on fewer ventures, they would become more efficient international competitors. As incentive, Roh announced that those chaebol that complied would be allowed to borrow freely to support their three selected core businesses. Those chaebol that refused to make a selection were to be denied access to bank credit.

Roh won a pyrrhic victory: the chaebol reluctantly agreed to designate their core businesses, but stymied the government by picking areas of specialization based on financial rather than efficiency criteria. For example, twelve of the thirty chaebol selected petrochemicals as a core area, knowing that this capital-intensive industry would maximize their borrowing potential. Given the nature of chaebol ownership and operation, it is doubtful that the state could ensure that funds borrowed by one subsidiary would not find their way to others in the same business group. Most analysts agree that if the government were to seriously attempt to financially isolate the various subsidiaries of a chaebol, the chaebol would likely respond by merging their noncore subsidiaries into their new core businesses.[22] In sum, this government initiative has also proven ineffectual.

While this struggle between the state and chaebol is far from resolved, what does seem clear is that the state no longer has the overwhelming power it once had to direct and if necessary discipline the chaebol. Even though it remains a powerful—probably the most powerful—political force in the country, it can no longer command and be confident that its commands will be obeyed.[23] Furthermore, as the chaebol gained greater freedom from the state, their activities became increasingly counterproductive in terms of the health of the South Korean economy.

The Erosion of State Power: Struggles over Trade

Further complicating South Korea's economic situation is the fact that the country's recent export success unintentionally produced new international pressures that threaten to undermine the South Korean state's ability to regulate trade. To understand this development, let us reconsider the condition of the South Korean economy in the period immediately following Chun's assumption of power. As discussed earlier, South Korea's 1979-1980 economic crisis forced the state to engage in massive foreign borrowing. As a result, total foreign debt rose from approximately 30 percent of GNP in 1978 to approximately 53 percent of GNP in 1982. In absolute terms, the country's foreign debt grew from $20.3 billion in 1979 to $40 billion in 1983. Moreover, this debt was increasingly short-term in nature, thereby requiring a quick payback.

The world economic slowdown led South Korea's major trading partners, the United States in particular, to further restrict imports,

TABLE 10.3
South Korean Trade with United States
(in billion U.S. dollars)

Year	Trade balance with United States
1981	-.4
1982	.3
1983	2.0
1984	3.6
1985	4.3
1986	7.3
1987	9.6
1988	8.6
1989	4.5
1990	2.4
1991	-.6

Source: Economic Planning Board.

adding to South Korea's foreign debt problems. Thus, South Korean exports subject to import restrictions in industrialized countries grew from 32.3 percent in 1981 to 42.9 percent in 1982. South Korean exports subject to antidumping measures, a specific form of protectionism, rose from 8.2 percent of total exports in 1981, to 12.4 percent in 1983, and to 17.9 percent in 1984.[24]

Chun was not only desperate for new financial aid and guaranteed access to U.S. markets, he also needed active U.S. political support to solidify his own rule. The Reagan administration was willing to offer Chun the assistance he sought, but, in exchange, it wanted the liberalization of the South Korean economy. Because some liberalization was in fact welcomed by Chun as a way to reduce inflation and discipline the chaebol, he willingly approved an increase in imports of select consumer goods and agricultural products. He also committed himself to a rapid increase in the percentage of goods classified as automatically approved for import. As a result, the number of goods on the automatically approved list jumped from 68.6 percent in 1980, to 74.5 percent in 1981, and 87.7 percent by 1985.[25] Chun, in turn, received what he wanted from the United States: significant political, economic, and military support.

As was true in the case of financial liberalization, however, South Korea talked a better trade liberalization game than it actually played. While some consumer markets were liberalized, it was the agriculture market that Chun was most willing to open. This strategy was designed to buy U.S. favor in the least damaging way for the chaebol who built their export success in concert with protected domestic markets. Even though the government increased the number of automatically approved goods, it continued to restrict the import of most manufactures through a number of special laws and tariffs. The government also continued to resist U.S. government demands for greater market freedom for U.S. banks and insurance companies.

By the mid-1980s, these trade practices had become a political issue in the United States. As Table 10.3 shows, South Korea's trade surplus with the United States had grown considerably over the decade, reaching over $4 billion dollars by 1985. Moreover, this trade surplus came at a time when the United States was struggling with its own rapidly growing trade deficit. Thus, even before South Korea's export machine swung into high gear in 1986, the U.S. government was seeking change in South Korea's trading policies.

South Korea continued to respond to U.S. pressures as it had before: it made promises and then found ways not to keep them. In 1985, for example, the government promised to lift import bans on 603 items, including color TVs, personal computers, and cars. The government announced, however, that these market-opening measures would only be phased in over a number of years, and that, as they took effect, would be offset by a number of new special tariffs.

U.S. anger and frustration with South Korean trade policy finally exploded in 1988. To reverse the trade patterns that had produced a South Korean trade surplus with the United States of $9.6 billion in 1987, the United States demanded import liberalization and a revaluation of the South Korean won. Its club in the negotiations was the Super 301 provision of the 1988 U.S. trade act, which required the U.S. trade representative to issue a report on the status of U.S. trade and identify "priority countries" considered to be unfair traders. According to the act, countries identified as unfair traders would be given three years to reform their trade practices or else face stiff trade sanctions. South Korea was a prime candidate for mention as a "priority" country; it was the country most often reported to the U.S. trade representative for unfair trade practices by U.S. corporations.[26]

U.S. threats of retaliation carried even more weight because of political developments internal to South Korea. Popular demands for the direct election of the president in South Korea had been building since 1985. By 1987, after millions of people had demonstrated in the streets, Chun was forced to yield and grant them their wish. Chun had already picked his chosen successor, former Army General Roh Tae Woo, but Roh was not well liked by most South Koreans because of his close ties to Chun. He and Chun were classmates at the same South Korean military academy, and Roh provided key military support for Chun when the latter was maneuvering for political power in December 1979. Unsure how the election would turn out, and thus what kind of political actions they might be forced to take, both Chun and Roh were eager to maintain positive relations with the United States. Under these conditions, capitulation to U.S. economic demands seemed by far the safest policy.

Roh took office in February 1988, and almost immediately agreed to allow the won to rise in value as well as liberalize the country's trade regime. This decision won him favor not only with the United States government but also with wealthy South Koreans who wanted greater access to foreign luxury goods. With South Korea's trade surplus setting new records, Roh no doubt also felt confident that these steps could be taken with little or no danger to the economy.

As we now know, Roh's confidence was not well founded. The higher value of the won, rising wages, Japanese reluctance to supply necessary components and technology, U.S. market restrictions, chaebol speculation, and import liberalization all took their toll on the South Korean economy. The merchandise trade surplus all but disappeared in 1989, and by 1990, the trade balance was back in deficit. The 1991 deficit was the biggest in South Korean history. Manufacturing profitability was also affected: profits as a percentage of sales fell from 2.5 percent in 1989, to 2.3 percent in 1990, and to 1.8 percent in 1991.[27] A Korea Development Bank survey reveals a similar downward trend in capital investment. Investment in manufacturing grew at a 27.9 percent average annual rate from 1986 to 1989, but by only 11.6 percent in 1991. The Korea Development Bank predicts that it will grow by only 2.2 percent in 1992. Investment in the heavy and chemical sector, which grew at an average annual rate of 29.1 percent over the three-year period of 1986-1989, is expected to grow by less than 1 percent in 1992.[28]

Almost overnight, South Korea seemed to enter a period of economic crisis. Exports, the key to South Korea's economy, were barely growing (actually shrinking in real terms), while imports, including imports for domestic consumption by the wealthy, were on the rise. Moreover, with land speculation fueling inflation, income inequality, and conspicuous consumption, political tensions were quickly heating up.

By late 1989, Roh was forced to admit that the South Korean economy was in serious trouble and, for the sake of his own political future, steps had to be taken to bring the situation under control. Risking U.S. anger, he began to reverse his previous policies. The won was devalued by approximately 6 percent in 1990, and a further 5 percent in 1991. He also launched a massive antiimport offense in April 1990.

The Office of National Tax Administration started investigating South Koreans who owned or sought to purchase foreign cars. Large department stores were also ordered to stop displaying imported luxury goods in their show windows as well as reduce floor space dedicated to foreign products. Hyundai Department Store, Lotte Shopping Center and Shinsegae Department Store, among the largest in South Korea, all immediately complied. Hyundai Department Store actually closed an entire floor of shops which had been selling foreign-brand garments. Lotte Department Store reduced the size of its foreign counters 43 percent and suspended all sales promotion efforts for imported goods. Shinsegae Department Store reduced its inventory of foreign products by about 75 percent.

Not long after, the Korea Trade Commission announced that it would begin investigations into whether imports of two hundred consumer products, including pens, cookies, and plates, were causing damage to domestic producers even though no formal complaints had yet been lodged. Foreign investment applications were also put on hold. Cargill, for example, has still not received a response to its 1988 application for permission to build a $30 million soybean-crushing mill. Past promises for liberalization were also forgotten, as the government reversed earlier agreements to ease restrictions on such foreign products as cigarettes, beef, and wine.[29]

These South Korean actions have indeed come at a high price

in terms of U.S. relations, with U.S. government and business leaders objecting strenuously to South Korea's antiimport campaign and currency policies. Nevertheless, in spite of all his efforts, Roh has so far been unable to reverse the country's economic decline. In particular, his antiimport campaign has yet to significantly reduce the rate of increase in imports. In 1991, for example, imports rose 16.8 percent compared to a rise in exports of only 10.5 percent. While it is certainly possible that state efforts to restrict imports will eventually succeed, it is also possible that the South Korean government will once again find it impossible to resist U.S. pressures for greater liberalization of trade and revaluation of the won.

While no one can predict the future course of U.S.-South Korean trade relations, there is no doubt that there has been a significant decline in the ability of the South Korean state to control trade activity. This decline also highlights the fact that U.S. willingness to support South Korean growth is more conditional than in the past. Thus, at the very time that South Korea faces increasingly serious economic problems, both domestic and international economic forces appear to have combined to undermine the ability of the state to respond.

The Structural Nature of South Korea's Economic Difficulties

The structural, and thus serious, nature of South Korea's current economic problems is now recognized by many within the South Korean government and business community. According to *Business Korea*, for example, a recent Ministry of Trade and Industry report on the nation's industrial health "blamed the current export problems on the lack of national competitiveness, not individual industries. The report notes that the entire export machine is breaking down."[30] The Korea Foreign Trade Association has also made its own examination of South Korea's trade problems, concluding that they are the result of a neglect of quality control, product design, customer service, and marketing. The following brief examination of three of South Korea's leading export industries—textiles, electronics, and automobiles—offers supporting evidence for this pessimistic view of South Korea's economic situation.[31]

TABLE 10.4
Apparel Exports
(in million U.S. dollars)

	1988		1989		1990		1991^P		1992^P	
	Amount	Growth (%)	Amount	Growth (%)	Amount	Growth (%)	Amount	Growth (%)	Amount	Growth (%)
Knitted apparel	3061	14.9	3082	0.7	2584	-16.2	2480	- 4.0	2406	- 3.0
Woven apparel	3747	15.6	3672	-2.0	3149	-14.2	3023	- 4.0	2947	- 2.5
Leather apparel	1419	31.4	1833	29.2	1733	- 5.5	1404	-19.0	1264	-10.0
Fur goods	222	-15.3	174	-21.6	133	-23.6	99	-25.6	84	-15.2
Total exports	8449	16.6	8761	3.7	7599	-13.3	7006	- 7.86	700	- 4.4

^{P} Projected.

Source: John Jie-Ae, "Korean Economy: Toothless Tiger?" *Business Korea*, (November 1991): 27-28.

Textiles

Once one of South Korea's most important export industries, apparel is fading fast. During the fifteen-year period from 1975 to 1989, apparel exports grew at an annual average rate of 12.1 percent a year. But, as Table 10.4 shows, overall apparel exports are now actually declining. The industry also faces serious domestic problems as a result of growing imports from low-wage Southeast Asian countries.

In general, South Korea's apparel problems are the result of a low technological base and considerably higher wages than competitor nations such as Indonesia, Thailand, and China. South Korean producers have sought to overcome their higher production costs by moving operations to Southeast Asian and Caribbean nations. This strategy is unlikely to help the South Korean economy, however, largely because profits earned overseas are rarely returned to Korea. As the *Korea Economic Weekly* explains:

> Since the late 1970s, a total of 1,200 Korean enterprises have incorporated affiliates abroad. Of this number, only about 10 percent have ever remitted home their profits from overseas operations, and moreover, their remitted amounts were very small, [industry] sources said.[32]

It is even doubtful that this strategy can save the South Korean apparel industry. South Korean firms, regardless of where they produce, are facing a very tough opponent: Japanese producers. Japanese producers have already faced the challenge South Korean producers now face. Unable to match the lower production costs of third world nations such as South Korea, they have responded by shifting their production of a variety of labor-intensive light manufacturing products, such as textiles, apparel, and shoes to countries such as Indonesia. Consequently, South Korean producers must now compete with more technically advanced Japanese producers who also have access to even cheaper labor. In short, it is difficult to see this industry once again becoming a leading export center. If South Korea is to maintain its export-driven growth, other industries must take the lead. Because consumer electronics was once thought to be such an industry, we will consider it next.

Electronics

The experience of the personal computer (PC) industry perhaps best illustrates the difficulties South Korean firms face in their quest to become international leaders in the export of advanced consumer electronics. Personal computer exports grew rapidly until 1989. From then on they have stagnated. In fact, sales abroad actually fell in 1990. South Korean PC producers are also losing market shares at home to cheaper and higher quality Taiwanese computers. International competition has forced prices so low that many South Korean producers now sell at a loss. The result is a major crisis in the South Korean computer industry:

> Korea's largest hard disk drive (HDD) producer, Oriental Precision, closed its doors recently. Koryo System, which earlier took over the debt-ridden Oriental Precision, also collapsed in mid-October [1991], pressured by snowballing financial debts. Other major computer makers such as Samsung Electronics Company, Hyundai Electronics Ind. and TriGem Computer are sharply reducing operation costs and promoting sales. They are being hurt by sluggish world demand, intensive competition at home and soaring wages. But the ultimate problem is, however, technology.[33]

South Korea's past success was based on low-cost assembly of foreign components. After three years of wage increases, however, average South Korean hourly wages are now higher than those in Taiwan, Singapore, and Hong Kong. Moreover, South Korea's dependence on imported technology has made it almost impossible for South Korean firms to boost their profits by introducing new higher-value products. When they tried to shift production to laptop and notebook computers, for example, most of their earnings ended up going to foreign suppliers—Japanese firms for liquid crystal displays, U.S. firms for central processing units, and Taiwanese firms for motherboards. South Korean firms have also tried to overcome their difficulties by establishing greater name recognition for their products. But because past South Korean production was largely undertaken as original equipment manufactured for major foreign firms, this has proven difficult.

South Korea's computer makers face even rougher times ahead as a result of a state decision to allow greater sales of American and Japanese personal computers in South Korea. In fact, new market openings now threaten the entire South Korean consumer electronics industry. The first significant liberalization came in 1989 when the South Korean government placed most consumer electronics on the automatic approval import list. The major exceptions were seven popular Japanese products whose importation the government continues to restrict through "import diversification" regulations. The result of this market opening: by 1990, foreign imports had 11 percent of total sales. Japanese products alone had a 6 percent market share.[34]

The real challenge to South Korea's consumer electronics industry lies ahead, however, as the South Korean government has committed itself to a partial opening of the country's retail market. Until now, Goldstar, Samsung, and Daewoo, South Korea's major producers of consumer electronics, were able to use their almost total monopolization of the country's retail network to dominate domestic sales. Even though foreign retail firms will be restricted by the size and number of stores they will be allowed to open, there is reason to believe that this new market opening, by offering greater visibility to foreign products, will have a devastating effect on the South Korean consumer electronics industry.

The Taiwanese experience is quite suggestive. Taiwan liberalized its consumer electronics distribution system in 1986. A year before liberalization, Taiwanese products accounted for 65 percent of all domestic sales. By the end of 1990, Japanese products had a 74 percent market share.[35]

Electronics is now South Korea's largest export sector, accounting for approximately 25 percent of all South Korean foreign sales. Yet while many South Korean consumer electronics producers remain strong competitors, current domestic and international trends make it highly unlikely that the industry can match its 1986-1988 record, a period during which exports grew by an average of 45 percent a year. In fact, as described above, the industry is now increasingly on the defensive. Without major advances in research and development and product innovation, it is difficult to see how this sector can be expected to drive the South Korean economy forward. And, as we will see next, much the same can be said about another of South Korea's key export industries: automobiles.

Automobiles

Automobiles, like electronics, was one of South Korea's leading export industries during the 1986-1988 period. As such, it seemed to suggest that Park's heavy and chemical industry plan had indeed enabled South Korea to successfully move beyond its past depend-ence on low-cost, labor-intensive, light manufacturing. However, much like consumer electronics, the South Korean automobile in-dustry now seems to be struggling to stay afloat.

South Korea's initial success in the automobile market was based on the export performance of the Hyundai Excel. Hyundai, however, soon found that competing against entrenched companies in a ma-ture market like the United States is not easy. Dependent upon low wages and foreign components and technology, Hyundai has yet to find an answer to rising domestic wages and costs of foreign parts and technology.

Hyundai's efforts to upgrade its production are also being frustrated by its weak technology base. For example: the Excel's transmission and engine are designed in Japan by Mitsubishi, who also produces the transmission. Hyundai is also dependent on foreign sources for styling designs. This dependence has made it difficult for Hyundai to improve its quality as well as offer U.S. consumers the constant model changes they demand. As a result, not only profit margins but sales as well have fallen.

While Hyundai attempted to maintain an independent production and marketing base, Daewoo followed a different strategy. In 1984, it concluded a joint venture agreement with General Motors to produce the Pontiac Lemans for export to the United States. The venture began with high hopes; "GM would marry engineering done at its German subsidiary to cheap Korean labor and American marketing know-how to produce a low-priced subcompact car."[36]

While promising on paper, the arrangement proved a failure. GM initially hoped to import into the United States between 80,000 and 100,000 Pontiac Lemans a year. The first Lemans came off the assemb-ly line in 1987, and U.S. sales rose quickly. But, after reaching a peak in 1988, exports have since fallen drastically. Fewer than 35,000 Lemans were sold in the United States in 1991.[37]

Citing rising labor costs and poor quality, GM is now seeking to dissolve its partnership with Daewoo. Daewoo, however, has its own complaints. When Daewoo concluded a deal to sell 7,000 cars to Eastern Europe in late 1988, GM tried to cancel it, claiming that such sales threatened its own European production. Although Daewoo was eventually allowed to complete the sale, GM forced it to agree not to pursue markets in regions already supplied by local GM subsidiaries. Later, when Daewoo developed its own sedan and asked GM to help market it in the United States, GM refused. As Daewoo discovered, joint ventures are no short cut to international competitiveness. Unable to gain the technology or marketing support it needed from GM, Daewoo is now forced to either find a new partner or begin the slow process of developing its own production and marketing capabilities.

In spite of these setbacks, South Korean auto producers continue to expand their production capacity. At the end of 1991, South Korean automobile producers had the capacity to build 2.2 million cars, up 17 percent from 1989. At the same time, estimated sales reached only 1.4 million cars. South Korean producers continue to count on exports to fill the gap. Yet, exports were lower in 1991 than in 1990. In fact, the 1991 total of 320,000 cars sold abroad compares quite unfavorably with 1988 exports sales of 576,000 cars.[38] As the *Los Angeles Times* explains:

> A lingering reputation for poor quality, combined with stagnating international markets and sky-rocketing wages in Korea, is stalling the growth of an industry that the nation once looked to as the engine of the Korean miracle.[39]

A Crisis in Economic Strategy

Although aware that South Korea's leading export industries are suffering from structural weakness, the state still remains committed to an economy driven by chaebol production for export. Its short-term strategy for renewed growth has thus largely been directed toward forcing chaebol investment into productive core business activities; lowering the value of the South Korean won; reducing imports; and driving down wages.

The state, however, has been only marginally successful in achieving its short-term goals. As we saw above, the chaebol have generally resisted state attempts to reduce their speculative and other nonproductive activities. While the government has forced down the value of the won, imports nevertheless continue to grow faster than exports. The state's only real short-term success has been to lower the rate of increase in nominal wages, from over 25 percent in 1989 to approximately 10 percent in 1991. This, however, required a major anti-labor offensive on the part of the state. For example, in March 1989 and then again in April 1990, over ten thousand riot police were ordered into action in a combined land, sea, and air operation to break strikes against Hyundai Heavy Industries in Ulsan. For 1992, the state announced that it would impose restrictions on those firms with more than 300 workers that raise wages above 5 percent. These restrictions include a loss of access to industrial estates and state property. Firms that face labor disputes as a result of the 5 percent wage limitation may receive special loans and tax breaks.

While temporarily forcing workers to accept lower wages, such actions have also accelerated the organization and politicization of the South Korean working class. In fact, as we will see in the next chapter, the dynamics of South Korean growth have worked to create an increasingly powerful mass-based social movement of farmers, women, the urban poor, students, environmentalists, and workers, thereby significantly threatening the ability of the state to continue to use repression to stimulate growth.

The state also has a long-term strategy to overcome the structural weakness of the South Korean economy: the creation of a new high-tech industrial core. According to a 1989 Ministry of Trade and Industry report, this new core will be built around microelectronics, mechatronics (computer-controlled machine tools), new materials development, biotechnology, optics, aircraft, and fine chemicals. Although South Korea currently runs a trade deficit in each of these seven industries, planners appear to believe that with strong government intervention, the chaebol can become international leaders in all seven. To accomplish this, the Ministry of Trade and Industry has called for a $38.8 billion spending program from 1990 to 1994. Approximately $16.4 billion is to be spent on research and development, with the government contributing 35 percent of the total. The remaining $22.4 billion is to be spent on new manufacturing facilities. While the chaebol are expected to undertake the investment, the government will support their efforts with subsidized loans. The government's plan also calls for the creation of five high-technology industrial complexes as well as new policy initiatives designed to attract foreign corporations willing to transfer core technologies to their South Korean production partners.[40]

It is hard to imagine that this long-term plan can succeed. While it is certainly possible to imagine individual chaebol profitably producing various high-tech components or products in joint venture with foreign capital, it seems highly unlikely that the state can succeed in creating an internationally competitive, high-technology sector capable of restoring South Korea's past export-driven rate of growth. The demands of the plan are enormous. For example, the percentage of South Korean exports originating in the seven targeted sectors is supposed to grow from its current level of 11 percent to over 40 percent by the year 2,000. As a result, South Korea's share of global high-technology trade is supposed to grow from 1.4 percent to 3.2 percent over the same time period.[41]

How likely is it that the state will succeed in making South Korea a leader in optics when it has yet to significantly redirect chaebol expenditures away from speculation and into productive investments in existing industries? How likely is it that the state can force foreign multinational corporations to transfer technology in microelectronics when it has so far been unsuccessful in achieving such a transfer in basic consumer electronics? And, how likely is it that foreign markets will be open to these higher value-added products when they are increasingly closed to more basic manufactures?

The state plan calls for massive new spending on research and development and manufacturing facilities. But as a Samsung research official recently commented: "Given the magnitude of the program, you have got to wonder where the money will come from."[42] The *Asian Wall Street Journal* notes that many analysts are skeptical "that the government would follow through on the commitment, citing past pledges to fund massive research and development programs that were never implemented."[43]

To appreciate South Korea's competitive disadvantage in these high-technology areas, it is worth noting that even though South Korean spending on research and development in 1991 was twice as high as in 1987, it was still less than what IBM alone spent in 1991 and one-fifteenth of what the Japanese spent.[44] Moreover, a lot of what South Korean firms consider research and development spending is actually money spent on reverse engineering attempts rather than basic research.

In summary, with structural problems at the root of South Korea's current economic difficulties, the South Korean economy faces difficult times ahead. Chaebol export growth was based largely on efficient use of low-cost labor in combination with imported foreign components and technology. Not surprisingly, as labor costs and currency rates rose, and Japanese and U.S. capitalists became more protective of their technology and markets, the South Korean export offensive faltered.

These negative developments were, as discussed above, largely generated by South Korea's recent export success. Moreover, this same success has also worked to undermine the power of the South Korean state in its relations with the chaebol, as well as foreign governments and corporations. Unwilling to consider a new development model, yet unable to control chaebol activity or regulate international trade as in the past, the state appears to have little choice but to seek to solve South Korea's economic problems by demanding greater sacrifices from the South Korean people, especially industrial workers and farmers.

Such a strategy has its limitations, however. As noted above, and as we will see in greater detail in the next chapter, popular resistance to the workings and logic of the South Korean political economy is growing stronger, thereby making it increasingly difficult for the state to impose its will on the population. This development makes it even less likely that the state can both maintain the existing political economy as well as create the framework for a new period of sustained growth.

CHAPTER 11

THE GATHERING STORM: POLITICAL TRENDS

As we have seen in earlier chapters, state domination over South Korean political life was essential to the "success" of South Korea's growth strategy. Military dictatorship ensured that there would be no effective opposition by farmers and workers to the state's economic policies. Thus, farm communities were destroyed, and basic workplace rights were denied in the interests of creating a low-cost and efficient industrial labor force.

In spite of three decades of rapid industrial growth, exploitation and repression continue to be central to the workings of the South Korean model. But while in the past the state had little trouble forcing the population to accept its will, today the South Korean people are far better able to defend their interests. This erosion of state political dominance is yet another important reason for believing that the South Korean model has finally exhausted its potential to support continued economic growth.

As we will see in this chapter, the social contradictions underlying South Korea's growth process rapidly matured during the decade of the 1980s, producing organized social movements which not only opposed South Korea's growth strategy but were also increasingly able to resist the state initiatives designed to sustain it. I will highlight this movement-building process by presenting, in turn, a brief description of the organizational and political development of farmers, the urban poor, environmentalists, women, and workers. But the political activity of these social movements represents something far more significant than just organized resistance to state power. As we will see in the final chapter, these social movements are rapidly building the organizational and political coherence necessary to offer and fight for a radically new and democratic vision of South Korean society.

The Farmers' Movement

Farmers began the 1980s in serious economic trouble. According to official government statistics, the percentage of rural households living in relative poverty rose from 3.4 percent in 1970, to 9.2 percent in 1976, and then to a still higher 11.2 percent in 1980.[1] Many farmers, unable to earn enough money to meet living expenses, were forced to sell their land and become tenant farmers. Thus, the percentage of farmers working other people's land soared from 27.8 percent in 1975 to 64.7 percent in 1985.[2]

Already battling for survival, farmers were hard pressed to survive the economic difficulties of the 1980s, which were made even worse by government policy. For example, in order to bring inflation under control in the early 1980s, Chun Doo Hwan not only cut government agricultural price supports, he greatly increased imports of foreign agricultural products. The latter policy was also designed to appease U.S. demands for more balanced trade.

This double-policy squeeze forced down domestic prices of grains, pork, and beef, as well as other agricultural products such as sesame seeds, red peppers, onions, pears, apples, and greenhouse-grown vegetables. In response, hundreds of thousands of farmers were forced to give up farming and leave for the cities. Those who remained were driven deeper into debt. While nominal farm income rose by 19 percent from 1980 to 1986, farm debt rose by over 39 percent. As a result, average farm household debt as a percentage of farm household income rose from 12.6 percent in 1980 to 36.6 percent in 1986.[3] By 1988, approximately 17 percent of total farm debt was being used to make payments on past debt, leading to a vicious debt trap.[4]

These state policies left South Korea heavily dependent on U.S. imports to meet domestic agricultural demand. By the end of 1986, South Korea's food self-sufficiency ratio fell to 47.7 percent.[5] In fact, with half of all food imports coming from the United States, South Korea became the third largest importer of U.S. agricultural products and the largest on a per capita basis.[6]

In desperation, South Korean farmers, beginning in 1984, launched a struggle against U.S. imports. The antiimport movement gained strength in 1986 with the formation of ten regional farmer organizations and the national headquarters of the Movement to Stop Importation. In 1987, farmer organizing took on still greater intensity. Building on the efforts of the previous year, farmer activists formed the National Association of Farmers. This organization enabled farmers to coordinate county-level activities nationwide for the first time since the Korean War. These activities included demonstrations and sit-ins in front of government offices to demand an end to agricultural imports and the irrigation tax, an increase in agricultural price supports, cancellation of farmer debts, and democratization of the government-run agricultural cooperative system.

Tenant farmers were particularly active, demonstrating for ownership of the land they farmed, particularly if it was owned by a major chaebol. More than three hundred farmers went to Seoul in August 1987, for example, and staged a month-long sit-in at Samyang Company shouting such slogans as "Return Our Land," and "Give Us Land, Otherwise Death." Similar demonstrations were organized against other chaebol, including Hyundai.[7]

Farmers also took up the larger national political struggle for democracy. Farmers combined their petition campaign for an increase in the price of rice with the national petition campaign for direct election of the president of South Korea. Farmer demonstrations for democratization of agricultural cooperatives were also enlarged to include demands for national democratization.

In 1988, farmers marched on the Ministry of Agriculture to demand cuts in irrigation taxes and tried to storm the U.S. Embassy to demonstrate against American pressure to further open South Korean agricultural markets. In February 1989, approximately 15,000 farmers from sixty counties demonstrated outside of the National Assembly building to demand an end to irrigation taxes, democratization of the cooperatives, and the banning of U.S. agricultural imports. When 4,000 police attempted to break up the demonstration, farmers fought back with firebombs and bamboo spikes. As *The Economist* noted: "Korea now has what it did not have before: a militant, organized body of farmers, pressing for protection, and willing to turn violent if they do not get it."[8]

The farmers movement was developing politically as well as organizationally during this period. Farmers were coming to understand that the farm crisis had its roots in their country's export-led growth strategy, and that as a matter of survival, they had to become more actively involved in the growing national struggle to change it. Farmer willingness to join with urban workers in a broader political movement, as well as worker willingness to support farmer demands, was encouraged by the strong continuing ties between the two social groups.

For example, many industrial workers, especially young women, moved to the cities from rural communities precisely in order to help their families maintain their farm. In fact, half of Seoul's population of over 10 million people was born in the countryside.[9] There was, as a result, a common basis upon which many workers and farmers could jointly oppose a system based on chaebol-controlled production of manufacturers for export and support a more regionally balanced and popularly controlled approach to development.

Giving concrete expression to this political development, farmers formed the National Farmer Movement Alliance in March 1989. Its declared goal, as expressed in its founding statement, was to place farmers at the forefront of the national struggle for democracy, improved living standards, and reunification.[10] In April 1990, a new nationwide alliance, the National Federation of Farmers Association, was organized to coordinate and advance farmer resistance to agricultural imports. Farmer recognition of the broader structural roots of South Korea's agricultural crisis was well illustrated by the remarks of Kwon Chong-Tae, the chairman of the group: "Farmers in Korea will no longer be victims of the urbanization and industrialization that have impoverished the rural areas." He also called upon South Korean farmers to join in the national struggle to end "economic exploitation by monopolistic capitalists at home and abroad."[11]

The South Korean farmers movement grew rapidly over the 1980s—from a number of isolated groups, to a network of organizations under the leadership of various regional committees, to a national formation. It has also become highly politicized, demanding not only changes in farm policy, but also wide-ranging changes in South Korea's existing political economy. Such a movement represents a major challenge to the South Korean government and its policy of sacrificing farmers in order to maintain open export markets for the chaebol.

The Urban Poor Peoples' Movement

Living and working conditions for the urban poor also worsened over the 1980s. As we saw in an earlier chapter, government policy played a major role in creating the urban poor, not only by forcing millions of people to migrate to the cities in search of employment, but also by refusing to provide basic social programs to support this urban population. Unfortunately, little has changed; the government continues to concentrate its financial resources on promoting chaebol production rather than providing basic services.

The South Korean state spends an amount equal to only 2.6 percent of the country's GNP on health, welfare, and social security. By contrast, Japan and the United States spend 12 percent and 13.8 percent, respectively. As Selig Harrison reports:

> Less than 2 percent of the elderly receive any form of social security. According to a recent study, the government spends only $390 million per year on all forms of welfare and would have to spend $1.3 billion "for every citizen to have a minimally adequate income" (defined as $32 per month). The study estimates that there are 4.3 million "poor and near poor" people earning less than $64 per month.[12]

More is involved than negligence, however. As we will see, government policy has itself negatively affected the living and working conditions of the urban poor. But, far from accepting their assigned role as passive victims of South Korea's industrialization, the urban poor have now developed their own organizations and, in concert with other social groups, advocate sweeping changes in South Korea's political economy.

Living Conditions

Housing remains a serious problem for the urban poor. In a 1988 report the government admitted that the nationwide supply of housing units was 40 percent below the number of households. In Seoul, approximately 24 percent of the population survives by either doubling or tripling up in rental housing, while another 20 percent live as illegal squatters.[13]

Recent government housing policy has only added to the housing problems of the poor. Early in the decade of the 1980s, the government launched a series of new "urban redevelopment projects." With the Asian Games (1986) and the Olympics (1988) in mind, the government decided to remove the urban poor from the Mokdong region which is on the way to Central Seoul from the airport.

Sanggyedong, in the northeastern part of Seoul, was one of the areas targeted for renewal. Approximately 1,500 households lived there, most having arrived during the 1960s from a previous relocation. The housing authorities succeeded in winning permission for the destruction of the Sanggyedong housing stock by convincing the owners that they would easily be able to purchase the new apartment units to be constructed. No arrangements were made for the renters. In fact, it was soon discovered that the housing authorities had deliberately understated the cost of the new units. None of the past owners or residents of Sanggyedong would be able to return.

With no alternatives available, residents, mostly renters, decided to resist the planned destruction of their existing housing. In March 1986, they formed a Committee for Planning and Action and organized a series of demonstrations and sit-ins to protest government plans to evict them. This resistance was only partially successful. While several hundred demonstrators were able to remain in the area throughout the winter, most of the housing was destroyed.

Warmer weather brought the demolition crews back to work. And, on April 14, thousands of police and thugs were mobilized for a military style "eviction" campaign which finally succeeded in driving the remaining residents out of their quarters. Similar operations followed in other neighboring areas on successive days.[14]

Many of those driven out of Sanggyedong retreated to Myongdong Cathedral, in the heart of Seoul, where, with others who had suffered a similar fate, they formed a combined committee to demand compensation from the government for their forced removal. They lived in tents, engaging in constant demonstrations and petition campaigns, and received extensive publicity and public support. Slowly, as a matter of survival, the urban poor were building their own political movement.

Public outrage over the brutality of the forced evictions finally pressured the government into negotiations with those living on the grounds of Myongdong Cathedral. But, before any agreement could be reached, the walls of one of the partially demolished buildings in Sanggyedong collapsed, killing a child named Oh Dong-Keun and injuring three others. Upon learning of the death, representatives from some twenty regions where forced evictions had recently occurred, came together and jointly planned a funeral service for the child. Before the funeral could take place however, some eight hundred combat police forcibly seized the body of the dead child from the mortuary where it was being held, and cremated it. Many urban poor were injured by the police in the resulting struggle over the body.

Days later, the following statement was issued by the coalition of urban poor which had formed to prepare for the funeral:

3.5 million urban poor people are rising in anger. Dong-Keun's death was not an accidental death. It was brought about by the forced eviction and demolition caused by the government and construction companies blinded by greed. We hold our anger and sadness and resolve to carry on an unshakeable struggle to prevent further tragedies of a second and third Dong-Keun.[15]

Forced evictions continued throughout the decade, with chaebol land speculation increasingly the main motive. With land scarce and valuable, no place was safe for the urban poor, especially in Seoul. The state-chaebol land operation is illustrated by the 1989 Sadangdong project which involved the government-approved forced relocation of approximately 2,500 poor families in order to create space for the construction of thirty new expensive high-rise apartments. The government offered each of the families approximately $1,200 as compensation, an inadequate sum for obtaining new housing.

When 300 families refused to move, hundreds of thugs were sent by the construction companies and government redevelopment agency to force them out. Two reporters from the *International Herald Tribune* described their removal procedure as follows: "Using steel pipes and sharp butcher knives the gangsters beat and threatened the people who refused to vacate their shacks. Police stood by, just watching the fight between them."[16] Several days later more than 2,000 riot police and special eviction teams returned to finish the job. They overpowered the residents who tried unsuccessfully to block the cranes and bulldozers being used to destroy their homes.

Employment Conditions

In spite of the general improvement in employment conditions over the 1980s, the central problem for the urban poor remains employment. From 1980 to 1987, there was a sharp increase in the percentage of workers classified as permanent employees (37.8 percent to 46.8 percent), and a fall in the number of self-employed (33.9 percent to 30.5 percent), unpaid family workers (18.8 percent to 13.4 percent), and daily workers (9.5 percent to 9.3 percent).[17] Nevertheless, as late as 1987, more than half of all South Korean workers continued to work as poorly paid non-permanent employees. The employment structure is even worse than these percentages might suggest, since the "permanent" worker category includes workers with only "temporary" employment contracts as well as those with longer-term "regular" contracts.

The ratio of South Korean wage earners—permanent and daily workers—to total workers was only 56.1 percent in 1987 as compared with 74.8 percent in Japan in 1986, and 87.5 percent in West Germany in 1985. Mining and manufacturing has experienced the biggest wage labor transformation of any sector in South Korea, with the ratio rising from 65.8 percent in 1963 to 83.8 percent in 1987. By comparison, the mining and manufacturing ratio for Japan was only marginally higher, 85.7 percent in 1986.[18] Thus, even though South Korea's mining and manufacturing employment structure still contains far more daily and temporary workers than does Japan's, the percentage of wage workers to total employment in the mining and manufacturing sector is quite similar in the two countries.

It is in the social overhead and service sectors, where the overall ratio of wage earners to total employees was only 60.9 percent in 1987, that we find the continuing basis for urban poverty. According to a Korea Development Institute study,

> the rate of employees [permanent and daily] in the SOC [social overhead capital] and services industry has remained at about the same level for the past two and a half decades, indicating a proportionate increase in self-employed and unpaid family workers. This result reflects the fact that due to the heavy emphasis of industrial policies on the pro-

motion of export industries, the formal and industrial sector of the tertiary industry did not expand as much as that of the secondary industry.[19]

Given South Korea's current economic strategy, it is likely that employment conditions for the urban poor will be slow to improve. First, since government plans are to modernize manufacturing, it is unlikely that the service sector will be able to command the resources necessary to modernize and significantly expand wage employment opportunities. Second, government plans for manufacturing are heavily weighted toward capital-intensive operations, thereby limiting the potential of the manufacturing sector to provide employment opportunities for those trapped in the low-paying service sector.

As with housing, many urban poor have also been forced to fight to defend their right to employment and survival. In July 1989, as part of a new urban renewal campaign, the government ordered all vendor stalls removed from the streets of Seoul and other cities. When leaders of the National Vendors Association, a mutual support group for the urban poor, protested the order, they were arrested. There are an estimated one million street vendors in South Korea (the majority women), with approximately 300,000 working in Seoul. Many of these vendors actively resisted the government's attempt to force them off the streets, resulting in "large-scale demonstrations involving thousands of poor men and women pitted against heavily armored police."[20]

The urban poor movement has also begun to find common cause with other social movements, especially labor. For example, the street vendors joined their protest activities against the government with those by teachers who were demonstrating against the government's refusal to recognize their newly formed teachers union. Similarly, the coleader of the recently formed National Organization of Urban Poor was arrested by the police for participating in the January 1990 founding rally for the illegal and militant Korea Trade Union Congress.[21] The urban poor and their struggle for better housing, social programs, and employment can no longer be ignored without cost to the government.

The Environmental Movement

For three decades the South Korean government has pursued growth with little or no regard for the environment. The result is a growing environmental crisis and an increasingly active environmental movement. Determined to halt the continuing destruction of the environment, this movement represents a serious challenge to South Korea's export-led growth strategy. And the government is clearly worried:

> National Assembly member Han Seung Soo, who stepped down as minister of trade and industry in March [1990], says there is a nationwide movement against the building of factories. "This will be a major problem which will restrict Korean growth in coming years."[22]

There were, according to press reports, seventy-three anti-pollution protests in the first seven months of 1990.[23] Most of those who took part in the demonstrations were low-paid industrial workers who live near factories and industrial dumps on the outskirts of Seoul and other industrial cities in the southeastern part of the country. But even white collar, middle-class residents of Seoul have begun to worry about the health effects of South Korea's growth strategy.

One major concern is air quality. The Seoul City government has recorded average sulphur dioxide levels in Seoul of .069 parts per million, 40 percent higher than legally permissible levels. These readings were more than five times higher than those recorded in Taipei and eight times higher than in Tokyo, two cities well known for air pollution.[24] Extremely high levels of sulphur dioxide have also been recorded in the South Korean industrial cities of Inchon, Pusan, Ulsan, Masan, and Changwon. This low air quality not only poses a threat to human beings, it also causes tremendous damage to farm crops produced in areas around these cities.

Water quality is another serious environmental problem. In late 1989, Seoul papers ran a series of articles documenting the fact that the city's drinking water was unsafe to drink.[25] These charges were supported by a June 1990 report to the National Assembly by the government Board of Audit and Inspection. The board checked water at eight water treatment plants and found it contaminated with triholomethane, a cancer-causing chemical.[26] As bad as conditions are in Seoul, water quality is generally lower around the southeastern industrial cities. As Walden Bello and Stephanie Rosenfeld report in their comprehensive critique of South Korea's growth strategy, "Large industrial complexes like the Masan Export Processing Zone and the massive Ulsan industrial complex discharge their effluents directly into the ocean. . . . "[27]

The causes of South Korea's environmental problems are not difficult to discover. Considering the problems of water pollution and toxic waste disposal, for example, a 1990 study by the Ministry of Environment and Seoul City government found that out of a sample of 373 companies, sixty-three were illegally dumping industrial waste. Among the violators were Hyundai Motor Service, Pfizer Korea, and Samsung.[28]

In response to public outcry over chaebol disregard for the environment and human health, the government recently passed a variety of new laws to stop the illegal dumping of hazardous waste. Unfortunately, given the state's commitment to growth at any price, little effort is actually put into enforcement. *South* magazine, for example, reports:

> The real story according to the Green Movement [of South Korea] is that many factories are routinely fitted with secret discharge pipes which are used for illegal midnight dumping even at state-owned enterprises. The EPA is considered to be underfunded and lacking in enough technically-qualified staff and therefore unable to implement a realistic waste-management monitoring system. . . .
>
> The government has been accused of failing to publish information on pollution and even its own Economic Planning Board has recently admitted that regulations are ignored not only by the private sector but also by government departments and state-owned companies.[29]

Faced with serious health-threatening conditions, made worse by government and chaebol determination to keep production costs to a minimum, those concerned with the environment have had no choice but to organize.[30] The first recognized environmental group, the Study Group of Pollution, came into existence in 1980. The members of this group were mostly engineers and scientists from Seoul National University and their activities were primarily directed toward raising awareness of environmental problems in the scientific community. The Korean Pollution Research Center (KPRC), founded in 1982 with strong church support, was the first group committed to community organizing.

The KPRC engaged in field studies in polluted areas and

helped local residents either resist the location of environmentally harmful industries in their communities or gain compensation for damages. One of its most significant efforts concerned health conditions around the Onsan Industrial Complex, an area with extensive nonferrous heavy metals industries. The KPRC investigated the "Onsan Illness," which struck 500 people in 1985. The KPRC was able to successfully demonstrate that the cause of this illness was contamination by heavy metals such as cadmium from local industry. The government, which initially discounted such claims, was eventually forced to relocate thousands of people.

In 1986, a new mass-based environmental organization, the Korean Anti-Pollution Civilian Movement Council, was formed. The following year, a new student-based environmental group, the Korean Anti-Pollution Movement Council, was established. In 1988, these two groups merged to create the Korean Anti-Pollution Movement Association, currently the largest and most active mass environmental movement in South Korea.

Although their concerns are national, the groups mentioned above are all centered and mostly active in Seoul. By the end of the decade, however, a number of independent regional environmental groups had also come into existence, largely as a result of local struggles led by workers, farmers, and fishermen: the Mokpo Green Movement Council was established in 1987, and the Pusan Anti-Pollution Civilian Movement Council, the Ulsan Anti-Pollution Movement Council, and the Kwangju Environmental and Anti-Pollution Movement Association were all formed in 1989. These groups are all multiclass, anti-chaebol, and grassroots in their orientation. Although formally independent of one another and the Seoul-based movement organizations, all of these groups share information and support each others' actions.

The environmental movement has already won a number of significant victories, blocking operation of a newly completed chemical plant in Kunsan on the west coast as well as construction of an industrial dump in Pusan. The government, however, appears determined not to allow environmental considerations to interfere with its industrialization program. It agreed in early 1991, for example, to allow DuPont to build a major joint venture titanium dioxide plant near Ulsan, even though the project was opposed by the government's own Environment Administration Office because of concerns over toxic waste disposal. The environmental movement has vowed to prevent the construction of the facility.

One of the most important new developments in the environmental movement has been its growing concern with nuclear power. South Korea relies on nuclear power for approximately 53 percent of its electricity, one of the highest levels of nuclear dependence in the world. The country currently has nine nuclear power plants, but the government has plans to build fifty more by the year 2030. These new plants are considered by the government to be absolutely essential for South Korea's continuing export growth.

Unfortunately, the existing plants were designed and constructed with little attention to quality and run with minimal attention to safety. There have been almost two hundred accidents, some serious enough to halt operations in seven different plants, as well as numerous claims of radiation leakage, all denied by the government. The country also faces a nuclear waste storage crisis. The temporary storage facilities which hold the country's waste are quickly running out of space, but the government has yet to begin construction of a permanent waste storage facility.[31] Recognizing the dangers that South Korea's nuclear program poses to the country, environmental groups have broadened their activities to include nuclear issues. They have targeted the nuclear industry for closure and, so far, successfully resisted government attempts to open any new plants.

Many struggles lie ahead between the government and those concerned with the health of the population and environment. With the government still committed to an economic strategy based on securing the most rapid industrial growth possible, it seems likely that the environmental movement will continue to grow in size and importance. Not surprisingly, this movement has also begun to join with other social movements in seeking a radical transformation of the South Korean political economy. As Kim Chi-ha, chairman of the Korean Environmental Council, explains: "The myth of limitless economic growth pounded into us by successive governments has devastated our precious land almost to the point where it no longer has the ability to heal."[32]

The Women's Movement

Unfortunately, the country's rapid economic growth has also done little to improve a woman's position in South Korean society. Married women, for example, continue to find it extremely difficult to obtain wage employment. Urban survey data from 1975 reveals that while almost 90 percent of all single women were employed as wage workers, less than 25 percent of married women (those married, divorced, or widowed) worked for wages. In rural areas, the overwhelming majority of working women were employed as unpaid family workers—62.2 percent of single women and 72.2 percent of women classified as married.[33]

The reason that single urban women continue to dominate wage employment is that South Korean employers believe that young unmarried women are more easily exploited. This is especially true in the textile and electronics industries where many of the women workers live in company-owned dormitories and are thus subject to direct employer monitoring. To maintain this system of social control, employers either fire women who marry or find ways to pressure them to resign. Many who lose their jobs for this reason are forced by economic necessity to seek employment in the service sector, often as self-employed or family workers.

Conditions remain far from acceptable even for those women who work for wages. Over 70 percent of all female wage workers in 1983 were employed in manufacturing, most in a few key export industries. Women comprised 68 percent of all textile workers, 77 percent of all clothing workers, 55 percent of all electronics workers, and 50 percent of all rubber workers.[34] Not only are these industries among the lowest paying in South Korea, women are also the lowest paid workers within the industry. Mid-1980s survey data, for example, reveals that in textile manufacturing, where the largest number of female wage workers were employed, women's average monthly wage was only 59.2 percent of men's monthly wage. In electronics, women earned only about 60 percent of what men earned.[35] These differences were largely the result of a highly segmented and discriminatory job structure.[36] In manufacturing as a whole, women's average monthly wage was still only 51 percent of that earned by male workers in 1987. In 1989, more than 60 percent of women workers received wages less than the government-designated minimum cost of living for a single female worker.[37]

Some young women who find it impossible to survive under these harsh employment conditions, turn to prostitution. Estimates are that there are between 800,000 and 1 million South Korean women who work in South Korea's sex industry. A number of these women work as prostitutes in cities surrounding the forty U.S. military bases which are spread throughout South Korea.[38]

Not surprisingly, women's oppression is not confined to the workplace. For example, under South Korea's male-dominated Family Law, the eldest male is always recognized as the head of the South Korean household. As a result, in cases of divorce, the husband is automatically given custody of all children and sole ownership of all immovable marital property. Even if the wife is allowed to raise the children, she is not allowed to make any major decision concerning their lives without her ex-husband's consent.

As I have illustrated in Part II, women fought courageously for their rights. Building on this history of resistance, women began in 1983 to form new grassroots organizations such as the Women's Hot Line to support battered women and the Korean Women Workers' Organization to coordinate women's struggles for greater workplace and trade union rights. In 1987, as part of the broader democratic revival, the Federation of Korean Women's Organizations was formed. An umbrella organization with twenty-five member groups, it has played a leading role in the fight to end sexual violence against women; close U.S. bases and end base-connected prostitution; reform the Family Law; and strengthen trade union rights. In sum, the dynamics of South Korean industrialization forced women to take up the fight for new work relations, social relations, and foreign relations. Such efforts also encouraged the women's movement to join with other social movements in demanding radical change in the country's economic and political institutions.

The Labor Movement

Workers, male and female, continue to pay a heavy price for South Korea's export-driven growth. Looking at working conditions, Barry

Renfrew, Seoul bureau chief for the Associated Press, found that:

> An average of five workers are killed and 390 are injured each day in every kind of workplace from huge factories and shipyards to backstreet sweatshops. According to government figures, in 1987 alone, 1,761 workers were killed in job-related accidents and 25,244 were maimed. From 1985 to 1987, the figures show that 5,139 workers were killed and 66,991 were maimed.[39]

Moreover, these figures only cover those industrial accidents which are officially reported to the government. The actual number of workers killed or injured could easily be twice as high. It is not difficult to explain why South Korea still has the highest industrial accident rate and the highest worker death rate in the world: the government will do nothing that might raise costs of production. The entire Ministry of Labor safety section, for example, has a staff of just thirteen people to enforce safety regulations nationwide.[40]

The nature of corporate and government complicity in maintaining a work regime threatening to worker health is illustrated by employment conditions at Wongjin Rayon, a company employing 1,600 workers in Taegu. Taegu is a major industrial city. Yet, the government labor office there has just one factory inspector for the entire city.[41]

Workers at Wonjin Rayon are regularly exposed to toxic chemicals in direct violation of government safety regulations. According to the law, for example, the workers at Wonjin Rayon should be fully equipped with special masks and gloves and never exposed to the toxic chemicals used by the firm for more than six hours a day. In actuality, workers receive no gloves and are forced to work shifts longer than twelve hours. Full ventilation of the work area is also required, but in order to save electricity, the company never uses ventilators. Windows are also kept shut to improve storage of the synthetic fibers.

Not surprisingly, many workers at Wonjin Rayon have suffered from serious illness. One such worker is Suh Young-sun, who is now fully paralyzed and brain damaged as a result of his exposure to high levels of carbon disulfide. Chung Hwan-san, who worked next to Suh, was also exposed. Although he continued to work in spite of growing physical problems, the company finally dismissed him in 1985. When he objected to his firing,

Wonjin Rayon gave him the equivalent of $9,000 in compensation, but told him that this money would be taken away if he lodged any formal complaint against the company. When he appealed to the local labor office for help, he was told that there was nothing he could do. He was warned against suing the company for additional compensation.

Low wages remain a serious problem for most South Korean workers. Government statistics reveal that in 1986, heads of urban worker households earned, on average, only about 63 percent of the amount needed to meet the government-determined minimum cost of living for a family of five. And among workers, manufacturing workers were the lowest paid. Even with large wage gains in 1988 and 1989, most working people still face a struggle just to survive. As the *Asian Wall Street Journal* explained in late 1989, "a spending binge by speculators and business tycoons has distorted the social statistics . . . most blue collar workers and salaried employees are losing ground in the face of an ever increasing cost of living, especially rising property prices . . . "[42]

The Rebirth of Labor Activism

Worker response to the oppressive conditions described above was initially limited by the repressive measures taken by Chun in the period immediately following his military takeover. However, by 1984, workers had regrouped sufficiently to be able to launch a new offensive. The Chunggye Garment Union reorganized and taxi drivers in Taegu, Pusan, Taejon, and Masan went on strike. Labor activity also resumed in the Seoul and Inchon areas among workers employed in metal, chemical, and fibers production.

Labor struggles in 1985 were even more significant. The key events of that year were the strikes against Daewoo Motors in Inchon and Daewoo Apparel Textile Company in the Kuro Industrial Area. The sit-down strike at Daewoo Motors, involving over 2,000 workers, represented three "firsts"; the first major strike against a chaebol; the first time since 1971 that male workers had taken the offensive in a major labor action; and the first time that workers had struck independently from the wishes of the existing official company union.[43] Also noteworthy was the fact that the president of Daewoo personally took part in the negotiations which ended the strike. The workers won a partial victory, gaining a wage increase. When the strike ended, however, the company had the strike leaders arrested.

The Kuro Industrial Area's struggle came one month later. In response to the arrest of union leaders at Daewoo Apparel Textile Company, workers began a sit-down strike. The company cut off all food, water, and electricity, and the police surrounded the plant. Much to the surprise of the company and police, more than one thousand workers from nine other factories in the industrial area went out in a sympathy strike. Students, church activists, and progressive political groups also marched in support.

Frightened by this social mobilization, the police, on the sixth day of the strike, allowed a group of thugs armed with steel pipes to enter the company facilities. The workers were severely beaten and then fired. Students, church, and movement activists present were also beaten, and many solidarity strikers were fired. The strike had been broken, but the Kuro struggle was another giant step forward for the labor movement. New levels of labor solidarity had been established, and relations between labor and non-labor groups had been strengthened.

These labor actions sent shock waves throughout the South Korean business community. As *Business Week* explained:

> Korea has enjoyed four years of steady growth and social stability since the turmoil of 1980, when troops ruthlessly crushed a popular uprising in Kwangju. But in the first six months of 1985, the Labor Ministry counted 146 labor disputes, twice the number last year. "A stable, diligent labor force has been one of the great attributes of the country," asserts Frederick C. Krause, executive vice-president of the American Chamber of Commerce in Korea. "Strikes were virtually unheard of. Now people will have to take a second look [before investing]."[44]

Labor activity slowed in 1986, but beneath the relative quiet, a labor movement was slowly being born. Gaining strength from the broader national struggle for democracy, the labor movement finally exploded into action in July 1987. The strike wave began with workers employed by the large chaebol in the industrial areas of Ulsan, Masan, Changwon, and Pusan and soon spread throughout the country to include manufacturing workers at small- and medium-sized businesses as well as white collar workers in health, finance, research, education, transportation, and tourism.

The total number of recorded labor disputes rose from 237 in 1986 to 3,749 in 1987. Over 3,200 strikes occurred between July and August of 1987 alone.[45] All of these strikes were illegal. South Korean labor law requires that workers notify government officials of a labor dispute and then accept a cooling-off period before calling a strike. In the past, corporations had taken advantage of this period to fire those workers trying to organize the strike. In this strike wave, however, the workers ignored the government and its laws. They struck first, and then offered to negotiate with the company. Workers also refused to limit their strike actions to company grounds as the law required; they marched and demonstrated outside of their factories, often smashing barricades placed by riot police.

The strike wave was so sudden and so explosive that the state and chaebol were thrown on the defensive. Both were clearly scared. As Mark Clifford, the South Korea corespondent for the *Far Eastern Economic Review*, explained at the time:

> An organized, powerful trade-union movement frightens both the economic mandarins and security officials. The mandarins worry about losing control over the economy. The security officials fear that a politicized trade-union movement would provide a vehicle for more radical views than the mainstream political system has previously tolerated.[46]

Most companies responded to this labor offensive by granting wage increases while bitterly resisting unionization. Companies often formed groups of thugs, called kusadae or "Save the Company Corps," to physically beat workers, especially those pressing for unionization. Beginning in early September, the government also swung into action against the workers. On September 4, thousands of combat police raided both the Hyundai shipyard in Ulsan and the Daewoo automobile plant in Inchon. Hundreds of workers were arrested. On September 18, Seoul police targeted over 8,000 people for investigation and possible arrest for their leadership role in labor activities. While such government and corporate actions succeeded in undermining many of the new unions, they did not succeed in breaking the new labor movement. In fact, the number of unions rose from 2,685 in December 1986 to 5,072 in June 1988.[47]

Even though the strike wave of 1987 was largely spontaneous, the solidarity lessons of 1985 had not been forgotten. Workers soon began to coordinate their actions regionally, industrially, and within the various subsidiaries of individual chaebol. This process was greatly accelerated in spring 1988, when workers launched a new strike wave and established a number of regionally structured democratic labor federations.

The Democratic Labor Movement Takes Shape

From January to May 1988, all of the major chaebol were again hit by massive strikes. The Daewoo and Hyundai groups were among the hardest hit by strikes, with their car, shipbuilding, and defense units all closed. Many workers were especially angry at Daewoo because of the enormous financial support its chairman had given the ruling party in the December 1987 elections. According to the government, manufacturers suffered nearly $1 billion in production losses and almost $300 million in export losses during the first five months of the year. Once again, however, the strike wave went far beyond industrial workers. Workers at insurance companies, banks, hospital workers, and newspapers all went out on strike demanding democratic unions, higher wages, and improved working conditions.

Even more important than the number of strikes was the degree of worker organization and coordination. In response to a new government and corporate offensive against workers, which included more kusadae and police violence, many workers joined their newly formed unions together into regional labor federations. In June 1988, for example, thirty-five trade unions based in the Inchon area formed the Inchon Regional Council of Trade Unions. The same month, fifteen trade unions formed the Seungnam Regional Council of Trade Unions.

These new regional labor federations have become the backbone of a new democratic labor movement. Their significance is illustrated by the birth and operation of the first regional labor federation to be established, that of the Masan-Changwon region. Masan and Changwon are geographically adjoining cities, each with a very different industrial specialization. Masan is home to a free-trade zone with a high concentration of foreign capital, light manufacturing, and low-paid female workers. Changwon is dominated by chaebol, heavy industry, and male industrial workers.

Under the circumstances, workers from the two cities could easily view each other as having separate or competing interests. But, because of the efforts of labor activists, workers in both cities developed a base of solidarity through joint participation in various hobby and interest clubs. As a result of this shared history, they were able to overcome their differences and join together for mutual benefit.

As the July-August 1987 strike wave came to a close and a counterattack against workers was launched by the state and corporations, Masan became a major battle zone. Many kusadae were organized to assault women workers and break their strikes and unions. In response, the workers of Changwon mobilized to oppose these attacks. They joined the workers of Masan in street battles to help the women defend their victories. The end result of this common struggle was that thirty newly formed democratic unions from both cities joined together in December 1987 to form the General Federation of Trade Unions in the Masan-Changwon Area.

The new federation immediately began a general education and outreach program to prepare for the struggles ahead, not only among workers, but also among the families of workers. The success of this program is reflected in the following description of the 1988 spring offensive:

> In the Spring of 1988, when the struggle for wage increase was at its height, Machang [Masan-Changwon] region, one worker-activist described, was like a "liberated zone" with slogans of workers piercing the spring sky in all parts of the industrial complex. Files of workers from different factories marched, with arms strongly linked, together, visiting different sites of strike actions. Workers encouraged each other in a strong sense of solidarity and determination.[48]

Common mealtimes were organized by the workers of the region, with such refreshments as "democratic coffee," "victory ginseng tea," and "unity milk" served after work at "strike-site refreshment houses" on factory grounds. The Masan-Changwon federation continues to organize summer training camps for union leaders, as well as year-round education programs on politics, labor laws, South Korean history, and the history of the South Korean labor movement. The federation also supports a strong cultural program in which workers and students join together to create new songs and plays responding to the themes of democracy and worker empowerment.

By July 1988, eight regional labor federations or councils had been formed. Reflecting the level of organizational and political development of the labor movement, these eight councils joined together to form the National Council of Labor Movement Organizations (NCLMO). The founding document of the NCLMO pledged the body to support the organizational efforts of workers to form "democratic genuine trade unions; to fight for the general rights of working people; and to consolidate links and relationships with other sectors of the democratization movement in order to struggle and campaign for the basic rights and political demands of the entire minjung [people]."[49]

At the same time another wave of strikes and union organizing took place in 1989. While the number of strikes declined from 1987 to 1989—3,749, 1,873, and 1,616, respectively—the average duration per strike increased—5.4 days, 13 days, and 18 days.[50] Moreover, the economic losses from the strikes also grew each year. A 100-day strike at Hyundai Heavy Industries in 1989 cost the company some $30 million dollars in profits. South Korea's three largest automobile companies claim that strikes lowered their production by 75,000 cars, worth some $1 billion dollars. Overall estimates are that strikes during the first half of 1989 cost South Korea some $4.5 billion in production losses.

The nature of worker demands was also changing. For example, Lho Joo Hyoung, writing for *Korea Business World*, commented that:

> As far as demands go, labor is likely to raise the ante. Last year [1988], the focus was better wages and the right to organize unions, but now workers want a say in how their companies are run. They're calling for equal control over personnel management and profit distribution. No longer do they think of a business as a personal asset subject to an owner's whims.[51]

While the great majority of unions associated with the NCLMO represent industrial workers, primarily at small- and medium-sized firms, unionization also spread to white collar workers. Hospital workers, researchers at government and private think tanks, newspaper reporters, bank workers, and workers at insurance and brokerage houses all began organizing unions. Perhaps the most significant white-collar union development was the May 1989 formation of the National Teachers' and Educational Workers' Union.

Teachers began to openly challenge the government-controlled education system in 1985 with the publication of a book calling for educational reform. The government quickly removed it from circulation. The following year, 500 teachers signed a petition calling for the right to form an independent teachers organization; self-governance in education; and reform of the country's exam-driven education system. To press their demands, teachers formed the National Teachers Association in 1987 and then the National Teachers' and Educational Workers' Union (NTEWU) in May 1989.

There had been no teachers' union in South Korea since 1961 when Park disbanded the existing union and ruled union organizing by teachers illegal. Viewing education as a key instrument of social control, the governments of Park Chung Hee, Chun Doo Hwan, and Roh Tae Woo all maintained a total monopoly on curriculum and teacher placement and evaluation; required teachers to represent government positions in the classroom as well as spy on their students; and supported an educational system where success is defined by student performance on government-written standardized tests. Not surprisingly, as the new teachers union itself explained:

> Teachers have been degraded to become propagandists for the regime. . . . Consequently, we have not met the nation's need for genuine education. . . . Because of the distorted education enforced by dictatorial regimes, we have lost our role as teachers and have become sellers of fragmentary knowledge and technicians in preparing pupils for examination. Who will call us teachers?[52]

The government has cracked down hard on the NTEWU and its supporters. After failing to prevent its founding congress, the government fired all teachers associated with the union. Over 1,600 teachers lost their jobs in the union's first year. One hundred teachers were imprisoned for demonstrating for the right to form a union. The stakes in this struggle between the government and teachers are enormous. The teachers proudly celebrate their own role as workers and call for a curriculum that honors both work and workers, a position that directly challenges both government authority and its strategy to divide white collar from blue collar workers.

Government Repression and Worker Resistance

Facing a declining economy and a growing labor movement, the government of President Roh Tae Woo began a new and more aggressive antilabor campaign. In March 1989, for example, it used force to break a strike of 5,000 Seoul subway workers and sent approximately 14,000 combat police to end a 109-day strike at the Hundai shipyard in Ulsan. Hundreds of workers were arrested.

In spite of this show of state resolve, South Korean workers continued to take steps to strengthen their movement. In January 1990 the NCLMO launched a new, more permanent organization, the Korea Trade Union Congress (KTUC). The KTUC has approximately 200,000 members, most of whom are employed in small- and medium-sized industrial firms. The goals of the KTUC as expressed in its founding declaration are as follows:

> On the basis of the mass union movement we will struggle towards achieving economic rights and unite with all the democratic peoples' movements which fight for economic and social reform, achieve fundamental changes of the current situation of workers, and pursue our struggle for democracy, self-reliance and peaceful national reunification.[53]

Recognizing the differences in the needs and conditions of workers employed in small- and medium-sized firms on the one hand and the largest firms on the other, sixteen of South Korea's largest workplace unions formed, in December 1990, the Conference of Large Factory Trade Unions. This new grouping included, among others, the unions established at Pohang Iron and Steel, Seoul Subway Corporation, Hyundai Heavy Industries, and Daewoo Shipyards. The Conference of Large Factory Trade Unions, with a current membership of approximately 100,000 workers, has pledged to work for the unity of all independent and democratic trade unions and support "joint activities on popular interests including prices, housing, taxes, and Uruguay Round negotiations."[54]

The government's response to these developments was a continuation of its war against workers. In April 1990, over 10,000 riot police were sent to the Hyundai shipyard in Ulsan to break another strike; again, hundreds of workers were arrested. Two days later, 2,400 riot police stormed Korea Broadcasting System headquarters in Seoul to end a 19-day strike by workers protesting the government's appointment of a former Chun Doo Hwan official as president.

Between January 1990 and July 1991, 848 trade unionists were arrested and kept in jail for periods ranging from a few weeks to a year or more. Of this total, 615 were leaders of unions associated with the KTUC. Nineteen out of the twenty-two members of the KTUC central committee were arrested several times.[55] According to one KTUC leader, "the repression against Chonnohyup (KTUC) compares with the treatment of workers' organizations in the 1920s under Japanese occupation."[56]

The Korean Trade Union Congress, the Conference of Large Factory Trade Unions, the white collar union federations, and the teachers union are currently on the defensive. The government's aggressive antiunion campaign has succeeded, for example, in significantly reducing the rate of increase in nominal wages in both 1990 and 1991. Manufacturing wages rose less than the rate of inflation in 1991. Yet, despite the repression, these new labor organizations continue to survive and strengthen their working relations. To the extent that South Korea's current economic strategy depends on sustained labor repression, there is every reason to believe that the labor movement will continue its advance, playing an even greater role in the struggle to create a new society based on popular empowerment.

One indication that this is happening was the turnout at the November 1991 Seoul rally organized by the KTUC among others, to commemorate the 1970 death of Chun Tae-il. Over 70,000 workers came from all over South Korea, making it, according to the Associated Press, "the largest dissident labor protest in South Korean history."[57] The government-supported FKTU had initially planned to hold its own rally, but cancelled it at the last minute when it became obvious that the attendance would be very low.

Conclusion

This attempt to highlight the development of several of South Korea's social movement groups was not meant to be exhaustive in terms of either experiences or groups. Rather, its purpose was to demonstrate how South Korea's own growth process produced an increasingly organized and powerful opposition movement. The result: the state no longer enjoys a position of unchallenged power over the population.

This change in power relations is especially significant given the developments discussed in the previous chapter. Unable to control the chaebol and international economic activity as in the past, the South Korean state appears committed to solving South Korea's growing economic crisis by demanding new sacrifices on the part of workers and farmers. As we have seen, the new social movements appear unlikely to accept these forced sacrifices. Both the South Korean economy and people face difficult times ahead.

CHAPTER 12

SOUTH KOREA
AT THE CROSSROADS

South Korea's economic strategy is fast losing its effectiveness. The international and domestic trends described in the previous two chapters have greatly weakened the power of the state and its ability to successfully respond to the country's growing economic problems. As a result, South Korea's rush to development appears to have reached its limits. Without significant change in strategy, South Koreans face a future in which continuing trade, production, and finance problems will lead to lower rates of growth, higher rates of inflation, greater income inequality and relative poverty, and social unrest.

Unable to turn back the hands of the clock, chaebol and state leaders are likely to respond to this new reality by gradually adjusting, separately and collectively, to the demands of global capitalism. The major chaebol are likely to accept a limited but secure position within the international division of labor by negotiating new agreements with U.S. and Japanese multinational corporations. Similarly, state leaders are likely to accept a more limited political and economic role, that of managing South Korea's integration into the world system. Greater reliance on international market forces would no doubt provide state officials with new opportunities for profit-making as well as new ways of disciplining South Korean workers and farmers. While accommodation with international capitalism appears to offer state and chaebol leaders their most attractive option, there is strong reason to believe that such a response would foreclose any possibility for South Korea to build upon its past industrial gains to create a more democratic and sustainable process of development. Like the great majority of people in other third world countries, South Koreans would find their choices and well-being limited by the logic of global profit maximization.

There is, of course, nothing inevitable about this outcome. In fact, as we will see, underlying the popular mobilization described in the previous chapter is a growing recognition that the only acceptable way to resolve South Korea's political and economic problems is through collective action designed to create a radically new South Korean political economy, one based on traditional socialist principles of popular empowerment.

Mainstream analysts do not give this socialist-oriented option the attention it deserves. The great majority of books and articles celebrating the South Korean "economic miracle" say little about the contradictory nature of the South Korean growth process and even less about South Korea's history of popular support for socialism. In fact, most of these books and articles give the impression that the goal of most South Koreans has always been the creation of a "capitalist democracy" based on U.S. institutions and values.

Whether by design or ignorance, these writers fail to mention that when Korea was divided into North and South most Koreans opposed not only the creation of a separate South Korea but its capitalist character as well. As I pointed out, the era of Japanese colonialism (1910-1945) gave rise to an anticapitalist progressive movement led by communists. Although repression by the United States and South Korean governments eventually destroyed that movement, its dream of a truly democratic, independent, and unified Korea never died. Finally, beginning in the early 1980s, a left movement has re-emerged in South Korea seeking to make this dream a reality. In this final chapter, I will describe the dynamics of its rebirth and consider its potential for success.

The Political Development
of the South Korean Opposition Movement

By the end of the Korean War in 1953, the left had been eliminated as a significant political force in South Korea. The Kwangju Uprising in 1980 was to mark its rebirth. Before we can appreciate the political impact of the Kwangju Uprising, however, we must briefly review the activities and political development of South Korea's opposition movement in the period bounded by these two events.

Progressive anti-government forces still existed in South Korea even after the end of the Korean War, but they were far less organized and radical than left opposition before the war. Even so, they faced tremendous state repression. For example, when the Progressive Party, which advocated socialist democracy, received two million votes in the 1956 presidential election, Syngman Rhee had its leader arrested and executed on the false charge of spying for North Korea. The party was ordered to disband.

When Rhee was finally driven from office by a student-led uprising in April 1960, students and workers once again resumed their activism. This popular mobilization was not, however, a direct continuation of the politics that had existed before the Korean War. Opposition to the regime was now led by students with no strong ideological position or organizational links to the population at large. Thus, while dissatisfaction with the regime was strong, it was also politically unfocused and disorganized. Reunification demands, however, continued to enjoy widespread support. Four days before a widely publicized meeting of students from North and South Korea was to take place, the military under Park Chung Hee seized power.

Park moved quickly to establish his political control by outlawing all public demonstrations and meetings; dissolving the National Assembly, political parties, and labor unions; and creating the Korean Central Intelligence Agency. These steps were manifestations of the new regime's slogan: "Victory over Communism." Recognizing that his government enjoyed little popular legitimacy, Park sought support for his rule through economic growth.

Powered by a state-directed program of export-led industrialization, the South Korean economy began a period of sustained and rapid growth. But, as we have seen, this growth failed to legitimatize the government in the eyes of many South Koreans. Beginning in the late 1960s, growing numbers of students, workers, farmers, urban poor, and religious activists began to resist the oppressive social changes that were part and parcel of the South Korean growth process.

Park responded to this challenge with heightened repression. When widespread fraud, bribery, and voter intimidation yielded only a slim victory over Kim Dae Jung in the 1971 presidential elections, Park decided that even sham democracy was too dangerous. He declared martial law in October 1972 and wrote a new constitution which made him a "legal" dictator. From this time until his assassination in 1979, Park ruled by means of presidential decrees that outlawed criticism of himself and his policies, and the KCIA, which routinely arrested and tortured dissidents.

Opposition to Park's regime, motivated largely by a liberal vision of "capitalist democracy," continued in spite of the dictatorship. Even more significantly, largely as a result of the efforts of student and religious activists, the various opposition movements slowly began to coalesce in the late 1970s. This important transformation was the result of a combination of factors: first, the self-immolation of Chun Tae-il shocked student and church activists into awareness of the desperate conditions faced by many workers and farmers; second, the process and pace of industrialization helped strengthen worker organizing and militancy; finally, civil disobedience and petition campaigns for democracy had achieved little but the arrest and torture of student and church activists.

These activists had hoped that their efforts would, by calling international attention to the lack of democracy in South Korea, force the government to liberalize its policies. Unfortunately, this strategy proved unsuccessful. As long as Park was able to ensure both growth and corporate profits, the South Korean government continued to enjoy the full support of both the United States and Japanese governments. This failure to attract international support eventually led many activists to conclude that only by supporting workers and farmers in their struggle for economic justice could they hope to bring about social reform.

As a result of this decision, many activists began to see the importance of expanding their original demands for formal political democracy to include the demands of workers and farmers for greater control over their own conditions of production. This awareness led to a far more radical and complete understanding of democracy. It carried with it a growing critique of South Korea's capitalist political economy as well as the pro-U.S. and pro-capitalist reform agenda of the liberal opposition movement's two main political leaders, Kim Dae Jung and Kim Young Sam. In fact, as we will see next, the objective realities of the democratic struggle—most dramatically the Kwangju Uprising—eventually led a critical mass of activists to reject the leadership of these two men and form an alternative movement based on far more radical principles.

The Kwangju Uprising and Anti-Americanism

As I mentioned earlier, student demonstrations in Kwangju were part of the national protest against the military takeover of General Chun Doo Hwan. When those students were viciously attacked by soldiers, citizens, outraged at the violence, joined with the students. The protestors seized arms and drove the troops from the city. A citizens committee, formed to negotiate a peaceful end to the confrontation, asked U.S. officials to serve as mediators. The officials declined to mediate, citing a commitment to neutrality in the internal affairs of South Korea. But the U.S. commander in South Korea revealed the true interests of the United States when he gave General Chun permission to use U.S.-controlled South Korean troops to "restore order" in Kwangju. Tens of thousands of South Korean troops assaulted the city. Over 2,000 Koreans died in the nine-day uprising.

To the shock of most South Koreans, President Jimmy Carter voiced support for Chun's actions and offered new loans to the Chun government. Not long after, Chun was invited to Washington, D.C., to become the first foreign leader to meet with newly elected President Ronald Reagan. The U.S. government justified its support for Chun on the grounds that a strong and stable South Korean government was necessary to protect the country from North Korean aggression. Japan also showed its support for the new South Korean government when Prime Minister Nakasone, on a visit to South Korea, offered Chun a substantial new aid package.

Kwangju and the events surrounding it were instrumental in moving many liberal anti-government activists to re-evaluate the role of the United States in contemporary South Korean politics and Korean history. These activists struggled to understand why the United States government had supported Chun. That led to other questions: why had the U.S. government supported Park?

Why had the United States opposed the Korean Peoples Republic and initiated the election process leading to the division of Korea? For many, a consistent set of answers began to emerge, leading to the conclusion that U.S. policy toward Korea was motivated not by a commitment to democracy but rather by a desire to maintain regional dominance. And because U.S. regional dominance was strengthened by division and dictatorship, the U.S. government created and continued to support both. This new understanding of U.S. policy led first to great anger directed against the U.S. government and then gradually to a broader anti-imperialist consciousness.

The most dramatic anti-American act since the end of the Korean War took place in December 1980 when the Kwangju branch office of the United States Information and Service Center (USIS) was burned down. Another attack took place in 1982, this time against the Pusan office of the USIS. Then, on May 23, 1985, seventy-five students from five universities occupied the library of the USIS office in Seoul. The students demanded that the U.S. government explain and apologize for its actions concerning Kwangju.

As student efforts were beginning to force a public debate over United States involvement in Korean affairs, farmers were also beginning to confront the United States. In 1985, for example, several hundred farmers tried to march on the U.S. embassy to protest U.S. attempts to increase beef and grain exports to South Korea. Students, viewing farmer protests as part of the broad struggle for national independence, occupied the office of the American Chamber of Commerce in Seoul to protest what they called "market terrorism."[1]

Anti-U.S. feelings were also aroused in the population by greater knowledge of the nature and extent of the U.S. military presence in South Korea. U.S. forces have had tactical nuclear weapons in South Korea since 1958. These weapons are under the complete operational control of the U. S. military; the South Korean government has absolutely no say over their location or use. Since 1976, the United States has also used South Korea as a location for annual war games, designated "Team Spirit," involving up to 200,000 U.S. and South Korean troops. Popular dissatisfaction with this situation grew substantially in the 1980s, however, as a result of a change in U.S. military policy.

During the presidency of Ronald Reagan, U.S. military planners adopted a new strategy based on the doctrine of "horizontal escalation." According to this strategy, the United States planned to respond to any military action by the Soviet Union with a counterstrike in a region of its own choosing. And, as it soon became clear, North Korea, Vietnam, and Asian Soviet cities were the preferred U.S. targets, to be hit with either nuclear, chemical, or conventional weapons from bases in South Korea, Guam, or Japan.

Given the U.S. government's almost total military freedom in South Korea, that country quickly became one of the most important forward locations for the projection of U.S. nuclear military power. The South Korean people became increasingly fearful that they would be drawn into a war, possibly a nuclear exchange, as a result of a conflict that they might have no involvement in or control over. The U.S. military presence thus raised, in yet another form, questions of South Korean sovereignty and subjugation to U.S. interests.

The Resurgence of the Left

It took only a few years after Kwangju for progressive sectors of South Korean society to fully understand that U.S. and Japanese policies in support of division and military dictatorship in South Korea were a direct result of the economic, political, and military interests of both countries. Since these foreign interests set limits on change in South Korea which were unacceptable to the democratic movement, many activists soon concluded that the struggle for democracy had to be broadened into a struggle for national liberation.

In response, a significant core of activists began forming anti-capitalist, anti-imperialist organizations in South Korea for the first time since the Korean War. In 1984, a number of workers who had been blacklisted after Chun seized power formed the Workers' Welfare Association (WWA) to help rebuild the South Korean labor movement. WWA leaders described their efforts as a continuation of the work of the 1940s left-led National Coalition of Korean Trade Unions.

In addition, some twenty-three organizations, including groups of writers and artists, intellectuals, workers (including the WWA), and farmers, women, and religious activists, formed the United Minjung [People's] Movement for Democracy and Unification (UMDU).

The UMDU projected a politics sharply at odds with that of the liberal movement led by Kim Dae Jung and Kim Young Sam. Calling for a new "people's constitution" with a leading political role for workers and farmers, it supported anti-capitalist structural changes in the South Korean economic system. It viewed United States and Japanese interests as obstacles to South Korean liberation and reunification of the peninsula and identified more closely with the peoples and struggles of the third world than with those of the advanced capitalist countries of the West. The formation of the UMDU was a major step forward for the progressive movement: it provided an organizational framework within which a common program of action could be developed and advanced, something that was lacking in the period immediately following Park's death.

The student movement also went through major changes during this period. Two radical groups emerged in 1986—Jamintu (the Struggle Committee for Anti-Imperialism) and Minmintu (the National Democratic Struggle Committee for Anti-Fascism). Both groups opposed the military dictatorship and imperialism and viewed the working class as the linchpin of successful revolutionary transformation of South Korean society. Although they worked closely, they differed on strategy, with the larger Jamintu stressing U.S. imperialism and Minmintu targeting the South Korean ruling class as the main enemy.

This multicentered left shared the priority of strengthening the labor movement and concentrated on organizing workers, supporting strikes, and demonstrating for labor reforms. They also agreed on the importance of increasing anti-U.S., anti-imperialist consciousness and carried out actions designed to highlight U.S. support for dictatorship and the continued division of the peninsula.

By 1985, WWA, UMDU, and radical student organizers realized a significant measure of success. Noteworthy in terms of labor struggles were the previously discussed Daewoo Motor Company and Kuro industrial area strikes. In the former, WWA activists played a leading role in organizing and guiding the strike action against an important South Korean joint venture with General Motors. In the Kuro action, both students and UMDU activists offered direct support to the women textile workers striking Daewoo Apparel. They also helped organize a national consumer boycott of Daewoo Apparel products. Student demonstrations also multiplied against

Chun and the United States: the largest occurred when over 80,000 students demonstrated against Chun and his visit to the United States.

The 1987 Election and
the Struggle for Power

Not only the government but also the mainstream opposition was greatly concerned by the left's organizational consolidation and growing influence among workers and students. Kim Dae Jung and Kim Young Sam were leading a joint campaign to force the government into allowing direct election of the president. Each of these leaders felt that he could win the election; each feared alternative actions which might undermine or deflect attention from their role in the campaign, particularly radical activities that stressed anti-U.S. and pro-working class themes.

The direct election campaign was being organized through a series of regional demonstrations designed to build support for a massive anti-government rally in Seoul. Partly in response to growing criticisms of the left by both Kim Dae Jung and Kim Young Sam, UMDU and student activists organized their own major demonstration in the industrial port city of Inchon on May 3, 1986. Thousands of students and industrial workers marched through the city shouting slogans against U.S. imperialism and military dictatorship and for a "people's revolution."

The demonstrators were attacked by police, and street battles raged throughout the afternoon and into the evening. The government expanded its response into a major antileft crackdown, and within days the entire leadership of the UMDU and student movement was either under arrest or underground. On May 8, the UMDU leadership issued a long statement in response to the government offensive, which reads in part:

> In world history, there has never been an instance where a dictatorial regime stepped down through dialogue or cooperation. There is no doubt about the fact that the vitalization of the people's movement is the only way to bring about the withdrawal of the dictatorship. The time has come for the NKDP (New Korea Democratic Party—the party of Kim Dae Jung and Kim Young Sam) instead of emphasizing the

fact that they are a conservative opposition party to truly understand what the Korean people really hope for, and to participate fully in the struggle to abolish military dictatorship from our land.[2]

Both the radicalism of the demonstration and the violence of its suppression shocked the nation. Government leaders tried to use the incident to isolate and destroy the left, but events surrounding the Inchon march turned out to spark public debate over many of the issues raised by the demonstrators—the U.S. and South Korean government's attitude toward reunification, the U.S. role in the Kwangju Uprising, South Korea's economic and political dependence on the United States, and the speed and nature of democratization.

The Inchon demonstration also triggered debate among left activists over whether they were moving so fast that they risked alienating key sectors of the population. Concluding that terms such as "imperialism" and a "people's revolution" did not yet have meaning for most people, many activists committed themselves to grassroots organizing around more accessible issues. They worked to build antifascist consciousness by organizing for the release of political prisoners, an end to torture and tear gas attacks, and freedom of press and assembly. To build anti-imperialist consciousness they organized to demand the removal of U.S. troops and nuclear weapons from South Korea and bring to an end the joint South Korean-U.S. war games. They also led independent initiatives for reunification. And they worked to advance understanding of and commitment to a people's revolution by supporting those initiatives that strengthened working-class, student, farmer, and urban poor organization.

This strategy also enabled the left and liberal opposition to renew their ties and form a coalition to continue the campaign launched by the two Kim's for constitutional reform and direct election of the president. It was the radical wing of this coalition (including UMDU, student, and church activists) that mobilized the millions of people who demanded democratic change during 1986 and 1987. Their efforts culminated in nineteen consecutive days of demonstrations following the ruling party's June 10, 1987, announcement that its presidential candidate would be Roh Tae Woo, former general and Chun's accomplice. During the largest demonstration, over 2 million people in thirty-four cities turned out to demand the release of all political prisoners, an end to the use of tear gas, freedom of assembly, and direct presidential elections.[3]

Finally, on June 29, Roh presented an eight-point proposal offering several concessions to the opposition, including direct election of the president, freeing of political prisoners, and open debate on reform of the constitution. Chun voiced his agreement with all eight points a few days later. Several thousand prisoners were in fact freed and Kim Dae Jung was released from house arrest.

But people remained angry. On July 9, for example, nearly one million people gathered in downtown Seoul for a memorial rally for a student killed by a tear gas cannister during the June demonstrations. Tens of thousands of people participated in rallies in other cities.

Ironically, it was at this point of popular victory that the left suffered a setback in its competition with the liberal opposition for leadership of the democratic movement. Although the left had powered the popular protests, the overwhelming desire of the population for an end to military dictatorship led most demonstrators to emphasize the demand for direct election of the president, thereby strengthening Kim Dae Jung's and Kim Young Sam's leadership positions. After the government promised concessions, the mass movement for the most part retreated to the sidelines to watch both of these politicians "battle" the government over constitutional reforms—and battle each other over who would oppose Roh in the elections. Left activists were powerless to influence these negotiations, which led to very modest constitutional revisions and the decision that both Kims would run against Roh.

In response to popular demands for an end to dictatorship, all of the presidential candidates promised significant change in the country's political and economic life. The ruling party's candidate, Roh Tae Woo, declared, for example, that: "The day when freedom and human rights could be slighted in the name of economic growth and national security has ended. The day when repressive force and torture in secret chambers were tolerated is over."[4] He also pledged to create an economy less dependent on exports and the chaebol. With the liberal opposition unable to unite around a single candidate, Roh Tae Woo succeeded in winning the election with only 36.6 percent of the vote.

Mainstream analysts celebrate this election victory as the triumph of liberal capitalist democracy. According to them, the public chose reform over revolution, and by selecting the ruling party candidate, they also demonstrated their basic support for South Korea's capitalist political economy. Although winning the right to directly elect the president was a significant victory for the South Korean people, there are many reasons for doubting this interpretation: the election took place before left forces were organized enough to affect the terms of political debate; the liberal opposition was bitterly divided; Roh also benefited from substantial election fraud and popular fears that the military might intervene again if the ruling party lost. Even more persuasive in casting doubt on the claim that the outcome of the voting demonstrated popular satisfaction with South Korea's system was the fact that after the election the left continued to gain in strength and support.

The Revolutionary Process
Regains Momentum

The left may have lost ground to the liberals, but the liberals lost the election to the government. Kim Dae Jung and Kim Young Sam responded to Roh's victory by blaming each other for their defeat and forming their own political parties, both of which did well in the 1988 National Assembly elections. Roh repeatedly broke his campaign promises for political and economic reforms, but both opposition leaders also disappointed many working people by failing to press for significant change. As popular disillusionment first with the government and then with the opposition spread, the left regained momentum.

The government's June 1987 concessions had not addressed labor issues and soon after their announcement workers launched a massive strike wave, averaging forty-four new strike actions per day from the end of June to the middle of September. Workers, undaunted by state and corporate violence, orchestrated a second strike wave in 1988. This time, with the support of student groups and mass movement organizations, workers moved beyond isolated strike actions to establish independent regional trade union councils which later joined with other labor groups to form the National Council of Labor Movement Organizations (NCLMO). As men-

tioned earlier, farmers, women, the urban poor, and citizens concerned about the environment also organized themselves and
pressed their demands through militant protest.

Dissatisfaction with both the regime and the liberal opposition
led these new organizations to move beyond demands for specific
reforms to raise a broader political agenda. The NCLMO, for example, declared its support for women's rights, structural transformation of the South Korean political economy, and reunification.
Organizations of farmers, urban poor, and women also joined in
the call for reunification, removal of U.S. troops and nuclear
weapons, and transformation of political and economic institutions.
Moreover, with each of these groups following labor's model of
organizing on a regional basis, activists were often able to unite all
the groups in a region and engage in joint political action.

Students also continued to pursue direct action in favor of
reunification. In May 1988, 10,000 students met at Korea University
and decided to send a letter to their counterparts in the North asking
for a June meeting in Panmunjom to discuss reunification. One
South Korean student leader was quoted by the *New York Times*
as saying:

> Our ultimate goal is not just blind unification, but achieving sovereignty
> under an independent regime. We have realized we can't have true
> democracy with a regime represented by military force and manipu-
> lated by a foreign, invasive force—the U.S.[5]

Students in the North agreed to the meeting, but Roh declared
it illegal. The South Korean government mobilized over 60,000 combat troops and successfully prevented students from the South from
meeting with thirteen designated North Korean student representatives. More than 800 South Korean students were arrested in
the process. The students succeeded, however, in forcing the first
widespread discussion in over twenty-five years on how and when
South Korea should pursue reunification with the North. Under
pressure, Roh had little choice but to publicly state his own support
for reunification. In July he issued a "Special Declaration on North-
South Relations" in which he said: "We have now come to a historic
point when we must achieve a breakthrough toward a lasting peace
and the reunification of the Korean peninsula."[6]

The victory in the 1987 election had shown the ruling party to be far more resourceful and flexible than many had predicted. But, as we have seen, this victory did not slow the organizational and political progress of the progressive movement. In January 1989, the South Korean left moved to consolidate and deepen this process by forming a new umbrella organization: the National Democratic Movement Federation (NDMF). Replacing the UDMU, which had been weakened by conflicts related to the 1987 presidential election, the NDMF represented an important political advance for several reasons. First, it was built on a structured base of mass organizations such as labor's NCLMO, the Federation of Korean Women's Organizations, and the Preparatory Committee of the National Farmers' Movement. Second, activists expressed their support for and willingness to follow a unified political program. Third, a majority of seats on the NDMF steering committee were given to worker, farmer, and urban poor representatives. Finally, the NDMF projected a more highly developed and radical politics than did the UDMU. As NDMF activists explained, the formation of this new organization "reconnects the break in continuity of the South Korean people's movement of the 1940s."[7]

Activists also intensified their reunification work. In a direct challenge to the government, Moon Ik Hwan, a past leader of the UMDU and senior advisor to the NDMF, secretly traveled to North Korea and met with Kim Il Sung in March 1989. In July, South Korean students, again in violation of South Korea's national security law, sent a representative, Im Soo Kyung, to the thirteenth annual World Youth and Student Festival hosted by North Korea. Both were arrested by the government on their return.

The Right Fights Back

Roh originally hoped to blunt any serious challenge to his rule by promoting a limited program of economic reform. However, this strategy became unworkable as the South Korean economy began to lose steam beginning in late 1988. As we saw earlier, the rate of growth of GNP in 1989 fell by almost 50 percent compared to what it had been in each of the three proceeding years. The merchandise trade surplus also fell sharply, from almost $9 billion in 1988 to less than $1 billion in 1989. And, with wages rising, the currency appreciating, foreign markets closing, and foreign technology being withheld, it soon became clear to Roh that South Korea was facing the possibility of a serious crisis.

In June 1989, Roh told his economic ministers that "our economic achievements of the past thirty years will burst like a bubble" if these negative trends are not reversed.[8] Faced with growing demands for action by business and political leaders, Roh finally abandoned any pretense at economic reform. As Mark Clifford, the South Korea specialist for the *Far Eastern Economic Review*, explained:

> Faced with trouble, the economic boffins reacted the way most people do: they reached back to the past. In South Korea, that means resurrecting the idea of Korea Inc. Big business groups, the much-maligned chaebol, are now expected to kick the export machine into high gear. Gone is the idea of domestic demand as the motor for the economy, gone is the idea of building up small and medium industries.[9]

This economic retrenchment had a political complement as well. Roh used Moon Ik Hwan's visit to North Korea to justify a massive crackdown on the South Korean left. As one publication concerned with Korean events related:

> Reports from South Korea indicate that more than 6,600 students, workers, and pro-democracy leaders have been detained during the past month's crackdown [June 1989], that more than 700 have been formally arrested for "political offenses" in the latest wave of repression that began in late April. Another 4,000, including almost all the leadership of the democratic coalition, Chonminryon (NDMF), are under police search or constant police surveillance.[10]

Roh also decided to use force to break labor's 1989 offensive. In March, for example, he sent more than 10,000 riot police to storm the Hyundai shipyards to end a strike; over seven hundred workers were arrested. Thousands of riot police were again sent to the Hyundai shipyards to smash another strike in 1990. Troops were also used to end a strike at the Korean Broadcasting System.

Even before workers officially formed their Korean Trade Union Congress (KTUC) in January 1990, Roh declared the organization illegal because, as he argued, "it is leading a vicious conflict with an ideology of class struggle for the liberation of labor."[11] The government's response to the formation of the KTUC was a virtual declaration of war against the new organization. The Home Affairs Ministry announced that it would place 337 additional intelligence agents in seventy-one major industrial complexes "in order to follow and investigate impure elements infiltrated into the workplace." The Ministry also announced plans to organize sixty-three riot police companies at key locations "for operations against illegal labor conflicts."

The Justice Ministry said, "Any time that there is a denunciation or accusation from the management side in relation to a labor dispute, the ministry will issue immediately a prior warrant of arrest against the accused and will execute the arrest." The Finance and Trade ministries declared that they would offer emergency funds to any firm facing illegal strikes. And the Labor Ministry announced a ban on all political strikes, defined as strikes where workers demand action from a government agency, such as release of arrested labor leaders.[12]

To further reassure the chaebol that he was committed to and capable of restoring stable economic and political conditions, Roh orchestrated in early 1990 a merger of his ruling party with opposition parties headed by Kim Young Sam and Kim Jong Pil to create an even larger new ruling party, the Democratic Liberal Party (DLP). With his party in control of approximately 70 percent of all seats in the National Assembly, Roh was free to push his agenda with no fear of parliamentary resistance.

Thus, on July 17, 1990, the DLP passed twenty-six different bills through the National Assembly in only thirty seconds. There were no formal hearings, debates, or votes. Among other things, these bills expanded state influence over the broadcast media as well as weakened the proposed local election process and civilian control over the military. The entire opposition resigned from the National Assembly, but with little impact on government policy.

The same process was repeated in May 1991. In response to growing mass demands for revision of the National Security Law, the DLP finally decided to take action. With hundreds of thousands of South Koreans protesting the April beating death of a college student by riot police, the DLP introduced and passed a revision of the country's National Security Law in thirty-five seconds. Again, there was no discussion, debate, or formal vote. The speaker of the National Assembly stood in the back of the meeting room, announced the name of the bill revising the National Security Law, declared it passed, and then left the room. The revisions were minor. For example, the phrase "an act that benefits the enemy organization" was changed to "an act committed knowing that it would disturb the security of the nation." What "to know" or "to disturb the security of the nation" meant was left undefined.[13]

The National Security Law remains a powerful political weapon in the hands of the state. The arrest rate of political prisoners is far higher under Roh than it was under Chun. More than 4,300 people were arrested during the first three years of Roh's rule, compared to a total of approximately 4,700 during the eight years Chun was in power. According to the Human Rights Committee of the Korean National Council of Churches, approximately 1,140 people were arrested and prosecuted for political offenses in 1991, an average of 3.1 a day as compared with an average of 1.6 a day during the Chun regime. Approximately 40 percent of South Korea's current political prisoners are in jail having been charged with violating the National Security Law. Those arrested are often subject to torture, including electric shock, rape, sleep deprivation, and beatings.[14]

Labor activists make up a substantial proportion of those arrested. In November 1991, the International Metal Worker's Federation unsuccessfully argued against South Korea's entry into the International Labor Organization, pointing out that "South Korea now has the highest number of worker representatives in prison of any country in the world. Attempts to organize free trade unions in companies such as Hyundai, Daewoo, and Samsung have met with repression."[15]

The Challenge Ahead

The government so far has succeeded in carrying out its repression of the left without arousing the population at large. One reason for its success is that Roh has been far more selective in his use of repression than was Chun. In general, institutions are less politicized and the media less controlled. People are also freer to voice their complaints, travel, and enjoy their wealth.

Another more important reason for the lack of political response to Roh's policies is that recent developments have caused many people to lose faith in the political process. For example, Roh's back-room negotiations with the leaders of two of the three opposition parties to form a new ruling party and his subsequent use of that party to control the National Assembly has left many South Koreans feeling disenfranchised and cynical. Decades of repression and the fear of chaos have also made people cautious about taking independent political action in opposition to the government. They understandably worry that such action might worsen the economic situation, endanger progress towards reunification, and possibly lead to a reimposition of military rule.

The current political passivity does not mean that most South Koreans are satisfied with the present state of affairs, however. Roh's approval rating stood at only 20 percent in 1991. People are worried about jobs, inequality, and poverty. They are angry that Roh has made no attempt to keep some of his most important campaign pledges, including his pledges to end police torture and spying, government corruption, government intervention in labor disputes, government favoritism toward the chaebol, and the system of presidential appointment of all governors and mayors. And they are angry that the various opposition parties continue to function more as political vehicles for their leaders than as representatives working for change.

The ruling elite, determined to hold on to power, is obviously unwilling to allow the economic and political reforms that it promised and the population wants. Yet, it is doubtful that the government's shift back to the policies of the past can ensure economic or political stability. It is unlikely, for example, that repression can bring long-term labor peace. It certainly offers no solution to South Korea's broader structural economic problems. Thus, while a majority of South Koreans have yet to endorse the struggle of the left to transform South Korea's political economy, worsening economic and political conditions may well lead many South Koreans to consider radical solutions to their country's problems. Their embrace of a progressive agenda will, however, ultimately depend upon whether the progressive movement can continue to grow and develop a practice and an alternative vision of society capable of inspiring people. As we see next, there are reasons to believe that the movement is capable of accomplishing these tasks.

The Character of the Movement

One reason for having confidence in the movement's ability to withstand government repression, broaden its base of support, and project an alternative political vision is its stable and diverse social foundation. Most important, the left is now anchored by a highly politicized and organized industrial working class. This source of strength gives the movement the political and economic centrality it has lacked since the 1940s. Moreover, while industrial workers provide the anchor, the movement is shaped by and draws its support from many other organized social groups, including farmers, women, the urban poor, environmentalists, students, artists, and religious activists. Especially noteworthy in terms of the movement's social composition is the role played by women. Women have won leadership positions in the labor, farmer, and urban poor people's movements. The Federation of Korean Women's Organizations has also helped to give women an independent voice in movement discussions and debates.

A second source of strength for the movement is its unity. The various social groups that structurally define the movement have demonstrated both respect as well as support for each other's struggles. For example, urban industrial workers and students have shown their solidarity with farmers in opposing U.S. farm imports. Worker struggles have also won strong support from other social movement groups. When the Korean Trade Union Congress was formed, more than twenty of the most important progressive organizations—including the National Farmers Alliance, the National Federation of Urban Poor, the National Democratic Movement Federation, The Federation of Korean Women's Organizations, the National Federation of Student Council Representatives, and the Korean Teachers' and Educational Workers' Union—issued the following joint statement:

> The ideological and violent repression of the government and monopoly conglomerates against the legitimate and rightful struggle of workers is a basic denial of the burning desire of 40 million Koreans. We will support and struggle together with the workers until they achieve their goal.[16]

Third, activists appear to understand and cultivate the role of community in their movement. They are creating a movement-building process that recognizes the importance of developing the human and political relations necessary to sustain as well as inspire a long-term struggle for social change. This commitment is expressed through the attention given to cultural activities. Workers, for example, regularly form cultural groups as one of their first actions after unionization. Union cultural groups in the same geographical region often join together and, with the assistance of movement artists, create new songs and plays celebrating their community and struggles. Such collaboration has, in turn, also influenced the work of growing numbers of writers, singers, actors, painters, and directors by providing them with new experiences, insights, and themes. The result of this interaction has been the development of a more stable and supportive political community as well as new forms of cultural expression that are politically energizing and empowering.

A fourth strength of the movement is its approach to organizing. Priority has been given to building strong grassroots organizations and close relations among organizations, an approach that has great potential to strengthen the political development and participation of those involved. As one measure of the movement's success, a new organization, the National Alliance for Democracy and National Reunification (NADNR), was formed in December 1991 to replace the National Democratic Movement Federation (NDMF). The NADNR represents an advance over the NDMF in that it includes more mass movement organizations and is committed to developing a unified, integrated leadership.

Of course, activists still have considerable work ahead if they are to succeed in building a politically strong and unified left. Among their most important challenges is the challenge to ensure that organizational structures and activities encourage political growth, open debate, and significant grassroots participation in decision-making. The fact that South Korea's various social groups have tended to develop on a regional basis has proven helpful in this regard by promoting experimentation, independent thinking, and a varied and multiple leadership base.

Basic Political Principles

Although the South Korean left has yet to develop its own well-defined political and economic program in response to the country's growing economic and political problems, it is united in seeking change based on the principles of democracy, national independence, and reunification. The challenge for the left, if it is to successfully shift the terms of national political debate, is to translate these broad principles into policies which both respond to people's immediate concerns as well as expand their sense of political possibilities.

The demand for democracy is the starting point for progressive activity in South Korea. Unlike the liberal opposition, democracy for the left means more than just direct elections and respect for basic civil and human rights. The Korea Trade Union Congress, for example, believes that workers, through their union, should have a significant role in managing enterprises, including wage, investment, and production decisions. The National Farmers' Alliance believes that the government-dominated agricultural cooperatives which shape the rural economy should be under direct farmer control. These demands for the "democratization" of basic economic institutions reflect the experiences of workers and farmers who have learned that economic growth under conditions they cannot control brings few benefits. One measure of popular receptivity to such traditional socialist-oriented demands: *The Asian Wall Street Journal* reported that the South Korean government has found it necessary to launch

> a think tank aimed at promoting capitalism, in response to what it views as growing support for leftist ideologies on campuses and work-places... [An Economic Planning Board official noted that] opposition groups have provided extensive education on socialism or communism to blue-collar workers, farmers, and students since the 1970s.[17]

One of the most important struggles for democracy in the terms highlighted above is that being waged by the Korean Teachers' and Educational Workers' Union. As noted earlier, successive military regimes have used the country's educational system to undermine opposition to their rule. To that end, the Ministry of Education has written all textbooks and dictated the content of all classes. Teachers have also been forced to monitor and report on the political views and activities of students. Long frustrated by these restrictions, as well as average secondary school class sizes of over fifty and the demands of preparing students to succeed in a highly competitive examination-based system, teachers decided in May 1989 to challenge the government's law against teacher unionization and form their own union to press for educational reform. Not surprisingly, teachers are demanding, among other things, greater freedom to write and select their own classroom material and restructure the country's educational curriculum.

What makes the teachers' union movement so exciting and important is that the union has directly tied these demands for greater teacher control over the education process (in other words workplace democracy) to the broader struggle to transform the society. For example, the union has argued that the country's education system, created under and in the interests of dictatorship, is unable to prepare students for the difficult job of creating democracy. Thus, teachers argue that they need greater independence from the state precisely to develop what they call a "meaningful" education, one that encourages students to be creative and responsible citizens rather than skilled examination-takers.

By raising the question of the purpose of education or, more precisely, the kind of education to best serve democracy, the union is directly challenging the government and the logic of the country's political economy. This challenge has been made explicit by the union's declaration that a "democratic" education should celebrate the values of participation and solidarity as well as the centrality of work and workers.

More concretely, teachers have actively defended political prisoners, helped the new democratic unions organize worker education classes, and taught workers labor history as well as basic reading and writing skills. They have set up regionally based outreach committees of union members to discuss the country's education problems with parents and students. Such efforts have been instrumental in building support among broad sections of the population for the union and education reform. They have also helped many people develop a more complete understanding of the meaning and importance of democracy as well as their own stake in the creation of a new society.

The demand for democracy, as exemplified by the actions of these teachers, may be the starting point for activists, but history has also taught the South Korean left that the struggle for democracy cannot be separated from the struggle for national independence and reunification. Kwangju made it clear that U.S. and Japanese government and corporate elites believe their interests in South

Korea are best protected by dictatorship and that division of the peninsula offers them a useful pretext for supporting the suppression of any significant challenge to the existing political economy.[18] Therefore, progress toward achieving national independence and reunification remains necessary to ensure the South Korean people the freedom to pursue the political and economic change they so desire. The recent heavy use of the National Security Law to repress political activists further highlights the importance and necessity of building a unified movement committed to all three principles.

As with its demand for democracy, the challenge for the left is to find a way to translate its call for national independence and reunification into policies capable of inspiring the population to action. Up to this point, the left has made considerable progress. Activists have significantly increased public awareness of the need to remove U.S. nuclear weapons and troops in order to strengthen the country's political independence and advance the reunification process. In fact many South Koreans acknowledge that without the efforts of student activists, reunification would still be a forbidden topic of discussion in the South.

The Terms of Struggle:
Creating a New Vision of Korean Society

As South Korea's economic crisis grew, the state tried to discredit the left by arguing that socialism, the only known alternative to South Korea's capitalist system, had been rejected wherever it was tried. While the South Korean movement never defined itself as socialist or its goal as the building of socialism in South Korea, its general political vision was certainly influenced by the socialist tradition. Thus, like movements throughout the world that seek to create alternatives to capitalism, it cannot escape the repercussions of the collapse of the former Soviet Union and the rejection of socialism by the countries of Eastern Europe. At the same time, because the movement in South Korea has never looked to these countries for a model of politics or economics, relying instead on its own experiences to define its strategy and vision, the South Korean government has achieved less with this tactic than it might have hoped.

The South Korean government instead has had more success in weakening support for the South Korean left when it raises the issue of the movement's relations with North Korea. The South Korean government charges the North Korean government with wanting to impose socialism on the people of the South through whatever means necessary and brands most movement activities in the South as North-Korean inspired. Continued uncertainty in the South about North Korea's intentions has enabled the South Korean government to raise doubts in some minds as to the intentions of the movement. The government has effectively used its propaganda against the North to justify its extensive use of the National Security Law against those in the progressive movement.

The movement has attempted to counter these attacks by pointing out that without its efforts there would be no progress toward reunification. It has also sought to argue that its approach to reunification, based on establishing direct contacts between people in North and South Korea, is the most likely to lead to the creation of a democratic and independent Korea. Unfortunately, the combination of North Korea's tightly controlled political system and the South Korean government's control of the media and all legal contacts with the North has greatly complicated movement attempts to demonstrate the virtues of this approach.

Until now the South Korean left has been reasonably successful in defending itself against charges that it is a mindless advocate of an outdated ideology or a dangerous front for North Korean interests. However, if it is to successfully lead a majority movement to transform South Korean society, it must do more than establish its independence and integrity. The state's decisive challenge remains unanswered: the movement must still convince a critical mass of people that it is possible to create a workable and attractive alternative to South Korea's current economic strategy.

Discussions and debates over issues relevant to answering this challenge continue. In broad terms, activists are united in opposing the country's current growth strategy in favor of one that is more domestically centered, regionally balanced, and environmentally sustainable. This new approach would give greater attention to producing affordable domestic goods with domestically developed technology and machinery rather than import-dependent, high-technology products for foreign markets. Export activity would also become more regionally centered as well as focused on a smaller range of technologically supportable products.[19]

Significantly, while activists are also in agreement that any new economic plan must be developed as part of the larger struggle to replace dictatorship with egalitarian and participatory structures of decision-making at the level of the state, community, and chaebol, many important issues concerning the restructuring of the South Korean political economy are only now being raised. For example, while there is general agreement to continue public direction of both domestic and international economic activity, there is no clear consensus how to ensure democratic participation in policy formulation. Some on the left advocate a planning system responsive to a strong National Assembly. Others propose creating a direct institutional link between key ministries and some association of national organizations representing the interests of important social groups such as women, youth, workers, environmentalists, farmers, and the urban poor.

Similarly, while many in the movement believe that democratic participation will require decentralizing existing state structures, it is unclear how these decentralized structures would operate. More specifically, it is unclear what decentralization would mean in terms of carrying out the kinds of activities currently under the jurisdiction of a ministry such as the Ministry of Trade and Industry. Related questions concern how best to organize production. Some activists support nationalizing the chaebol to create powerful public enterprises with institutionalized worker participation. Others would prefer to break up the chaebol into a number of independent private firms, again with strong institutional support for worker participation in management.

Obviously, answers to these questions cannot be decided on in the abstract but must emerge out of the process of transformation itself. What is exciting—but unfortunately little known outside of South Korea—is that an organized left is beginning to raise and debate such issues in the context of an increasingly popular struggle to transform South Korean society. With the ruling elite in South Korea apparently committed to a program that is unlikely to win majority support or satisfactorily address the nation's political and economic problems, these debates can be expected to grow in both intensity and significance. If the movement proves effective in translating its principles into a coherent and integrated program of action through perhaps a new political party, the terms of national political debate can be expected to radically shift to the left. At that point, the ideological struggle feared by the South Korean government would fully be joined.

Korean revolutionaries have engaged in and lost struggles before. But as Kim San commented in the lead quote to this book, "history keeps a fine accounting." I offer no predictions about the outcome of the contemporary South Korean struggle except to say that among the factors that will loom large in history's ongoing accounting are the ability of the South Korean left to build and lead a mass-based, democratic movement and the flexibility of the South Korean ruling class. Because the international political and economic environment will undoubtedly also leave its heavy mark, those of us concerned with creating democratic and sustainable development can also have an effect. By helping to challenge the myth of capitalism's triumph in South Korea, we can influence the international environment in ways bound to strengthen the position of those working for progressive change inside as well as outside South Korea.

NOTES

Introduction

1. Thomas Kamm, "South Americans Push Sales of State Assets in Swing to Capitalism," *Wall Street Journal*, 9 July 1991.
2. Staffan Burenstam Linder, *The Pacific Century: Economic and Political Consequences of Asian-Pacific Dynamism* (Stanford, CA.: Stanford University Press, 1986), p. 54.
3. Quoted in Bruce Cumings, *The Origins of the Korean War: Liberation and The Emergence of Separate Regimes, 1945-47* (Princeton, NJ: Princeton University Press, 1981), p. 200.

1: Acknowledging the Primacy of State Intervention

1. Tony Michell, *From a Developing to a Newly Industrialized Country: The Republic of Korea, 1961-82* (Geneva: International Labor Organization, 1988), p. 19.
2. Ibid., p. 10.
3. Ibid., p. 11.
4. Bela Balassa, "The Role of Foreign Trade in the Economic Development of Korea," in *Foreign Trade and Investment: Economic Development in the Newly Industrializing Asian Countries*, ed. Walter Galenson (Madison, WI: University of Wisconsin Press, 1985), p. 141.
5. Ibid., p. 142.
6. Stephan Haggard, *Pathways from the Periphery: The Politics of Growth in the Newly Industrializing Countries* (Ithaca, N.Y.: Cornell University Press, 1990), p. 55.
7. Balassa, *The Role of Foreign Trade*, p. 141.
8. Before 1983, the World Bank, in recognition of the special status of a number of oil-exporting third world countries, divided middle-income countries into two groups, according to whether they were oil importers or oil exporters. Since South Korea is an oil importer and had,

by 1980, achieved middle-income status for oil-importing countries, I use country averages for this classification as a reference point for evaluating South Korea's structural transformation and relative economic performance. The World Bank now divides middle-income countries into two groups solely on the basis of their per capita Gross National Product: lower middle income and upper middle income. South Korea has been classified as an upper-middle-income country since 1983.

9. "The Koreans Are Coming," *Business Week*, 23 December 1985.

10. Jie-Ae Sohn, "Crossing Over," *Business Korea* 8, no. 12 (June 1991).

11. "Brave New World: Why Have the Economic Fortunes of Latin America and Asia Diverged So Dramatically," *Far Eastern Economic Review* (September 1990): 13.

12. Bela Balassa and John Williamson, *Adjusting to Success: Balance of Payments Policy in the East Asian NICS* (Washington, D.C.: Institute For International Economics, June 1987), pp. 2-3.

13. Ibid., p. 11.

14. Ibid., p. 13.

15. Ibid., p. 14.

16. Ibid., pp. 14-15.

17. Ibid., p. 15.

18. Ibid., p. 16.

19. As quoted in Gordon White and Robert Wade, "Developmental States and Markets in East Asia: An Introduction," in *Developmental States in East Asia*, ed. Gordon White (New York: St. Martin's Press, 1988), p. 4.

20. As quoted in Linder, *The Pacific Century*, p. 41.

21. Alice H. Amsden, *Asia's Next Giant: South Korea and Late Industrialization* (New York: Oxford University Press, 1989), p. 139.

22. Byung-Nak Song, *The Rise of the Korean Economy* (New York: Oxford University Press, 1990), pp. 101-102.

23. Karl Schoenberger, "If It's Fancy, Don't Market It in Seoul," *Los Angeles Times*, 11 September 1990.

24. Michell, *From a Developing to a Newly Industralized Country*, p. 53.

25. Walden Bello and Stephanie Rosenfeld, *Dragons in Distress: Asia's Miracle Economies in Crisis* (San Francisco: Institute for Food and Development Policy, 1990), p. 59.

26. Song, *The Rise of the Korean Economy*, p. 118.

27. Michell, *From a Developing to a New Industralized Country*, p. 91.

28. Amsden, *Asia's Next Giant,* p. 90. The main reason for the disagreement over South Korea's fiscal policy is that the South Korean government has an exceptionally complex budget structure. Looking only at the government general account, as do most economists, it appears that the South Korean government consistently runs a surplus. However, the South Korean government also maintains over fifteen different

special budget accounts as well as a number of off-budget accounts. When all of these accounts are included in the budget calculation, as they should be, we find that the South Korean government regularly runs a deficit. See Michell, *From a Developing to a Newly Industrialized Country*, p. 69.

29. Amsden, *Asia's Next Giant*, p. 116. These sales figures overstate the extent of chaebol activity because they include the value of inputs purchased from non-chaebol firms. However, because many "independent suppliers" are in fact secretly owned by or under the control of the chaebol, the overstatement is probably slight. Looking at shipment figures for manufacturing, which are a reasonably good proxy for value added, we still find concentration high and increasing. The top ten business groups raised their share of total shipments from 21.2 percent in 1977 to 30.2 percent in 1982. See ibid., p. 122.
30. Bello and Rosenfeld, *Dragons in Distress*, p. 63.
31. Ibid., p. 232.
32. Robert Wade, "State Intervention in 'Outward-looking' Development: Neoclassical Theory and Taiwanese Practice," in *Developmental States in East Asia*, p. 39.
33. Bello and Rosenfeld, *Dragons in Distress*, p. 232.
34. Wade, "State Intervention in 'Outward-looking Development: Neoclassical Theory and Taiwanese Practice," p. 49.
35. Ibid., p. 50.
36. For further discussion of the differences between the Latin American and East Asian experiences see White and Wade, "State Intervention in 'Outward-looking Development: Neoclassical Theory and Taiwanese Practice," and Peter Evans, "Class, State, and Dependence in East Asia: Lessons for Latin Americanists," in *The Political Economy of the New Asian Industrialism*, ed. Frederic C. Deyo (Ithaca, N.Y.: Cornell University Press, 1987).
37. For a discussion of the economic and political problems facing both Taiwan and South Korea, see Bello and Rosenfeld, *Dragons in Distress*. South Korea's situation will, of course, be addressed more fully in this book.

2: The Structure and Function of State Planning

1. This period will be discussed in more detail in Chapter 6.
2. These figures are based only on economic assistance. According to conservative estimates, total military aid for the period from 1946 to 1976 was approximately $6.8 billion compared to total economic aid of $5.7 billion. See Thorkil Casse, *The Non-Conventional Approach to Stability: The Case of South Korea: An Analysis of Macro-Economic Policy 1979-84* (Copenhagen: Center for Development Research, 1985), p. 21.

3. For a discussion of the political logic behind Rhee's economic policies see Haggard, *Pathways from the Periphery*, pp. 54-60.

4. As quoted in ibid., p. 58.

5. Stephan Haggard, Byung-Kook Kim, and Chung-In Moon, "The Transition to Export-led Growth in South Korea: 1954-1966," *Journal of Asian Studies* 50, no. 4 (November 1991): 855.

6. Ibid., p. 856.

7. Joungwon A. Kim, *Divided Korea: The Politics of Development, 1945-1972* (Cambridge, MA: Harvard University Press, 1976), p. 209.

8. Interestingly, there was considerable support within the military for an economic plan based on state ownership and principles of self-reliance. In fact, a group of colonels developed a draft plan that, according to some involved in the process, was essentially a "socialist" plan. It was shredded by the coup leadership for fear that U.S. officials might see it; unfortunately, no copies remain. I am indebted to David Satterwhite for this point as well as my general understanding of the politics behind the development and implementation of South Korea's first Five Year Plan. For a more complete presentation and analysis of the politics of the period, see his forthcoming book, *The Politics of Economic Development: Coup, State, and the Republic of Korea's First Five Year Plan (1962-1966)* (Seattle, WA: University of Washington Press, 1993).

9. "Economic Planning Board: Looking for a New Role," *Business Korea* (August 1991): 18.

10. Song, *The Rise of the Korean Economy*, p. 141.

11. "Economic Planning Board: Looking for a New Role," *Business Korea* (August 1991): 19.

12. Michell, *From a Developing to a Newly Industrialized Country*, p. 20.

13. Amsden, *Asia's Next Giant*, p. 7.

14. Richard Luedde-Neurath, "State Intervention and Export-Oriented Development in South Korea," in *Developmental States in East Asia*), p. 76.

15. Ibid., p. 76.

16. Amsden, *Asia's Next Giant*, p. 17.

17. Michell, *From a Developing to a Newly Industrialized Country*, p. 66.

18. The Korea Foreign Traders' Association was founded under the name Korea Traders' Association. It took its current name in 1988.

19. Michell, *From a Developing to a Newly Industrialized Country*, p. 66.

20. Haggard, Kim, and Moon, "The Transition to Export-led Growth in South Korea; 1954-1966,"pp. 860-61.

21. George E. Ogle, *South Korea: Dissent within the Economic Miracle* (New Jersey: Zed Books Ltd. in association with International Labor Rights Education and Research Fund [Washington, D.C.], 1990), pp. 31-32.

22. Michell, *From a Developing to a Newly Industrialized Country*, p. 63.

3: Policy Implementation:
State Direction of National Economic Activity

1. Paul Kuznets, "The Dramatic Reversal of 1979/1980: Contemporary Economic Development in Korea," *Journal of Northeast Asian Studies* 1, no. 3 (1982): 85.
2. Leroy P. Jones and Il Sakong, *Government, Business, and Entrepreneurship in Economic Development: The Korean Case* (Cambridge, MA: Harvard University Press, 1980), p. 296.
3. Ibid., pp. 69-70.
4. Luedde-Neurath, "State Intervention and Export Oriented Development in South Korea," p. 75.
5. Jones and Sakong, *Government, Business, and Entrepreneurship in Economic Development*, p. 101.
6. Ibid., p. 104.
7. Amsden, *Asia's Next Giant*, p. 94.
8. Ibid., p. 76.
9. Song, *The Rise of the Korean Economy*, p. 91.
10. Michell, *From a Developing to a Newly Industrialized Country*, p. 43.
11. Larry Westphal, "The Republic of Korea's Experience with Export-Led Industrial Development," *World Development* 6, no. 3 (1978): 348.
12. Michell, *From a Developing to a Newly Industrialized Country*, p. 41.
13. Jung-en Woo, *Race to the Swift: State and Finance in Korean Industrialization* (New York: Columbia University Press, 1991), p. 193.
14. Ibid., p. 166.
15. World Bank, *Korea: Managing the Industrial Transformation*, Vol. 2 (Washington, D.C.: World Bank, 1987), p. 103.
16. Amsden, *Asia's Next Giant*, p. 55.
17. World Bank, *Korea*, p. 10.
18. Ibid., p. 25.
19. Ibid., p. 26.
20. Ibid., p. 27.
21. Ibid., p. 31.
22. Ibid., p. 29.
23. "Industrial South Korea," *Far Eastern Economic Review*, 19 July 1984, p. 43.
24. Damon Darlin, "Korea's 30 Biggest Firms Told to Shrink," *Wall Street Journal*, 30 April 1991, p. A12.
25. Richard M. Steers et al., *The Chaebol: Korea's New Industrial Might* (New York: Harper and Row, 1989), p. 37.
26. As quoted in Sam Jameson, "Families Still Keep Grip on S. Korea's Conglomerates," *Los Angeles Times*, 10 December 1990, p. D4.
27. George E. Ogle, *South Korea: Dissent within the Economic Miracle* (London: Zed Press in association with International Labor Rights Education and Research Fund [Washington, D.C.], 1990), p. 70.

28. Jones and Sakong, *Government, Business, and Entrepreneurship*, p. 357.
29. Amsden, *Asia's Next Giant*, p. 276.
30. Jones and Sakong, *Government, Business, and Entrepreneurship*, p. 358.
31. Amsden, *Asia's Next Giant*, p. 269.
32. Ibid., pp. 286-87.
33. Ogle, *South Korea*, p. 40.
34. Song, *The Rise of the Korean Economy*, p. 100.
35. Ogle, *South Korea*, p. 40.
36. Bello and Rosenfeld, *Dragons in Distress*, p. 52.
37. This development will be discussed in more detail in Chapter 10.
38. Jones and Sakong, *Government, Business, and Entrepreneurship*, p. 141.
39. Ibid., p. 143.
40. Song, *The Rise of the Korean Economy*, pp. 118-19.
41. Michell, *From a Developing to a Newly Industrialized Country*, p. 33.
42. Data presented in this and the following two paragraphs are drawn from the discussion in Jones and Sakong, *Government, Business, and Entrepreneurship*, pp. 148-54.
43. Hyun-Chin Lim, *Dependent Development in Korea, 1963-1979* (Seoul: Seoul National University Press, 1985), p. 110.
44. Song, *The Rise of the Korean Economy*, p. 97.
45. Lim, *Dependent Development in Korea*, p. 111.
46. Song, *The Rise of the Korean Economy*, pp. 144-45.
47. Amsden, *Asia's Next Giant*, p. 298.
48. Ibid., p. 302.
49. Ibid., p. 317.
50. "How South Korea Scares Japan," *The Economist*, 14 May 1988.
51. Amsden, *Asia's Next Giant*, p. 297.
52. Song, *The Rise of the Korean Economy*, p. 118.
53. Tony Michell, "Domestic Bliss: Lessons From Korean Economic Development 1962-82," *Euro Asia Business Review* 2, no. 2 (1983): 26.
54. Song, *The Rise of the Korean Economy*, p. 118.

4: Policy Implementation:
State Regulation of International Economic Activity

1. "A Survey of South Korea," *The Economist*, 21 May 1988.
2. Luedde-Neurath, "State Intervention and Export-Oriented Development in South Korea," pp. 78-79.
3. Ibid., p. 79.
4. Ibid., p. 81.
5. Karl Schoenberger, "If It's Fancy, Don't Market It in Seoul."
6. For more information on the South Korean automobile industry see Chapter 8 of Bello and Rosenfeld, *Dragons in Distress* and Sung-Hwan Jo, *The Car Industry in the Republic of Korea*, International Employ-

ment Policies Working Paper No. 22 (Geneva: International Labor Organization, August 1988).

7. Jo, *The Car Industry in the Republic of Korea*, p. ii.
8. As quoted in "The Government Turns Thumbs Down," *Korean Economic Report* (September 1990): 37.
9. Schoenberger, "If It's Fancy, Don't Market It in Seoul."
10. Ibid.
11. Damon Darlin, "South Korea Regresses on Opening Markets, Trade Partners Say," *Wall Street Journal*, 12 June 1990.
12. Ibid.
13. Luedde-Neurath, "State Intervention and Export-Oriented Development in South Korea," p. 81.
14. Bohn-young Koo, "The Role of Direct Foreign Investment in Korea's Recent Economic Growth," in *Foreign Trade and Investment* , p. 178.
15. Russell Mardon, "The State and the Effective Control of Foreign Capital: The Case of South Korea," *World Politics*, no. 43 (October 1990): 121.
16. Ibid., p. 122.
17. Ibid., p. 129.
18. Lim, *Dependent Development in Korea, 1963-1979*, pp. 114-15.
19. Ibid., p. 114.
20. Mardon, "The State and the Effective Control of Foreign Capital," p. 117.
21. Luedde-Neurath, "State Intervention and Export-Oriented Development in South Korea," pp. 86-87.
22. Mardon, "The State and the Effective Control of Foreign Capital," p. 134.
23. These case studies are based largely on information presented in Mardon, "The State and the Effective Control of Foreign Capital."

5: Japanese Imperialism, the State, and Class Struggle

1. Amsden, *Asia's Next Giant*, p. 3.
2. Song, *The Rise of the Korean Economy*, p. 239.
3. For example, see "Learning from South Korea," my review of Amsden's book, *Asia's Next Giant* in *Monthly Review* 42, no. 4 (September 1990).
4. Bruce Cumings, *The Origins of the Korean War: Liberation and The Emergence of Separate Regimes, 1945-47* (Princeton, NJ: Princeton University Press, 1981), p. 10.
5. Ki-baik Lee, *A New History of Korea*, trans. Edward W. Wagner with Edward J. Shultz (Cambridge, MA: Harvard University Press, 1984), p. 287.
6. Herbert P. Bix, "Regional Integration: Japan and South Korea in America's Asian Policy," in *Without Parallel*, p. 180.
7. Lee, *A New History of Korea*, p. 314.
8. Ibid., p. 319.

9. Bruce Cumings, "American Policy and Korean Liberation," in *Without Parallel*, p. 49.

10. Lee, *A New History of Korea*, p. 348.

11. Ibid., p. 351.

12. Ibid., p. 349.

13. Ibid.

14. Bruce Cumings, "The Origins and Development of the Northeast Asian Political Economy: Industrial Sectors, Product Cycles, and Political Consequences," in *The Political Economy of the New Asian Industrialization*, p. 45.

15. Lee, *A New History of Korea*, pp. 354-55.

16. Ibid., p. 358.

17. Dae-Sook Suh, *The Korean Communist Movement, 1918-1948* (Princeton, NJ: Princeton University Press, 1967), p. 202.

18. Cumings, *The Origins of the Korean War*, pp. 11-12.

19. For further discussion of this point see Bruce Cumings, "The Origins and Development of the Northeast Asian Political Economy: Industrial Sectors, Product Cycles, and Political Consequences."

20. Lee, *A New History of Korea*, p. 317.

21. Nym Wales and Kim San, *Song of Ariran: A Korean Communist in the Chinese Revolution* (1941; San Francisco: Ramparts Press, 1972), p. 82.

22. Cumings, *The Origins of the Korean War*, p. 19.

23. Bong-youn Choy, *A History of the Korean Reunification Movement: Its Issues and Prospects* (Peoria, IL: Research Committee on Korean Unification, Institute of International Studies, Bradley University, 1984), p. 25.

24. Suh, *The Korean Communist Movement*, p. 132.

25. Urban Industrial Mission, *Short History of South Korea's Labor Movement: Historical Overview and Some Information on Current Developments* (Inchon, South Korea: Urban Industrial Mission, 1988), p. 2.

26. Ibid., pp. 2-3.

27. Ibid., p. 5.

28. Cumings, *The Origins of the Korean War*, p. 30.

29. Ibid., p. 28.

30. Ibid.

6: U.S. Imperialism, the State, and Class Struggle

1. As quoted in Bong-youn Choy, *A History of the Korean Reunification Movement*, p. 10.

2. As quoted in ibid.

3. Cumings, "American Policy and Korean Liberation," p. 46.

4. As quoted in Choy, *A History of the Korean Reunification Movement*, p. 11.

5. Cumings, *The Origins of the Korean War*, p. 77.

6. Choy, *A History of the Korean Reunification Movement*, p. 36.

7. Cumings, *The Origins of the Korean War*, p. 95.
8. Ibid., p. 270.
9. As quoted in ibid., p. 200.
10. Choy, *A History of the Korean Reunification Movement*, p. 52.
11. Ibid., p. 57.
12. Jon Halliday, "The United Nations and Korea," in *Without Parallel*, p. 116.
13. Halliday and Cumings, *Korea: The Unknown War*, p. 41.
14. Ibid., p. 85.
15. Ibid., p. 146.
16. Ibid., p. 200.
17. Ibid., pp. 210-11.
18. James B. Palais, "'Democracy' in South Korea, 1948-72," in *Without Parallel*, p. 326.
19. Kim, *Divided Korea*, p. 209.

7: U.S. and Japanese Influence on the Organization and Performance of the South Korean Economy

1. Gavan McCormack, "Japan and South Korea, 1965-1975: Ten Years of 'Normalization,'" in *Korea, North and South: The Deepening Crisis*, ed. Gavan McCormack and Mark Selden (New York: Monthly Review Press, 1978), p. 174.
2. See Tony Michell, "Administrative Traditions and Economic Decision Making in South Korea," *IDS Bulletin* 15, no 2 (1984).
3. As quoted in Michell, *From a Developing to a Newly Industrialized Country*, p. 11.
4. Kim, *Divided Korea*, p. 258.
5. Cumings, "The Origins and Development of the Northeast Asian Political Economy: Industrial Sectors, Product Cycles, and Political Consequences," p. 67.
6. James Stentzel, "Seoul's Second Bonanza," *Far Eastern Economic Review*, 30 July 1973, p 43.
7. Frank Baldwin, "America's Rented Troops: South Koreans in Vietnam," *Bulletin of Concerned Asian Scholars* (October-December 1975): 39.
8. Stentzel, "Seoul's Second Bonanza," p. 43.
9. Kim, *Divided Korea*, p. 264.
10. Ibid., p. 264.
11. Thorkil Casse, *The Non-Conventional Approach to Stability: The Case of South Korea—An Analysis of Macro-Economic Policy, 1979-84* (Copenhagen: Center for Development Research, 1985), p. 65.
12. Nakano Kenji, "Japan's Overseas Investment Patterns and FTZs," *AMPO: Japan-Asia Quarterly Review* 8 (1977): 33.

13. Ibid., p. 37.
14. As quoted in Tsuchiya Takeo, "Masan: An Epitome of the Japan-ROK Relationship, *AMPO: Japan-Asia Quarterly Review* 8, no. 4 and 9, nos. 1 and 2 (1977): 61.
15. As quoted in ibid., p. 59.
16. Bix, "Regional Integration: Japan and South Korea in America's Asian Policy," p. 217.
17. For more discussion of the Japanese role in South Korea's industrialization see Kenji, "Japan's Overseas Investment Patterns and FTZs," p. 48, and McCormack, "Japan and South Korea, 1965-1975: Ten Years of 'Normalization,' " p. 179.
18. Paul Ensor, "Two Way Trade-off," *Far Eastern Economic Review*, 6 March 1986.
19. Paul Ensor, "Caught in the Machine," *Far Eastern Economic Review*, 18 September 1986, p. 63.
20. Bello and Rosenfeld, *Dragons in Distress*, p. 114.
21. As quoted in Ensor, "Caught in the Machine," *Far Eastern Economic Review*, 18 September 1986, p. 62.
22. Ibid. p. 62; "Machinery Imports Culprit of Trade Deficit with Japan," *Korea Times*, 1 August 1991.
23. Steven Brull, "Success Breeds High-Tech Skinflints, S. Koreans Say," *Los Angeles Times*, 19 July 1990, p. D3.
24. "Is Japan a Reluctant Supplier?," *Business Korea* (July 1990): 77.
25. Damon Darlin, "Korean Technology Lag May Spell Trouble for Economy's Recovery," *Asian Wall Street Journal Weekly*, 6 August 1990.
26. Ibid.
27. As quoted in "Japan Reluctant to Transfer Technologies to Korea," *Korea Herald*, 18 September 1990.
28. Leslie Helm, "Curing a Copycat Syndrome," *Los Angeles Times*, 8 April 1991.
29. Damon Darlin, "Korea's Goldstar Faces a Harsh New World under Democracy," *Wall Street Journal*, 8 November 1989.
30. "Japanese Investment in Korea: A Rocky Marriage," *Business Korea* (July 1990).
31. Mark Clifford, "Goodbye to All That," *Far Eastern Economic Review*, 13 December 1990, p. 64.
32. Chung-In Moon, "Irony of Interdependence: Emerging Trade Frictions between South Korea and the United States," in *Alliance under Tension: The Evolution of South Korean-U.S. Relations*, ed. Manwoo Lee, Ronald D. McLaurin, and Chung-In Moon (Boulder, CO: Westview Press, 1988), p. 52.
33. "In Search of a Better Balance," *Business Korea* (July 1989): 16.
34. As quoted in Ramon Moreno, "Exchange Rates and Trade Adjustment in Taiwan and Korea," *Economic Review, Federal Reserve Bank of San Francisco*, no. 2 (Spring 1989): 30.

35. Joseph P. Manguno, "Korean VCR Makers' Invasion of U.S. Backfires as Profit Margins Disappear," *Wall Street Journal*, 5 April 1989.
36. "Export Profit Margins Decreasing," *Korea Economic Weekly*, 16 September 1991, p. 1.
37. Leslie Helm, "A Bumpier Road Ahead," *Los Angeles Times*, 18 March 1991.
38. "Mexico, A New Economic Era," *Business Week*, 13 November 1990, p. 103.
39. Ibid., p. 104.

8: The Political Economy of Growth and Crisis: 1961 to 1972

1. Kim, *Divided Korea*, p. 234.
2. Ibid., p. 232-34.
3. U.S. House of Representatives, *Investigation of Korean-American Relations* (Washington, D.C.: U.S. Government Printing Office, 1978), p. 227.
4. Kim, *Divided Korea*, pp. 240-41.
5. Jung-en Woo, *Race to the Swift: State and Finance in Korean Industrialization* (New York: Columbia University Press, 1991), p. 107.
6. Kim, *Divided Korea.*, p. 257.
7. Ibid., p. 264.
8. U.S. House of Representatives, *Investigation of Korean-American Relations*, p. 242.
9. Ibid., p. 243.
10. Ibid., p. 234.
11. Christian Institute for the Study of Justice and Development, *Social Justice Indicators in Korea*, 2nd ed. (Seoul: Minjungsa, 1987), p. 91.
12. Bernie Wideman, "The Plight of the South Korean Peasant," in *Without Parallel: The American-Korean Relationship Since 1945*, p. 276.
13. Kim Chang Soo, "Marginalization, Development and the Korean Workers' Movement," *AMPO: Japan-Asia Quarterly Review* 9, no. 3 (July-November 1977): 22.
14. McCormack, "The South Korean Economy: GNP versus the People," in *Korea, North and South: The Deepening Crisis*, p. 103.
15. Woo, *Race to the Swift*, p. 105.
16. Ibid., p. 126.
17. U.S. House of Representatives, *Investigation of Korean-American Relations*, p. 24.
18. Amsden, *Asia's Next Giant*, p. 76
19. Ogle, *South Korea*, p. 43.
20. Wideman, *Without Parallel*, p. 274.
21. Soo, "Marginalization, Development and the Korean Workers' Movement," p. 29.
22. Ibid., p. 31.
23. Young-ock Kim, *The Position of Women Workers in Manufacturing Industries in South Korea: A Marxist-Feminist Analysis*, Working

Paper—Sub-Series on Women's History and Development No. 6 (Ithaca, N.Y.: Cornell University Press, 1986), p. 40.
24. Ibid., p. 50.
25. As quoted in Jang Jip Choi, *Labor and the Authoritarian State: Labor Unions in South Korean Manufacturing Industries, 1961-1980* (Seoul, South Korea: Korea University Press, 1989), pp. 127-28.
26. As quoted in ibid., p. 125.
27. Ogle, *South Korea*, p. 20.
28. Bernie Wideman, "Korean Chauvinism," *Far Eastern Economic Review*, 5 March 1973, p. 5.
29. As quoted in Wideman in "The Plight of the South Korean Peasant," p. 299.
30. Kim, *Divided Korea*, p. 279.
31. As quoted in Sugwon Kang, "The Politics and Poetry of Kim Chi-ha," *Bulletin of Concerned Asian Scholars* 9, no. 2 (1977): 4.
32. Gerhard Breidenstein, "Capitalism in South Korea," in *Without Paralle*, p. 257.
33. Choi, *Labor and the Authoritarian State*, p. 88.
34. U.S. House of Representatives, *Investigation of Korean-American Relations*, pp. 39-40.
35. "Busy Jailers," *Far Eastern Economic Review*, 28 May 1973.

9: The Political Economy of Growth and Crisis: 1973 to 1981

1. Michell, *From a Developing to a Newly Industrialized Country*, p. 74.
2. Amsden, *Asia's Next Giant*, p. 116.
3. Woo, *Race to the Swift*, p. 155.
4. Ibid., p. 133.
5. Song, *The Rise of the Korean Economy*, pp. 60-61. Inflation is measured by the GNP deflator.
6. Stephen Haggard and Chung-In Moon, "The South Korean State in the International Economy: Liberal, Dependent, or Mercantile?" in *The Antinomies of Interdependence: National Welfare and the International Division of Labor*, ed. John Gerard Ruggie (New York: Columbia University Press, 1983), p. 176.
7. Woo, *Race to the Swift*, p. 142.
8. Haggard and Moon, "The South Korean State in the International Economy," pp. 176-77.
9. Tim Shorrock, "South Korea: The New Regime Brings More Repression, and a Return to Reprocessing Goods for Sale in Japan and the U.S.," *Multinational Monitor* (June 1981): 20.
10. As quoted in Haggard and Moon, "The South Korean State in the International Economy," p. 181.
11. UNCTAD Secretariat, *Fibres and Textiles: Dimensions of Corporate Marketing Structures* (New York: United Nations, 1980), p. 240.
12. Amsden, *Asia's Next Giant*, p. 100.

13. Russell G. Kincaid, "Korea's Major Adjustment Effort," *Finance and Development* (December 1983): 21.
14. As quoted in T.K., *Letters from South Korea*, ed. Sekai, translated by David L. Swain (Tokyo: Iwanami Shoten Publishers, 1976), pp. 26-27.
15. Hagen Koo, "The Political Economy of Income Distribution in South Korea: The Impact of the State's Industrialization Policies," *World Development* 12, no. 10 (1984): 1036.
16. Ibid., p. 1030.
17. Kim Dae Jung, *Mass-Participatory Economy* (Lanham, Md.: University Press of America, 1985), p. 37.
18. Asia Watch Committee, *Human Rights in Korea* (Washington, D.C.: Asia Watch, 1985), p. 171.
19. Amsden, *Asia's Next Giant*, p. 196.
20. Choi, *Labor and the Authoritarian State*, p. 303. One of the more serious problems with the consumer price index as a measure of cost of living is that it does not include housing costs, one of the biggest and fastest-growing categories of consumer expenditure.
21. Michell, *From a Developing to a Newly Industrialized Country*, pp. 110-111.
22. Jip, *Labor and the Authoritarian State*, p. 301.
23. Ibid., pp. 302-4.
24. Ibid., p. 304.
25. Ibid., p. 302.
26. Kim, *The Position of Women Workers in Manufacturing Industries in South Korea*, pp. 50-51.
27. *On Korean Laborers: A Perspective Paper and Data Base* (Seoul, South Korea), p. 48.
28. Bello and Rosenfeld, *Dragons in Distress*, p. 24.
29. As quoted in Kim Chang Soo, "Marginalization, Development and the Korean Workers' Movement," p. 34.
30. Christian Institute for the Study of Justice and Development, *Social Justice Indicators in Korea*, p. 122.
31. As quoted in Annette Fuentes and Barbara Ehrenreich, *Women in the Global Factory* (Boston: South End Press, 1983), p. 22.
32. U.S. House of Representatives, *Investigation of Korean-American Relations*, p. 39.
33. Choi, *Labor and the Authoritarian State*, p. 80.
34. Ibid., p. 129.
35. Ogle, *South Korea*, p. 86.
36. Soo, "Marginalization, Development and the Korean Workers' Movement," p. 37.
37. As quoted in Ogle, *South Korea*.
38. Bello and Rosenfeld, *Dragons in Distress*, p. 85.
39. T.K., *Letters from South Korea*, p. 85.
40. Korea Christian Alliance for Democracy and Reunification, *A Time to Breakdown, and a Time to Build: The People's Movement for Self-*

Reliant National Independence, Genuine Democracy and National Reunification (Seoul: 1989), p. 12.

41. Asia Watch Committee, *Human Rights in Korea*, p. 30.
42. Michael A. Launius, "The State and Industrial Labor in South Korea," *Bulletin of Concerned Asian Scholars* 13, no. 4 (1984): 6.
43. Asia Watch Committee, *Human Rights in Korea*, p. 37.
44. "Labor Problems: Long Term Peace Prospect Looks Poor," *Far Eastern Economic Review*, 19 July 1984, p. 74.
45. Launius, "The State and Industrial Labor in South Korea," pp. 8-9.
46. As quoted in "Buying Time for Change," *Far Eastern Economic Review*, 12 November 1982, p. 40.
47. As quoted in Choi Sung-il, "Anti-Americanism in South Korea: From Kwangju to Reunification," a paper presented at the 1991 annual meeting of the American Political Science Association, Washington, D.C., *Los Angeles Times*, 8 August 1980, p. 3.
48. As quoted in Bong-youn Choy, *A History of the Korean Reunification Movement: Its Issues and Prospects*, p. 147.
49. Woo, *Race to the Swift*, p. 187.

10: The Gathering Storm:
Economic Trends

1. Clyde Haberman, "South Korea's Future Pivots on Role Chun Chooses," *Oregonian*, 12 April 1987, p. A3.
2. See Amsden, *Asia's Next Giant*, p. 132, and "Industrial South Korea," *Far Eastern Economic Review*, 19 July 1984, p. 43.
3. Amsden, *Asia's Next Giant*, p. 116.
4. "Industrial South Korea," *Far Eastern Economic Review*, 19 July 1984, p. 43.
5. Christian Institute for the Study of Justice and Development, *Social Justice Indicators in Korea*, pp. 21-22.
6. Ibid., p. 22.
7. Woo, *Race to the Swift*, p. 197.
8. As quoted in ibid., p. 199.
9. Bello and Rosenfeld, *Dragons in Distress*, p. 73.
10. See Selig S. Harrison, "Is South Korea Going to Be the Next Philippines?" *New York Times*, 25 January 1987; and Susan Moffat, "Koreans Test Democratic Institutions By Pressing Demands in Chun Inquiry," *Asian Wall Street Journal Weekly*, 21 November 1988.
11. Interestingly, Roh Tae Woo, the current president, was head of the Ministry of Home Affairs at the time many of these frauds took place.
12. Woo, *Race to the Swift*, p. 200.
13. See, for example, the editorial, "Dubious Image of Korean Economy," *Business Korea* (February 1991): 7.
14. For purposes of comparison with the inflation figures given in Chapter

9, the 1991 rate of inflation, as measured by the GNP deflator, was officially 10.9 percent, the highest in ten years.

15. Woo, *Race to the Swift*, pp. 200-201.

16. Karl Schoenberger, "Speculators Fuel Real Estate Fever in South Korea," *Los Angeles Times*, 18 March 1990.

17. Ibid.

18. Bello and Rosenfeld, *Dragons in Distress*, p. 71.

19. As quoted in Joseph P. Manguno, "Middle Class Anger Focuses on Economic Woes," *Asian Wall Street Journal Weekly*, 14 May 1990, p. 2.

20. Joseph P. Manguno, "Spiraling Property Costs Dash Dreams of Young Koreans to Buy a First Home," *Asian Wall Street Journal Weekly*, 23 October 1989, p. 18.

21. As quoted in "Denying Crisis, Roh Tries Another Tack to Restore Confidence in the Economy," *Asian Wall Street Journal Weekly*, 14 May 1990, p. 2.

22. Sohn Jie-Ae and Cho Sun-young, "Building Strength for World Prominence," *Business Korea* (May 1991).

23. Adding to the complexity of the state-chaebol relationship is the fact that: "Many chaebol families . . . have succeeded in establishing alliances by marriage with the nation's power elite. Children of the late President Park, former President Chun Doo Hwan and President Roh have married sons or daughters of big businessmen. The newspaper *Dong-A Ilbo* says 25 of Korea's top 100 business groups enjoy 'marriage alliances' with current or former government leaders. "See Sam Jameson, "Families Still Keep Grip on S. Korea's Conglomerates," *Los Angeles Times*, 10 December 1990.

24. Woo, *Race to the Swift*, p. 188.

25. Ibid., p. 188.

26. Eduardo Lachica, "Korea Launches Offensive to Ward Off U.S. Trade Sanctions," *Asian Wall Street Journal Weekly*, 17 April 1989.

27. "Korean Manufacturers' Earnings," *Wall Street Journal*, 12 June 1992.

28. "Capital Investment Growth Poised For Slowdown During 1992: KDB," *Korea Economic Weekly*, 25 May 1992.

29. Damon Darlin, "South Korea Regresses on Opening Markets, Trade Partners Say," *Wall Street Journal*, 12 June 1990, p. A7.

30. Kim Jin-Moon, "Building a New Image," *Business Korea* (December 1991): 29.

31. See Chapters 6, 7, and 8 of Bello and Rosenfeld, *Dragons in Distress*, for a more detailed examination of these three industries.

32. "Overseas Korean Operations Remitting Little of Profits," *Korea Economic Weekly*, 16 September 1991, p. 16.

33. "Computer Makers Facing Worst of Times," *Korea Economic Weekly*, 14 October 1991, p. 19.

34. Sohn Jie-Ae, "Strong Image, Weak Underbelly," *Business Korea* (September 1991): 25.

35. Ibid.

36. Damon Darlin and Joseph B. White, "GM Venture in Korea Nears

End, Betraying Firm's Fond Hopes," *Wall Street Journal*, 16 January 1992, p. A1.

37. Ibid.
38. Leslie Helm, "A Bumpier Road Ahead," *Los Angeles Times*, 18 March 1991, p. D1.
39. Ibid.
40. "Seoul Unveils Plan to Develop Nation's High-Tech Industries," *Asian Wall Street Journal Weekly*, 16 October 1989.
41. Sam Jameson, "South Korea Plans Major Push Into High-Tech Fields," *Los Angeles Times*, 11 December 1989, p. D9.
42. As quoted in "Seoul Unveils Plan to Develop Nation's High-Tech Industries," *Asian Wall Street Journal Weekly*, 16 October 1989.
43. Ibid.
44. Leslie Helm, "Curing a Copycat Syndrome," *Los Angeles Times*, 8 April 1991.

**11: The Gathering Storm:
Political Trends**

1. "South Korea: An Impromptu Performance," *The Economist*, 18 August 1990, p. 16.
2. "Justice for the Alienated," *Activity News: Newsletter of the National Council of Churches* (March-April 1990): 2.
3. Christian Institute for the Study of Justice and Development, *Social Justice Indicators in Korea*, p. 95.
4. Bello and Rosenfeld, *Dragons in Distress*, p. 86.
5. Christian Institute for the Study of Justice and Development, *Lost Victory: An Overview of the Korean People's Struggle for Democracy in 1987* (Seoul: Minjungsa, 1988), p. 254.
6. Bello and Rosenfeld, *Dragons in Distress*, p. 88.
7. Christian Institute for the Study of Justice and Development, *Lost Victory*, pp. 258-59.
8. "South Korea: An Impromptu Performance," *The Economist*, 18 August 1990, p. 17.
9. Susan Moffat, "Korea Farmers Ready to Wage Fierce Battle Against U.S. Imports," *Asian Wall Street Journal Weekly*, 23 January 1989.
10. Kim Ae-dai, "The Farmers' Movement in South Korea," *Korea Report* 3, no. 1 (July 1989): 22.
11. As quoted in "National Farmers' Organization Formalized," *Korea Update*, no. 98-99 (May-June 1990): 13.
12. Selig H. Harrison, "A Chance for Detente in Korea," *World Policy Journal* (Fall 1991): 608.
13. Bello and Rosenfeld, *Dragons in Distress*, p. 39.
14. Christian Institute for the Study of Justice and Development, *Lost Victory*, pp. 95-96.
15. As quoted in ibid., p. 97.

16. Peter Leyden and David Bank, "Evictions Threaten the Poverty-Stricken," *International Herald Tribune*, 5 July 1989, p. 9.

17. Choongsoo Kim, *Labor Market Developments of Korea in Macroeconomic Perspectives*, KDI Working Paper No. 8909 (Seoul: Korea Development Institute, April 1989), p. 53.

18. Ibid., p. 16.

19. Ibid., pp. 16-17.

20. "Thousands of Street Vendors Fight to Protect Livelihood," *Korea Update*, no. 92 (August 1989): 7.

21. "Despite Ban, Chonnohyop Founded January 22,"*Korea Update*, no. 96 (January-February 1990): 5

22. Mark Clifford, "Kicking Up a Stink," *Far Eastern Economic Review*, 18 October 1990, p. 72.

23. Ibid.

24. Ibid.

25. Ibid.

26. "Highlighting Health to Cover Up Contamination?" *Business Korea* (September 1990): 54.

27. Bellow and Rosenfeld, *Dragons in Distress*, pp. 101-2.

28. Clifford, "Kicking Up a Stink," p. 72.

29. "Curbing a Pollution Economy," *South* (February 1991): 20-21.

30. The following history of environmental activism is largely informed by the work of Su-Hoon Lee. For a more complete discussion see his paper with David A. Smith, "Antisystemic Movements in South Korea: The Rise of Environmental Activism," which was presented at the 15th PEWS Conference, University of Hawaii, March 28-30, 1991.

31. Bellow and Rosenfeld, *Dragons in Distress.*, pp. 108-109.

32. As quoted in "Curbing a Pollution Economy," p. 21.

33. Kim, *The Position of Women Workers in Manufacturing Industries in South Korea*, p. 47.

34. Ibid., p. 50.

35. *On Korean Laborers: A Perspective Paper and Data Base* (Seoul, 1988), p. 48.

36. Ibid., p. 49.

37. *Women Take the Forefront: Women's Movement in South Korea* (Washington, D.C.: Korea Information and Resource Center, August 1991).

38. Liz McGregor, "Women's Slow Progress," *International Herald Tribune*, 5 June 1989, p. 10.

39. Barry Renfrew, "Korea's Growth Takes a Toll on Workers," *Asian Wall Street Journal Weekly*, 9 January 1989, p. 11.

40. Ibid., p. 11.

41. Peter Maass, "Success of Korean Economy Comes at High Cost for Workers," *Oregonian*, 30 April 1989, p. A7.

42. Steven Jones, "Asia Grows Wealthier, but Disparities Widen," *Asian Wall Street Weekly*, 27 November 1989.

43. Ogle, *South Korea*, p. 111.

44. "The Unrest That Could Stall Seoul's Growth Engine," *Business Week*, 5 August 1985, p. 40.
45. Damon Darlin, "Labor Unrest Poses Threat to Economic Stability," *The Asian Wall Street Journal Weekly*, 26 February 1990.
46. Clifford, "Labor Strikes Out," *Far Eastern Economic Review*, 27 August 1987, p. 16.
47. Darlin, "Labor Unrest Poses Threat to Economic Stability."
48. Christian Institute for the Study of Justice and Development, "Transitional Conjuncture," *Korean Situationer*, no. 12 (June-August 1988, p. 29.
49. Ibid., p. 15.
50. Darlin, "Labor Unrest Poses Threat to Economic Stability."
51. Lho Joo Hyoung, "Workers' Power," *Korea Business World* (June 1989): 28.
52. Chunkyojo, *Movement for a Genuine Education* (Seoul: Chunkyojo [Korean Teachers' and Educational Workers' Union], date unknown), p. 5.
53. As quoted in "Korea in the 80's: Decade of the Workers," *Asian Labor Update*, no. 1 (February-April 1990): 9.
54. "Unions of 16 Large Plants Form Alliance," *Korea Labor: Monthly Newsletter of the Korea Research and Information Center* (Seoul), no. 4 (December 1990): 6.
55. "Korea: An Achievement That We Still Exist," *Asian Labor Update*, no. 6 (January 1992): 2.
56. Ibid., p. 1.
57. As quoted in ibid., p. 3.

12: South Korea at the Crossroads

1. For an insightful discussion of the rise of anti-Americanism in South Korea, see Tim Shorrock, "The Struggle for Democracy in South Korea in the 1980s and the Rise of Anti-Americanism," *Third World Quarterly* (October 1986).
2. As quoted in ibid., p. 1216.
3. The events of June are well described in Christian Institute for the Study of Justice aqnd Development, *Lost Victory*, pp. 101-22.
4. As quoted in Jae Jung Suh, "Roh Tae Woo's Human Rights Record," *Korea Report* 10 (February-March 1990): 19.
5. As quoted in David Easter, "Students March for Reunification; Police Arrest 800," *Guardian*, 22 June 1988.
6. As quoted in Ogle, *South Korea*, pp. 165-66.
7. As quoted in Marian Louie, "South Korean Mass Movement Mushrooms," *Frontline*, 3 July 1989.
8. As quoted in Paul H. Kreisberg, "Democracy Adds to Strife over Korean Economy," *Los Angeles Times*, 12 July 1989.
9. Mark Clifford, "The Return of Korea Inc.," *Far Eastern Economic Review*, 28 December 1989.

10. "Crackdown in Korea," *Korea Update* 91 (July 1989): 3.
11. As quoted in Easter, "South Korea Blames Labor for Economic Woes."
12. Ibid.
13. "National Security Law Revisions Railroaded in 35 Seconds," *Korea Report* 13 (August-September 1991): 3.
14. "1991 Korea Human Rights Situation," *Korea Update* 105 (January 1992): 7.
15. As quoted in "ILO Admits South Korea," *Korea Update* 105 (January 1992): 8.
16. As quoted in "Chonnohyup Supporters Association Formed," *Korea Update* 97 (March 1990): 17.
17. "Seoul Is Launching Two Bodies to Study Economic Policy," *Asian Wall Street Journal Weekly*, 10 July 1989, p. 11.
18. Although the U.S. government is said to have engaged in behind-the-scenes maneuvering in support of Roh's call for direct election of the president in 1987 over Chun's plan to renew military dictatorship, there is strong reason to believe that this U.S. endorsement of democracy over dictatorship was made only for tactical reasons, based on the fear that a continuation of military dictatorship at that time might trigger an uncontrollable social revolution. The U.S. government did everything possible to weaken and discredit the democratic movement's direct election campaign before finally shifting positions at the last minute to bolster Roh's credentials as a reformer and help him get elected.
19. See the concluding chapter in Bello and Rosenfeld, *Dragons in Distress*, for a valuable discussion of an alternative economic strategy for South Korea, Taiwan, and Singapore that is quite similar to the one highlighted here for South Korea.

BIBLIOGRAPHY

Activity News: Newsletter of the National Council of Churches. "Justice for the Alienated." March-April 1990.

Ahn, Junghyo. *White Badge: A Novel of Korea.* New York: Soho Press, 1989.

Amsden, Alice H. *Asia's Next Giant: South Korea and Late Industrialization.* New York: Oxford University Press, 1989.

Asia Watch Committee. *Retreat from Reform: Labor Rights and Freedom of Expression in South Korea.* Washington D.C.: Asia Watch, 1990.

————. *Human Rights in Korea.* Washington D.C.: Asia Watch, 1985.

Asian Labor Update. "Korea in the 80s: Decade of the Workers." No. 1, February-April 1990.

————. "Korea: An Achievement That We Still Exist." No. 6, January 1992.

Asian Wall Street Journal Weekly. "Denying Crisis, Roh Tries Another Tack to Restore Confidence in the Economy." 14 May 1990.

————. "Seoul Is Launching Two Bodies to Study Economic Policies." 10 July 1989.

————. "Seoul Unveils Plan to Develop Nation's High-Tech Industries." 16 October 1989.

Balassa, Bela. "The Role of Foreign Trade in the Economic Development of Korea." In *Foreign Trade and Investment: Economic Development in the Newly Industrializing Asian Countries,* ed. Walter Galenson. Madison, WI: University of Wisconsin Press, 1985.

Balassa, Bela, and John Williamson. *Adjusting to Success: Balance of Payments Policy in the East Asian NICs.* Washington D.C.: Institute for International Economics, June 1987.

Baldwin, Frank. "America's Rented Troops: South Koreans in Vietnam." *Bulletin of Concerned Asian Scholars.* October-December 1975.

Bank of Korea. *Economic Statistics Yearbook.* Seoul: Bank of Korea, various years.

————. *Quarterly Economic Review.* Seoul: Bank of Korea, various years.

Bello, Walden, and Stephanie Rosenfeld. *Dragons in Distress: Asia's Miracle Economies in Crisis.* San Francisco, CA: Institute for Food and Development Policy, 1990.

Bix, Herbert P. "Regional Integration: Japan and South Korea in America's Asian Policy." In *Without Parallel: The American-Korean Relationship Since 1945*, ed. Frank Baldwin. New York: Pantheon Books, 1974.

Breidenstein, Gerhard. "Capitalism in South Korea." In *Without Parallel: The American-Korean Relationship Since 1945*, ed. Frank Baldwin. New York: Pantheon Books, 1974.

Brull, Steven. "Success Breeds High-Tech Skinflints, S. Koreans Say." *Los Angeles Times*, 9 July 1990.

Business Korea. "Economic Planning Board: Looking for a New Role." August 1991.

————. "Dubious Image of Korean Economy." February 1991.

————. "Its Time to Pay the Price for Dependency on Foreign Knowhow." February 1991.

————. "Highlighting Health to Cover Up Contamination?" September 1990.

————. "Is Japan a Reluctant Supplier?" July 1990.

————. "Japanese Investment in Korea: A Rocky Marriage." July 1990.

————. "In Search of a Better Balance." July 1989.

————. "The Chaebol Draw Fire." June 1989.

Business Week. "Mexico, A New Economic Era." 13 November 1990.

————. "Korea's Powerhouses Are Under Siege." 20 November 1989.

————. "Has the Korean Miracle Run Out of Magic." 3 July 1989.

————. "The Koreans Are Coming." 23 December 1985.

————. "The Unrest That Could Stall Seoul's Growth Engine." 5 August 1985.

Casse, Thorkil. *The Non-Conventional Approach to Stability: The Case of South Korea—An Analysis of Macro-Economic Policy, 1979-84*. Copenhagen: Center for Development Research, 1985.

Cho, Sun-Young. "Fear of Social Malaise Sparks Restrictions." *Business Korea*, September 1990.

Choi, Jang Jip. *Labor and the Authoritarian State: Labor Unions in South Korean Manufacturing Industries, 1961-1980*. Seoul: Korea University Press, 1989.

Choi, Sung-il. "Anti-Americanism in South Korea: From Kwangju to Reunification." Paper presented at annual meeting of American Political Science Association, Washington, D.C., 1991.

Choy, Bong-youn. *A History of the Korean Reunification Movement: Its Issues and Prospects*. Peoria, IL: Research Committee on Korean Unification, Institute of International Studies, Bradley University, 1984.

Christian Institute for the Study of Justice and Development. "Transitional Conjuncture." *Korean Situationer*, no. 12, June-August 1988.

————. *Lost Victory: An Overview of the Korean People's Struggle for Democracy in 1987*. Seoul: Minjungsa, 1988.

————. *Social Justice Indicators in Korea* (2nd ed.). Seoul: Minjungsa, 1987.

Chunkyojo. *Movement for a Genuine Education.* Seoul: Chunkyojo (Korean Teachers' and Educational Workers' Union), date unknown.

Clifford, Mark. "Goodbye to All That," *Far Eastern Economic Review.* 13 December 1990.

————. "Kicking Up a Stink." *Far Eastern Economic Review,* 18 October 1990.

————. "The Return of Korea Inc." *Far Eastern Economic Review,* 28 December 1989.

————. "Appearances Are Deceptive." *Far Eastern Economic Review,* 11 February 1988.

————. "Labor Strikes Out." *Far Eastern Economic Review,* 27 August 1987.

Cumings, Bruce. "The Origins and Development of the Northeast Asian Political Economy: Industrial Sectors, Product Cycles, and Political Consequences." In *The Political Economy of the New Asian Industrialization,* ed. Frederic C. Deyo. Ithaca, NY: Cornell University Press, 1987.

————. *The Origins of the Korean War: Liberation and the Emergence of Separate Regimes, 1945-47.* Princeton, NJ: Princeton University Press, 1981.

————. "American Policy and Korean Liberation." In *Without Parallel: The American-Korean Relationship Since 1945,* ed. Frank Baldwin. New York: Pantheon Books, 1974.

Darlin, Damon, and Joseph B. White. "GM Venture in Korea Nears End, Betraying Firm's Fond Hopes." *Wall Street Journal,* 16 January 1992.

Darlin, Damon. "Korea's 30 Biggest Firms Told to Shrink." *Wall Street Journal,* 30 April 1991.

Darlin, Damon. "Korean Technology Lag May Spell Trouble for Economy's Recovery." *Asian Wall Street Journal Weekly,* 6 August 1990,

————. "South Korea Regresses on Opening Markets, Trade Partners Say." *Wall Street Journal,* 12 June 1990.

————. "Labor Unrest Poses Threat to Economic Stability." *Asian Wall Street Journal Weekly,* 26 February 1990.

————. "Korea's Goldstar Faces a Harsh New World Under Democracy." *Wall Street Journal,* 8 November 1989.

Easter, David. "South Korea Blames Labor for Economic Woes." *Guardian,* 4 April 1990.

————. "Students March for Reunification; Police Arrest 800." *Guardian,* 22 June 1988.

The Economic Planning Board. *Major Statistics of Korean Economy.* Seoul: Economic Planning Board, various years.

————. *Social Indicators in Korea, 1987.* Seoul: Economic Planning Board, 1987.

The Economist. "South Korea: An Impromptu Performance." 18 August 1990.

————. "A Survey of South Korea." 21 May 1988.

————. *"How South Korea Scares Japan."* 14 May 1988.

Ensor, Paul. "Caught in the Machine." *Far Eastern Economic Review*, 18 September 1986.

————. "Two Way Trade-off." *Far Eastern Economic Review*, 6 March 1986.

Evans, Peter. "Class, State, and Dependence in East Asia: Lessons for Latin Americanists." In *The Political Economy of the New Asian Industrialization*, ed. Frederic C. Deyo. Ithaca, NY: Cornell University Press, 1987.

Far Eastern Economic Review. "Brave New World: Why Have the Economic Fortunes of Latin America and Asia Diverged So Dramatically?" September 1990.

————. "Industrial South Korea." 19 July 1984.

————. "Labor Problems: Long Term Peace Prospect Looks Poor." 19 July 1984.

————. "Buying Time for Change." 12 November 1982.

————. "Busy Jailers." 28 May 1973.

Fuentes, Annette, and Barbara Ehrenreich. *Women in the Global Factory*. New York: Institute for New Communications, South End Press, 1983.

Haberman, Clyde. "South Korea's Future Pivots on Role Chun Chooses." *The Oregonian*, 12 April 1987.

Haggard, Stephan. *Pathways from the Periphery: The Politics of Growth in the Newly Industrializing Countries*. Ithaca, NY: Cornell University Press, 1990.

Haggard, Stephan, and Chung-In Moon. "Liberal, Dependent or Mercantile? The South Korean State in the International System." In *The Antinomies of Interdependence*, ed. John Ruggie. New York: Columbia University Press, 1983.

Haggard, Stephan, Byung-Kook Kim, and Chung-In Moon. "The Transition to Export-led Growth in South Korea: 1954-1966." *Journal of Asian Studies* 50, no. 4, November 1991.

Halliday, Jon. "The United Nations and Korea." In *Without Parallel: The American-Korean Relationship Since 1945*, ed. Frank Baldwin. New York: Pantheon Books, 1974.

Halliday, Jon, and Bruce Cumings. *Korea: The Unknown War*. New York: Pantheon Books, 1988.

Hamilton, Clive. *Capitalist Industrialization in Korea*. Boulder, CO: Westview Press, 1986.

Hansen, Henrik. "Fierce Competition and Tighter Regulations." *Business Korea* (August 1991).

Harrison, Selig S. "A Chance for Detente in Korea." *World Policy Journal* 8, no. 4, Fall 1991.

————. "Dateline South Korea: A Divided Seoul." *Foreign Policy*, no. 67 (Summer 1987).

————. "Is South Korea Going to Be the Next Philippines?" *New York Times*, 25 January 1987.

Hart-Landsberg, Martin. "Economic Growth and Political Struggle in South Korea." *Labor, Capital, and Society* 23, no. 2 (November 1990).

————. "Learning from South Korea—A Review of Asia's Next Giant: South Korea and Late Industrialization by Alice H. Amsden." *Monthly Review* 42, no. 4 (September 1990).

————. "South Korea: Looking at the Left." *Monthly Review* 41, no. 3 (July-August 1989).

————. "South Korea: The Miracle Rejected." *Critical Sociology* 15, no. 3 (Fall 1988).

————. "South Korea: The Fraudulent Miracle." *Monthly Review* 39, no. 7 (December 1987).

Helm, Leslie. "Curing a Copycat Syndrome." *Los Angeles Times*, 8 April 1991.

————. "A Bumpier Road Ahead." *Los Angeles Times*, 18 March 1991.

International Monetary Fund. *International Financial Statistics, Supplement on Trade Statistics*. Supplement series, no. 15. Washington, D.C.: International Monetary Fund, 1988.

————. *International Financial Statistics, Supplement On Output Statistics*. Supplement series, no. 8. Washington, D.C.: International Monetary Fund, 1984.

Jameson, Sam. "Familes Still Keep Grip on S. Korea's Conglomerates." *Los Angeles Times*, 10 December 1990.

————. "South Korea Plans Major Push into High-Tech Fields." *Los Angeles Times*, 11 December 1989.

Jo, Sung-Hwan. *The Car Industry in the Republic of Korea*. International Employment Policies Working Paper No. 22. Geneva, Switzerland: International Labor Organization, August 1988.

Johnson, Chalmers. "Political Institutions and Economic Performance: The Government-Business Relationship in Japan, South Korea, and Taiwan." In *The Political Economy of the New Asian Industrialization*, ed. Frederic C. Deyo. Ithaca, NY: Cornell University Press, 1987.

Jones, Leroy P., and Il Sakong. *Government, Business, and Entrepreneurship in Economic Development: The Korean Case*. Cambridge, MA: Harvard University Press, 1980.

Jones, Steven. "Asia Grows Wealthier, but Disparities Widen." *Asian Wall Street Journal Weekly*, 27 November 1989.

Kamm, Thomas. "South Americans Push Sales of State Assets in Swing to Capitalism." *Wall Street Journal*, 9 July 1991.

Kang, Sugwon. "The Politics and Poetry of Kim Chi-ha." *Bulletin of Concerned Asian Scholars* 9, no. 2 (1977).

Kenji, Nakano. "Japan's Overseas Investment Patterns and FTZs." *AMPO:*

Japan-Asia Quarterly Review 8, no. 4 and 9, nos. 1 and 2 (1977).

Kim, Ae-dai. "The Farmers' Movement in South Korea." *Korea Report* 3, no. 1 (July 1989).

Kim, Chang Soo. "Marginalization, Development and the Korean Workers' Movement." *AMPO: Japan-Asia Quarterly Review* 9, no. 3 (July-November 1977).

Kim, Choongsoo. *Labor Market Developments of Korea in Macroeconomic Perspectives.* KDI Working Paper No. 8909. Seoul: Korea Development Institute, April 1989.

Kim, Dae Jung. *Mass-Participatory Economy.* Lanham, MD: University Press of America, 1985.

Kim, Eun Mee. "From Dominance to Symbiosis: State and Chaebol in Korea." *Pacific Focus* 3, no. 2 (Fall 1988).

Kim, Jin-Moon. "Building a New Image." *Business Korea,* December 1991.

Kim, Joungwon Alexander. *Divided Korea: The Politics of Development, 1945-1972.* Cambridge, MA: Harvard University Press, 1976.

Kim, Kwang Suk. "Lessons from South Korea's Experience with Industrialization." In *Export-Oriented Development Strategies,* ed. Vittorio Corbo, Anne O. Krueger and Fernando Ossa. Boulder, Co.: Westview Press, 1985.

Kim, Young-ock. *The Position of Women Workers in Manufacturing Industries in South Korea: A Marxist-Feminist Analysis.* Working Paper—Sub-Series on Women's History and Development, No. 6. Ithaca, NY: Cornell University Press, 1986.

Kincaid, Russell G. "Korea's Major Adjustment Effort." *Finance and Development,* December 1983.

Kiva, Aleksei. "Socialist Orientation: Reality and Illusions." *International Affairs,* July 1988.

Koo, Bohn-young. "The Role of Direct Foreign Investment in Korea's Recent Economic Growth." In *Foreign Trade and Investment: Economic Development in the Newly Industrializing Asian Countries,* ed. Walter Galenson. Madison, WI: University of Wisconsin Press, 1985.

Koo Hagen. "The Political Economy of Income Distribution in South Korea: The Impact of the State's Industrialization Policies." *World Development* 12, no. 10 (1984).

Korea Christian Alliance for Democracy and Reunification. *A Time to Breakdown, and A Time to Build: The People's Movement for Self-reliant National Independence, Genuine Democracy and National Reunification.* Seoul: Christian Alliance for Democracy and Reunification, 1989.

Korea Economic Journal. "Imported Cars Challenge Local Markets." 31 July 1989.

Korea Economic Weekly. "Capital Investment Growth Poised For Slowdown During 1992: KDB." 25 May 1992.

————. "Computer Makers Facing Worst of Times." 14 October 1991.

————. "Export Profit Margins Decreasing." 16 September 1991.

————. "Overseas Korean Operations Remitting Little of Profits." 16 September 1991.

————. "Corporate Non-Productive Expenses Ever Increasing." 16 September 1991.

Korea Herald. "Japan Reluctant to Transfer Technologies to Korea." 18 September 1990.

Korea Information and Resource Center. *Women Take the Forefront: Women's Movement in South Korea.* Washington, D.C.: Korea Information and Resource Center, August 1991.

Korea Labor: Monthly Newsletter of the Korea Research and Information Center (Seoul, South Korea). "Unions of 16 Large Plants Form Alliance." No. 4 (December 1990).

Korea Report. "National Security Law Revisions Railroaded in 35 Seconds." Vol. 5, nos. 1 and 2 (August-September 1991).

————. "Distribution of Wealth: A Critical Issue in South Korea." Vol. 1, no. 4 (September-October 1987).

Korea Times. "Machinery Imports Culprit of Trade Deficit with Japan." 1 August 1991.

Korea Update. "ILO Admits South Korea." No. 105 (January 1992).

————. "1991 Korea Human Rights Situation." No. 105 (January 1992).

———— "National Farmers' Organization Formalized." Nos. 98 and 99 (May-June 1990).

————. "Chonnohyup Supporters Association Formed." No. 97 (March 1990).

————. "Despite Ban, Chonnohyop Founded January 22." No. 96 (January-February 1990).

————. "Thousands of Street Vendors Fight to Protect Livelihood." No. 92 (August 1989).

————. "Crackdown in Korea." No. 91 (July 1989).

————. "Over 2,000 Riot Police and Peak-Kol-Dan in Sadangdong Re-development Area." No. 91 (July 1989).

The Korean Economic Report. "The Government Turns Thumbs Down." September 1990.

Kreisberg, Paul H. "Democracy Adds to Strife over Korean Economy." *Los Angeles Times,* 12 July 1989.

Kuznets, Paul. "The Dramatic Reversal of 1979/1980: Contemporary Economic Development in Korea." *Journal of Northeast Asian Studies* 1, no. 3 (1982).

Lachica, Eduardo. "Korea Launches Offensive to Ward Off U.S. Trade Sanctions." *Asian Wall Street Journal Weekly,* 17 April 1989.

Launius, Michael A. "The State and Industrial Labor in South Korea." *Bulletin of Concerned Asian Scholars* 13, no. 4 (1984).

Lee, Byung Jong. "Five Korean Automakers Protest Samsung's Plan for Car Factory." *Asian Wall Street Journal Weekly*, 16 July 1990.

Lee, Ki-baik. *A New History of Korea*, translated by Edward W. Wagner with Edward J. Shultz. Cambridge, MA: Harvard University Press, 1984.

Lee, Su-Hoon, and David A. Smith. "Antisystemic Movements in South Korea: The Rise of Environmental Activism." Paper presented at the 15th PEWS Conference, University of Hawaii, March 28-30, 1991.

Lehner, Urban C. "With Japan's Backing, Indonesia Gains a Larger Role in Regional Economy." *Wall Street Journal*, 10 January 1992.

Leyden, Peter, and David Bank. "Evictions Threaten the Poverty-Stricken." *International Herald Tribune*, 5 July 1989.

Lho, Joo Hyoung. "Workers' Power." *Korea Business World*, June 1989.

Lim, Hyun-Chin. *Dependent Development in Korea, 1963-1979*. Seoul: Seoul National University Press, 1985.

Linder, Staffan Burenstan. *The Pacific Century: Economic and Political Consequences of Asian-Pacific Dynamism*, Stanford, CA: Stanford University Press, 1986.

Louie, Marian. "South Korean Mass Movement Mushrooms." *Frontline*, 3 July 1989.

Luedde-Neurath, Richard. "State Intervention and Export-Oriented Development in South Korea." In *Developmental States in East Asia*, ed. Gordon White. New York: St. Martin's Press, 1988.

————. *Import Controls and Export-Oriented Development: A Reassessment of the South Korean Case*. Boulder, CO: Westview Press, 1986.

Maass, Peter. "Success of Korean Economy Comes at High Cost for Workers." *Oregonian*, 30 April 1989.

Manguno, Joseph P. "Middle Class Anger Focuses on Economic Woes." *Asian Wall Street Journal Weekly*, 14 May 1990.

————. "Spiraling Property Costs Dash Dreams of Young Koreans to Buy a First Home." *Asian Wall Street Journal Weekly*, 23 October 1989.

————. "Korean VCR Makers' Invasion of U.S. Backfires as Profit Margins Disappear." *Wall Street Journal*, 5 April 1989.

Mardon, Russell. "The State and the Effective Control of Foreign Capital: The Case of South Korea." *World Politics*, no. 43 (October 1990).

McCormack, Gavan. "Japan and South Korea, 1965-1975: Ten Years of Normalization." In *Korea, North and South: The Deepening Crisis*, ed. Gavan McCormack and Mark Selden. New York: Monthly Review Press, 1978.

————. "The South Korean Economy: GNP versus the People." In *Korea, North and South: The Deepening Crisis*, ed. Gavan McCormack and Mark Selden. New York: Monthly Review Press, 1978.

McGregor, Liz. "Women's Slow Progress." *International Herald Tribune*, 5 June 1989.

Michell, Tony. *From a Developing to a Newly Industrialized Country: The Republic of Korea, 1961-82*. Geneva, Switzerland: International Labor Organization, 1988.

————. "Administrative Traditions and Economic Decision Making in South Korea." *IDS Bulletin* 15, no. 2 (1984).

————. "Domestic Bliss: Lessons from Korean Economic Development 1962-82." *Euro Asia Business Review* 2, no. 2 (1983).

Moffat, Susan. "Korea Farmers Ready to Wage Fierce Battle Against U.S. Imports." *Asian Wall Street Journal Weekly*, 23 January 1989.

————. "Koreans Test Democratic Institutions by Pressing Demands in Chun Inquiry." *Asian Wall Street Journal Weekly*, 21 November 1988.

Moon, Chung-In. "Irony of Interdependence: Emerging Trade Frictions Between South Korea and the U.S." In *Alliance under Tension: The Evolution of South Korean-U.S. Relations*, ed. Manwoo Lee, Ronald D. McLaurin, and Chung-In Moon. Boulder, CO: Westview Press, 1988.

Moreno, Ramon. "Exchange Rates and Trade Adjustment in Taiwan and Korea." *Economic Review*. Federal Reserve Bank of San Francisco, no. 2 (Spring 1989).

Ogle, George E. *South Korea: Dissent within the Economic Miracle*. New Jersey: Zed Books Ltd. in association with International Labor Rights Education and Research Fund [Washington D.C.], 1990.

On Korean Laborers: A Perspective Paper and Data Base. Author and publisher unknown. Seoul, Korea, 1988.

Palais, James B. "'Democracy' in South Korea, 1948-72." In *Without Parallel: The American-Korean Relationship Since 1945*, ed. Frank Baldwin. New York: Pantheon Books, 1974.

Renfrew, Barry. "Korea's Growth Takes a Toll on Workers." *Asian Wall Street Journal Weekly*, 9 January 1989.

Satterwhite, David. "The Politics of Economic Development: Coup, State, and the Republic of Korea's First Five Year Plan (1962-1966)." Ph.D. dissertation. University of Washington, forthcoming.

Schoenberger, Karl. "If It's Fancy, Don't Market It in Seoul." *Los Angeles Times*, 11 September 1990.

————. "Speculators Fuel Real Estate Fever in South Korea." *Los Angeles Times*, 18 March 1990.

Shim, Jae Hoon. "Militants Speak Out." *Far Eastern Economic Review*, 10 July 1986.

Shorrock, Tim. "The Struggle for Democracy in South Korea in the 1980s and the Rise of Anti-Americanism." *Third World Quarterly*, October 1986.

————. "South Korea: The New Regime Brings More Repression, and a Return to Reprocessing Goods for Sale in Japan and the U.S." *Multinational Monitor*, June 1981.

Simmons, Robert R. "The Korean Civil War." In *Without Parallel: The American-Korean Relationship Since 1945*, ed. Frank Baldwin. New York: Pantheon Books, 1974.

Sohn Jie-Ae. "Korean Economy: Toothless Tiger?" *Business Korea*, November 1991.

————. "Strong Image, Weak Underbelly." *Business Korea*, September 1991.

————. "Crossing Over." *Business Korea*, June 1991.

Sohn Jie-Ae and Sun-Young Cho. "Building Strength for World Prominence." *Business Korea*, May 1991.

Song, Byung-Nak. *The Rise of the Korean Economy*. New York: Oxford University Press, 1990.

Soo, Han Seung. "South Korea's Model Development." *Asian Wall Street Journal Weekly*, 23 October 1989.

South. "Curbing a Pollution Economy." February 1991.

Steers, Richard M., Yoo Keun Shin, and Gerardo R. Ungson. *The Chaebol: Korea's New Industrial Might*. New York: Harper and Row, 1989.

Stentzel, James. "Seoul's Second Bonanza." *Far Eastern Economic Review*, 30 July 1973.

Stone, I. F. *The Hidden History of the Korean War*. New York: Monthly Review Press, 1952.

Suh, Dae-Sook. *The Korean Communist Movement, 1918-1948*. Princeton, NJ: Princeton University Press, 1967.

Suh, Jae-Jung. "Roh Tae Woo's Human Rights Record." *Korea Report* 3, nos. 2 and 3 (February-March 1990).

T.K. *Letters From South Korea*, trans. David L. Swain, ed. Sekai. Tokyo: Iwanami Shoten Publishers, 1976.

Takeo, Tsuchiya. "Masan: An Epitome of the Japan-ROK Relationship." *AMPO: Japan-Asia Quarterly Review* 8, no. 4 and 9, nos. 1 and 2, 1977.

Teal, Greg. "The State, the Labor Process, and Industrial Health and Safety in South Korea." *Labor, Capital and Society* 21, no. 2 (November 1988).

UNCTAD Secretariat. *Fibres and Textiles: Dimensions of Corporate Marketing Structures*. New York: United Nations, 1980.

Urban Industrial Mission. *Short History of South Korea's Labor Movement: Historical Overview and Some Information on Current Developments*. Inchon, South Korea: Urban Industrial Mission, 1988.

U.S. House of Representatives, Committee on International Relations. *Investigation of Korean-American Relations*. Washington, D.C.: U.S. Government Printing Office, 1978.

Wade, Robert. "State Intervention in 'Outward-looking' Development: Neoclassical Theory and Taiwanese Practise." In *Developmental States in East Asia*, ed. Gordon White. New York: St. Martin's Press, 1988.

Wales, Nym, and Kim San. *Song Of Ariran: A Korean Communist in the Chinese Revolution*. San Francisco: Ramparts Press, 1972 (originally published in 1941 by John Day Co.).

Wall Street Journal. "Korean Manufacturers' Earnings." 12 June 1992.

————. "South Korea's Trade Gap Reached a Record in 1991." 6 January 1992.

Westphal, Larry. "The Republic of Korea's Experience with Export-led Industrial Development." *World Development* 6, no. 3 (1978).

White, Gordon, and Robert Wade. "Developmental States and Markets in East Asia: an Introduction," in *Developmental States in East Asia*, ed. Gordon White. New York: St. Martin's Press, 1988.

Wideman, Bernie. "The Plight of the South Korean Peasant." In *Without Parallel: The American-Korean Relationship Since 1945*, ed. Frank Baldwin. New York: Pantheon Books, 1974.

————. "Korean Chauvinism." *Far Eastern Economic Review*, 5 March 1973.

Woo, Jung-en. *Race to the Swift: State and Finance in Korean Industrialization*. New York: Columbia University Press, 1991.

World Bank. *Korea: Managing the Industrial Transition*, Vol. 2. Washington, D.C.: World Bank, 1987.

————. *World Development Report*. Washington, D.C.: World Bank, various years.

INDEX